THE LIBRARY OF WORLD AFFAIRS

Editors:

George W. Keeton

and

Georg Schwarzenberger

Number 68

FOREIGN INVESTMENTS AND INTERNATIONAL LAW

BY THE SAME AUTHOR

Das Völkerbunds-Mandat für Palästina, Stuttgart 1929.
Die Kreuger-Anleihen, Munich and Leipzig 1931.
Die Internationalen Banken für Zahlungsausgleich und Agrarkredite, Berlin 1932.
Die Verfassung der Spanischen Republik, Königsberg 1933.
William Ladd, London 1935—2nd ed. 1936.
The League of Nations and World Order, London 1936.
Making International Law Work (together with G. W. Keeton), London 1939—2nd ed. 1946.
Power Politics. A Study of World Society, London 1941—3rd ed. 1964 (German ed. 1955—Spanish ed. 1960).
International Law and Totalitarian Lawlessness, London 1943.
International Law as Applied by International Courts and Tribunals, First published London 1945—Vol. I: *General Principles*, 3rd ed. 1957; Vol. II: *The Law of Armed Conflict*, 1968; Vol. III: *The Law of International Institutions* (in preparation).
A Manual of International Law, London 1947—5th ed. 1967 (German ed. 1949).
The Fundamental Principles of International Law, Recueil, Hague Academy of International Law, 1955—Vol. 87.
The Legality of Nuclear Weapons, London 1958 (transl. into German, Italian and Spanish, 1958–59).
The Frontiers of International Law, London 1962.
The Inductive Approach to International Law, London 1965.
The Principles and Standards of International Economic Law, Recueil, Hague Academy of International Law, 1966—Vol. 117.

FOREIGN INVESTMENTS
AND
INTERNATIONAL LAW

BY

GEORG SCHWARZENBERGER

of Gray's Inn, Barrister-at-Law
Professor of International Law in the University of London
Director, London Institute of World Affairs

LONDON
STEVENS & SONS
1969

*Published in 1969 by
Stevens & Sons Limited
of 11 New Fetter Lane
London — Law Publishers
and printed in Great Britain
by The Eastern Press Limited
of London and Reading*

SBN 0420 42120 3

AUSTRALIA
The Law Book Company Ltd.
Sydney : Melbourne : Brisbane

GREAT BRITAIN
Stevens & Sons Ltd.
London

INDIA
N. M. Tripathi Private Ltd.
Bombay

ISRAEL
Steimatzky's Agency Ltd.
Jerusalem : Tel Aviv : Haifa

NEW ZEALAND
Sweet & Maxwell (N.Z.) Ltd.
Wellington

PAKISTAN
Pakistan Law House
Karachi

U.S.A. AND CANADA
Frederick A. Praeger Inc.
New York : Washington

TO

GEORGE W. KEETON

IN FRIENDSHIP

PREFACE

THE status and protection of investments abroad are central and perennial, but ever-changing themes of International Economic Law.

In one way or another, these problems have concerned me for forty years. My interest in them dates from the late twenties when I studied the impact of the Soviet Union on International Law, and was surprised to find that this impact was considerably less than that of International Law on the Soviet Union. When, at about the same time, I examined the legal aspects of the activities of Ivan Kreuger and his transnational match empire, I was again confronted with the limitations imposed by international law on the discretion of the States parties to such government contracts. This became even more evident from the study of the practice of international courts and tribunals and the post-1945 policies of nationalisation and decolonisation. Thus, the time has come to gather together the various strands of earlier studies and present them as a coherent whole.

The book is addressed to three categories of readers:

(1) The growing number of students, especially on the postgraduate level, of International Economic Law.

(2) Practitioners in the field who have taught me more than I can ever hope adequately to acknowledge about their particular concerns. Yet, it was they who, over the years, have pointed out to me that, between catching planes and attending board meetings here, there and everywhere, they are far too busy to keep up to date with the wider aspects and literature relating even to their own work.

(3) Politicians, civil servants, bankers, investors and interested laymen who would like to make up their own minds on the significance of the growing number of multilateral draft conventions put before them as more or less adequate safeguards against the risks besetting property abroad in our time.

This book owes a great deal to information supplied, with surprising willingness, by governmental and private quarters in capital-exporting and capital-importing countries alike. In any case involving the communication of confidential information, the mutual understanding was clear. It was that these sources of information would not be cited, and I should remain a free agent to check and cross-check the information received in the quasi-judicial spirit in which I consider research work should be carried out. Thus, the debt of gratitude I owe to helpers in this category can be expressed only in this generalised form.

As in the past, I have been greatly assisted by the active co-operation—academic, critical, editorial and technical—of a team of friends and colleagues in the Faculty of Laws of University College, London and the London Institute of World Affairs: E. D. Brown, Bin Cheng, Margaret Homewood, Julie Ann Howard, Zainy Jamal, F. Parkinson, A. Sutton, L. G. Taylor and M. Youssefian. My colleagues Brown and Sutton have carried the burden of preparing the tables and indices and seeing the book through the press. Again, it was a pleasure to co-operate in the production of this book with the publishers and printers.

As a modest tribute, this book is dedicated to Professor G. W. Keeton on his retirement from his appointments as Professor of English Law in the University of London and Vice-Provost and Head of the Department of Law of University College, London. The fact that the dedication can be repeated in the words of the first edition of *Power Politics* (1941) is sufficient outward evidence of the fact that this friendship has stood the test of time. Moreover, nobody knows better than I that, without Professor Keeton's initiative and sustained support, I should never have had the opportunity of introducing and developing at University College London International Law and Relations on the interdisciplinary basis on which, in the last thirty years, these subjects have there become established, nor of creating a niche for International Economic Law as a distinct field of postgraduate academic studies in the College and the University of London.

G. S.

UNIVERSITY COLLEGE, LONDON

November 27, 1968

CONTENTS

PART TWO

MULTILATERAL APPROACHES

CONCLUSIONS

TABLE OF CASES

TABLE OF TREATIES

TABLE OF PUBLIC CONTRACTS

TABLE OF UNITED NATIONS RESOLUTIONS

ABBREVIATIONS

A	Series A, containing the Judgments and Orders of the Permanent Court of International Justice, 1923–30
A/B	Series A/B, containing the Judgments, Orders and Advisory Opinions of the Permanent Court of International Justice, 1931–40
A.I.O.C.	Anglo-Iranian Oil Company
A.J.C.L.	*American Journal of Comparative Law*
A.J.I.L.	*American Journal of International Law*
A.S.I.L. Proceedings ..	*Proceedings of the American Society of International Law*
A.V.R.	*Archiv des Völkerrechts*
Acta Scandinavica ..	*Acta Scandinavica Juris Gentium*
Am.Bar Assn.J.	*American Bar Association Journal*
Annuaire de l'Institut ..	*Annuaire de l'Institut de Droit International*
Annuaire français ..	*Annuaire français de droit international*
Annuaire suisse	*Annuaire suisse de droit international*
Annual Digest	*Annual Digest and Reports of Public International Law Cases*, 1929–55
Arbitration J.	*Arbitration Journal*
B.D.I.L.	C. Parry (ed.), *A British Digest of International Law*, 1965–
B.F.S.P.	*British and Foreign State Papers*
B.I.L.C.	C. Parry (ed.), *British International Law Cases*, 1964–67
B.P.I.L.	Lauterpacht, E. (ed.), *British Practice in International Law*, 1963– . See also under *Contemporary Practice*
B.Y.I.L.	*British Yearbook of International Law*
C.L.P.	*Current Legal Problems*
C.M.L.R.	*Common Market Law Review*
Calif.L.R.	*California Law Review*
Can.Y.B.I.L.	*Canadian Yearbook of International Law*
Cheng, B., *General Principles of Law* ..	Cheng, B., *General Principles of Law as applied by International Courts and Tribunals*, 1953
Cmd.	Command Papers (United Kingdom), 1919–56
Cmnd.	Command Papers (United Kingdom), 1956–
Col.J.Transnational Law ..	*Columbia Journal of Transnational Law*
Col.L.R.	*Columbia Law Review*
Conflict Resolution ..	*Journal of Conflict Resolution*
Contemporary Practice ..	E. Lauterpacht (ed.), *The Contemporary Practice of the United Kingdom in the Field of International Law*, 5 I.C.L.Q. (1956)—10 (1961) and supplements covering 1962 (1962–63). *See also under* B.P.I.L.
Cornell L.Q.	*Cornell Law Quarterly*
Domke Symposium ..	Sanders, P. (ed.), *International Arbitration: Liber Amicorum for Martin Domke*, 1967
E.C.H.R.	European Court of Human Rights
ECOSOC	United Nations Economic and Social Council
E.E.C.	European Economic Community
E.F.T.A.	European Free Trade Association
Erler Festgabe	*Wirtschaft und Atomenergie im internationalen Recht*, 1965
F.C.N. Treaties	Treaties of Friendship, Commerce and Navigation
FF	*Feuille féderale* (Swiss)
f.o.b.	free on board
Federal Bar J.	*Federal Bar Journal*
Fundamental Principles ..	Schwarzenberger, G., *The Fundamental Principles of International Law*, 87 Hague *Recueil* (1955)
GATT	General Agreement on Tariffs and Trade
Gen.Ass.Res.	Resolution of the General Assembly of the United Nations
Grotius Transactions ..	*Transactions of the Grotius Society*
Gutzwiller Festgabe ..	*Jus et Lex, Festgabe für Max Gutzwiller*, 1959
H.C.Deb.	House of Commons, Parliamentary Debates (*Hansard*)
H.L.Deb.	House of Lords, Parliamentary Debates (*Hansard*)

Hackworth Digest ..	Hackworth, G. H., *Digest of International Law*, 1940–44 (8 vols.)
Hague *Recueil*	*Recueil des Cours, Académie de Droit International de la Haye*
Harv.Bus.Rev.	*Harvard Business Review*
I.B.R.D.	International Bank for Reconstruction and Development
I.C.J.	International Court of Justice
I.C.J.Y.B.	International Court of Justice, *Yearbook*
I.C.L.Q.	*International and Comparative Law Quarterly*
I.C.S.I.D.	International Centre for the Settlement of Investment Disputes
I.D.A.	International Development Association
I.E.L.	International Economic Law
I.F.C.	International Finance Corporation
I.L.A.	International Law Association
I.L.M.	*International Legal Materials*
I.L.Q.	*International Law Quarterly*
I.L.R.	*International Law Reports*, 1950–
I.M.F.	International Monetary Fund
Ind.Op.	Individual Opinion
Indian J.I.L.	*Indian Journal of International Law*
Indian Y.B.I.A.	*Indian Yearbook of International Affairs*
Inductive Approach ..	Schwarzenberger, G., *The Inductive Approach to International Law*, 1965
J.B.L.	*Journal of Business Law*
J.P.L.	*Journal of Public Law*
J.W.T.L.	*Journal of World Trade Law*
Janssen Festschrift ..	Kraenzlin, E., and Mueller, H. E. A. (eds.), *Der Schütz des privaten Eigentums im Ausland: Festschrift für Hermann Janssen*, 1958
Keesing's Archives ..	*Keesing's Contemporary Archives. Weekly Diary of World Events*
Kreuger-Anleihen ..	Schwarzenberger, G., *Die Kreuger-Anleihen*, 1931
L.J.	*Law Journal*, for instance, *Georgetown L.J.*
L.Q.R.	*Law Quarterly Review*
L.R.	*Law Review*, for instance, *Harvard L.R.*
Ll.L.R.	*Lloyd's List Law Reports*
Liber Amicorum A. Bagge	*Liber Amicorum of Congratulations to Algot Bagge*, 1956
Liber Amicorum J.P.A. François (1959) ..	*Varia Juris Gentium, Liber Amicorum J.P.A. François*, 1959 (2 vols.)
Lillich (1962)	R. B. Lillich, *International Claims: Their Adjudication by National Commissions*, 1962
—— (1965)	——, *The Protection of Foreign Investment. Six Procedural Studies* (1965)
—— (1967)	——, *International Claims: Postwar British Practice* (1967)
M.A.T.	Mixed Arbitral Tribunal (the references are to the *Recueil des décisions des tribunaux arbitraux mixtes*, 1921–30)
M.L.R.	*Modern Law Review*
Manual	Schwarzenberger, G., *A Manual of International Law* (5th ed.—1967)
Mélanges Gidel	P. Vellas (ed.), *Mélanges en l'honneur de Gilbert Gidel*, 1961
Mélanges Guggenheim ..	Lalive, P., and Freymond, J. (eds.), *Recueil d'Études de Droit International en Hommage à Paul Guggenheim*, 1968
Mélanges Kollewijn-Offerhaus	*De Conflictu Legum. Essays Presented to R. D. Kollewijn/J. Offerhaus*, 1962
Mélanges Rolin	J. Baugniet and Others (eds.), *Problèmes de droit des gens, Mélanges offerts à Henri Rolin*, 1964
Mélanges Séfériadès ..	Ecole de Sciences Politiques "Panteois," *Mélanges Séfériadès*, 1961 (2 vols.)
Mich.L.R.	*Michigan Law Review*
Minnesota L.R.	*Minnesota Law Review*
Most - Favoured - Nation Standard	Schwarzenberger, G., *The Most-Favoured-Nation Standard in British State Practice*, 22 B.Y.I.L. (1945)
N.Y.U.L.Q.R.	*New York University Law Quarterly Review*
Netherlands R.I.L. ..	*Netherlands Review of International Law*
O.E.C.D.	Organisation for Economic Co-operation and Development
O.E.E.C.	Organisation for European Economic Co-operation
Ö.Z.Ö.R.	*Österreichische Zeitschrift für Öffentliches Recht*
P.C.A.	Permanent Court of Arbitration

Power Politics	Schwarzenberger, G., *Power Politics. A Study of World Society* (3rd ed.) 1964
Principles of I.E.L. ..	Schwarzenberger, G., *The Principles and Standards of International Economic Law*, 117 Hague *Recueil* (1966)
R.D.I.L.C.	*Revue de droit international et de législation comparée*
R.G.D.I.P.	*Revue générale de droit international public*
R.I.A.A.	United Nations, *Reports of International Arbitral Awards*, 1948–
Répertoire Français ..	Kiss, A. Ch., *Répertoire de la pratique française en matière de droit international public*, 1962–
Scritti Perassi	*Scritti di diritto internazionale in onore di Tomaso Perassi*, 1957 (2 vols.)
Sep. Op.	Separate Opinion
Strupp-Schlochauer ..	Strupp, K., *Wörterbuch des Völkerrechts*, 1960–62 (4 vols.), edited by H.-J. Schlochauer
T.A.N.U.	Tanzanian African National Union
The Frontiers	Schwarzenberger, G., *The Frontiers of International Law*, 1962
T.I.A.S.	*United States, Treaties and Other International Acts Series*
U.A.R.	United Arab Republic
U.K.	United Kingdom
U.N.	United Nations
U.N.C.T.A.D.	United Nations Conference on Trade and Development
U.N.I.D.O.	United Nations Industrial Development Organisation
U.N.T.S.	United Nations Treaty Series
U. Pa. L.R.	*University of Pennsylvania Law Review*
Univ. Chicago L.R. ..	*University of Chicago Law Review*
Virg. J.I.L.	*Virginia Journal of International Law*
Vol. I	Schwarzenberger, G., *International Law as Applied by International Courts and Tribunals*, Vol. I (General Principles), 3rd ed., 1957
Vol. II	Schwarzenberger, G., *International Law*, Vol. II (The Law of Armed Conflict), 1968
Whiteman Digest ..	Whiteman, M. M., *Digest of International Law*, 1963–
Y.B.W.A.	*Year Book of World Affairs*
Z.A.I.P.R.	*Zeitschrift für ausländisches und internationales Privatrecht*
Z.A.Ö.R.V.R.	*Zeitschrift für ausländisches öffentliches Recht und Völkerrecht*

INTRODUCTION

CHAPTER 1

FUNDAMENTALS

"Property and law are born together. Before the laws there was no property: take away the laws, all property ceases."
Jeremy Bentham, *Principles of the Civil Code* (1786).

SIX matters are best dealt with in this introductory Chapter: the governing rules of international customary law on the protection of foreign investments; the objects of the book; the complexities of the problems discussed; their methodological implications; the major assumptions made in this study and, finally, questions of terminology.

1—THE GOVERNING RULES OF INTERNATIONAL CUSTOMARY LAW

The issues to be considered under this head fall into three groups: the major rules of international customary law applicable to all types of foreign investment; the special problems connected with public or State contracts as, for instance, oil and mineral concessions, and the doubts raised regarding continued reliance on the traditional rules of international customary law in this field.

(a) The Major Rules

The applicable law can be stated in two well-established rules of international customary law:

(1) *State Property.* In principle, the property of sovereign States situated abroad is immune from the jurisdiction of the territorial sovereign.

In the law of peace, minor exceptions apply to immovable State property abroad and, on the domestic level, a number of States have restricted the application of the rule by the introduction of functional and other tests of their own.[1]

The rule is one of the law of peace. In a *status mixtus* between peace and war in unorganised international society, this rule—like any other

[1] See, for instance, B.D.I.L. (First Phase), Vol. 7, pp. 118–120; B.I.L.C., Vol. 3, p. 275 *et seq.*; *Whiteman Digest*, Vol. 6 (1968), p. 553 *et seq.*; *Répertoire français*, Vol. 3 (1965), p. 315 *et seq.*

On the relations between sovereign immunity and the United States Act of State doctrine, see R. A. Falk, *The Role of Domestic Courts in the International Legal Order* (1964), p. 64 *et seq.*; Lillich (1965), p. 3 *et seq.*; K. R. Simmonds, 14 I.C.L.Q. (1965), p. 452 *et seq.*; E. F. Mooney, *Foreign Seizures: Sabbatino and the Act of State Doctrine* (1967) and, further, the *Manual*, pp. 453–454 and 461–463. See also 3 I.L.M. (1964), pp. 381 and 1075; 4 *ibid.* (1965), pp. 578, 636, 988, 1018 and 1209; 5 *ibid.* (1966), p. 477; 6 *ibid.* (1967), pp. 871 and 898, and 7 *ibid.* (1968), pp. 23–24.

rule of international customary law—is subject to the law of reprisals and, in a state of war, specialised rules apply between enemy States and between belligerent and neutral States.[2]

(2) *Private Property.* In principle, private property is subject to the municipal law of the sovereign State in which it is situated.

In accordance with the minimum standard of international customary law applicable to foreign property, such property may be expropriated only in the public interest, without unjustifiable discrimination, and on payment of full or adequate, prompt and effective compensation.

What constitutes expropriation and justifiable interference with foreign property cannot be determined in the abstract. On these matters, as on the quantum and modalities of the payment of the compensation due, the minimum standard of international law continuously and imperceptibly varies with the changing views held on these matters by the preponderant number of subjects of international law.[3]

By this standard, interference with foreign property by taxation or measures of monetary policy such as devaluation of the national currency, on a footing of *de jure* and *de facto* equality, does not normally constitute an interference amounting to expropriation and calling for compensation. Yet, in particular circumstances, such action, as well as other forms of interference, may amount to creeping nationalisation.[4] Similarly, while some forms of discrimination appear unjustified, others may be considered to be permissible under the minimum standard.[5] Finally, much of the disagreement in the Doctrine of international law on the quantum and modalities of damages due in the case of an otherwise lawful expropriation is due to the relativity and subjectivity of the minimum standard which, in its elasticity and self-adaptability, represents one of the characteristic features of international customary law.[6]

International adjudication cannot give objectivity to an inherently subjective standard, but merely provide finality for any particular dispute. Yet, notwithstanding this reservation, relevant decisions of international Courts and tribunals appear to constitute the most authoritative evidence

[2] See, further, Vol. II, pp. 38, 63, 308 and 549 *et seq.*

[3] Helpful checks on recent trends are provided by discussions such as those on the international effects of nationalisation at the Siena Session of the *Institut de Droit International* during the litispendence of the *Anglo-Iranian Oil Company* case before the I.C.J. (44 (II) *Annuaire de l'Institut* (1952), p. 251 *et seq.*) and at the New York Conference of the International Law Association, following the nationalisation by Egypt of the Suez Canal Company (*Report of the 48th Conference* (1958), pp. 130 *et seq.* and 654–655), and the Report in *The New York Times*, September 8, 1958.
See also below, pp. 7 and 65 *et seq.*

[4] See below, pp. 95 and 162, and, further, 6 B.D.I.L., pp. 350–351, and G. C. Christie, 38 B.Y.I.L. (1962), p. 307 *et seq.*

[5] See below, pp. 120, and 163 *et seq.*

[6] See, further, *Fundamental Principles*, p. 372 *et seq.*

available on the subject. Thus, against this background, the expropriation rule set out above has been formulated.[7]

(b) Public Contracts

The specialised rules of international law applicable to public contracts between subjects and objects of international law can be stated in six propositions:

(1) In substance, if not necessarily in form, public contracts are consensual engagements between subjects and objects of international law. The presumption is in favour of these contracts being governed by municipal law. In such cases, it depends on the municipal law in question whether transactions in this category are to be construed as contracts or unilateral acts and as pertaining to the field of private or public law.[8]

(2) It is a matter of the intention of the contracting parties whether the law of the contract is to be the municipal law of the State party to the contract, that of any other State, an abstraction from municipal law such as the general principles of law recognised by civilised nations or a system of quasi-international law.[9]

(3) If parties stipulate for the application of international law, this may mean one of two things. Either the subject of international law concerned intends—effectively or otherwise [10]—to bestow on the other

[7] See, for instance, the Judgment of the Permanent Court of International Justice on *Certain German Interests in Polish Upper Silesia* (Germany-Poland—1926), Series A 7, pp. 21–22 and 42; Cheng, *General Principles*, pp. 37 *et seq.* and 122–123; Vol. I, p. 200 *et seq.*; the cases and literature listed in *Banco Nacional de Cuba* v. *Sabbatino et al.* (1962—Court of Appeals), 35 I.L.R., p. 11, at pp. 17–18, and in B. A. Wortley, *Expropriation in International Law* (1959), pp. 34–35.

[8] See 4 *Répertoire Français* (1962), p. 287 *et seq.*, *Whiteman Digest*, Vol. 8 (1967), p. 1071 *et seq.*; for the relevant case law, Vol. I, p. 146 *et seq.*, and 5 C.L.P. (1952), p. 312 *et seq.*; for earlier statements of the law, *Kreuger-Anleihen* (1931), p. 9 *et seq.*, and (*contra*) F. A. Mann, 21 B.Y.I.L. (1944), p. 11 *et seq.*, and, further, H. Mosler, *Wirtschaftskonzessionen bei Aenderung der Staatshoheit* (1948), p. 65 *et seq.*; K. S. Carlston, *Law and Organisation in World Society* (1962), p. 10 *et seq.*; Th. T. F. Huang, 51 A.J.I.L. (1957), p. 289 *et seq.*; H. O. Calvert, 1 *University of Malaya L.R.* (1959), p. 265 *et seq.*; F. A. Mann, 35 B.Y.I.L. (1959), p. 34 *et seq.*; Ch. M. Spofford, 113 Hague *Recueil* (1964), p. 197 *et seq.*; W. Wengler, *Völkerrecht*, Vol. 2 (1964), p. 1017, n. 1; H. Cattan, *The Law of Oil Concessions in the Middle East and North Africa* (1967), p. 4 *et seq.*; M. El-Sayed, *L'Organisation des Pays Exportateurs de Pétrole* (1967), p. 71 *et seq.*, and, for an East German view, G. Brehme, *Souveränität der jungen Nationalstaaten über Naturreichtümer* (1967), p. 175 *et seq.*, especially on relevant Communist literature.

The relevant passage in the decision of June 25, 1963, of the Saudi Arabian Council of Ministers, limiting the use of arbitration clauses in government contracts, also deserves to be noted: "The law applicable to disputes to which the State is a party shall be determined in accordance with the established general principles of international law, the most important of which is the principle of the application of the law pertaining to the place of execution. Government agencies may not choose any foreign law to govern their relationship with such individuals, companies or private organisations (Section 3—3 I.L.M. (1964), p. 45). See also below, p. 151, note 75.

[9] See, further, below, p. 13, note 34, and A. Verdross, 18 Y.B.W.A. (1964), p. 230 *et seq.*

[10] In a legal system which is as individualistic as is international law in unorganised international society, any limitation of the right of existing subjects to grant recognition to certain categories of objects of international law only cannot be presumed. Yet, any such act of recognition is purely relative and does not commit any third parties. See, further, *Fundamental Principles*, p. 228 *et seq.*

party international personality for purposes of particular contractual relations or, in all probability, the parties agree to apply to the contract international law by way of analogy and, thus, subject it to a régime of quasi-international law.[11]

(4) A lawfully concluded public contract is a property or " vested " right in the technical meaning attached to the term by the Permanent Court of International Justice.[12] If the other party is a foreign national, his contractual rights, like any other property rights,[13] are protected by international law against confiscation by the State party to the contract.

(5) In the case of a public contract subject to the municipal law of the State party to it, but not protected by express undertakings against the future exercise of legislative powers or administrative discretion, the State party to the contract may interfere with the contract on grounds of public interest.[14] A renunciation of the future exercise of these powers cannot be presumed. Yet, in such a contingency, it must grant full, prompt and effective compensation. Otherwise, such interference amounts to a tortious act under international law.[15]

(6) If in a public contract which, otherwise, is subject to the law of the State party to it, the other party has been promised freedom from future legislative or administrative interference, such a promise crystallises the relations between the parties on the basis of the municipal law as it existed at the time when the public contract was made.

Under a particular municipal law, State organs may be prohibited from entering commitments of this type. Yet, if, in fact, they do so in relation to foreign nationals, they are presumed to have acted constitutionally and within the limits of their authority. In principle, foreign nationals cannot be expected to doubt the word of the highest authorities of a sovereign State. Any purported repudiation of their obligations by such State organs amounts to an elementary breach of good faith, an act of *venire contra factum proprium.*[16]

There is only an apparent exception to the rule. If the incapacity of State organs to enter a public contract or to undertake certain obligations is common knowledge or has been specifically brought to the attention of the other party before the conclusion of the contract, the State party to the contract incurs no tortious liability under international law. The other party's actual or imputed knowledge rules out any breach of good faith in this respect.

Every State has the right to expect that its nationals abroad will be treated in good faith. If a State breaks its obligations of non-interference

[11] See *loc. cit.* in note 9 above.
[12] See above, p. 5, note 7, and, further, 5 C.L.P. (1952), p. 312, n. 52.
[13] See below, p. 17.
[14] See above, p. 4, and below, pp. 161–162.
[15] See above, p. 4.
[16] See further, *Fundamental Principles*, p. 290 *et seq.*

with a public contract which it has concluded with foreign nationals, it acts in bad faith and contravenes the minimum standard of international law in favour of such foreign nationals and the general principles of law recognised by civilised nations.[17]

If the parties to a public contract agree to submit the contract to a legal system other than that of the State party to the contract, this intention further strengthens the case of the other party against unilateral interference by the State concerned. It emphasises even more clearly the intention of the contracting parties to take the contract out of the context of the municipal law, present and future, of the State party to the consensual engagement.

(c) A Vanishing Consensus?

In a recent United Nations document it has been suggested that there is a "vanishing consensus" on the rules of international customary law for the protection of foreign investments.[18] It has also been argued that the ordinary rules of international law on expropriation do not apply to cases of profound or large-scale social change, resulting in general policies of nationalisation [19]; that the existing law on the subject has been profoundly affected by the population explosion among the subjects of international law [20] and that, in contemporary international law, the quantum of compensation due in cases of expropriation is more correctly expressed in terms such as adequate [21] or partial,[22] rather than full, compensation.

[17] See, *loc. cit.* in note 16 above and, further, Vol. I, p. 562 *et seq.*

[18] United Nations. Department of Economic and Social Affairs. *The External Financing of Economic Development* (1968—E.68.II. D.10), Section 84 (p. 31).

Similarly, the United States Supreme Court in *Banco Nacional de Cuba* v. *Sabbatino* (1964): "There are few if any issues in international law today on which opinion seems to be so divided as the limitations on a State's power to expropriate the property of aliens" (376 U.S. 398, at p. 428—1964).

[19] S. Friedman, *Expropriation in International Law* (1953), p. 206 *et seq.*; K. Katzarov, *The Theory of Nationalisation* (1964), p. 349 *et seq.*; I. Brownlie, *Principles of Public International Law* (1966), p. 437; C. F. Amerasinghe, *State Responsibility for Injuries to Aliens* (1967), p. 121 *et seq.*

For an intermediate view see M. Sørensen (ed.), *Manual of Public International Law* (1968), p. 485 *et seq.*

See further, *Kreuger-Anleihen* (1931), p. 39 *et seq.*; I. Foighel, *Nationalisation* (1957), p. 16 *et seq.*, and G. Fouilloux, *La Nationalisation et le droit international public* (1962), p. 474 *et seq.*

[20] See below, pp. 9 and 185 *et seq.*

[21] See, for instance, the Note communicated by the Minister of the United Kingdom to the Rumanian Minister for Foreign Affairs on September 7, 1948, which is instructive on this point and other matters of principle: "His Majesty's Government considers that compensation in the form of bonds on the fund of nationalised industry apparently redeemable from the eventual profits of the individual nationalised undertakings, cannot be considered to provide the prompt adequate and effective compensation which accepted principles of international law require. While His Majesty's Government does not dispute the right of a sovereign power to expropriate interests subject to its jurisdiction and belonging to British subjects, it must, nevertheless, refuse to recognise the validity of such expropriations when they are discriminatory in their nature and effects and when provisions for equitable evaluation and for prompt, adequate and effective compensation are not provided by the expropriating Government. In view of the nature of

(*ctd. overleaf*)

[22] For footnote, see p. 8.

The issues at stake in these controversies affect merely the always fluctuating contents of the minimum standard of international customary law regarding the protection of foreign property. The burden of proof regarding any asserted change in the established contents of the minimum standard lies on those who assert that, in any respect, the preponderant number of subjects of international law have ceased to accept the traditional standard as law. The fact that most of the contemporary subjects of international law are poor, and that a good many of them are hardly "viable" in economic terms or prefer to default on their obligations is scarcely an acceptable substitute for evidence of a changing *convictio juris.*

(1) *Specialised Rules for Nationalisation*? In principle, it is left to every sovereign State to decide for itself on its internal political, social and economic structure. This is the quintessence of the rules governing the principle of sovereignty. Yet, the difference between political and legal sovereignty in international relations is that, under international law, a sovereign State may *exercise* its sovereignty only subject to compliance with all other rules of international law.[23]

It is difficult to see why the mere scale of expropriation measures, as compared with individual acts of expropriation, or the rise of new ideologies should by themselves exempt such policies of nationalisation from the operation of the governing rules of international customary law. Similarly, even a whole series of bilateral agreements, embodying settlements of claims for the nationalisation of property rights on a footing of partial compensation, hardly constitutes by itself evidence of any change in the relevant rules of international customary law. British treaty practice—like that of other capital-exporting States—suggests that such treaties are the result of complex and highly pragmatic considerations, but

(*Note 21 ctd.*)
the Rumanian legislation and its application to United Kingdom interests, His Majesty's Government therefore reserves all rights of British subjects and demands either restitution or prompt, adequate and effective compensation for the properties nationalised under that legislation, as also the satisfaction of British financial claims in general, including some £20,000,000 of bonded debts."

The trend towards further vagueness in compromise formulas which mean all things to all men is illustrated by related terms such as "appropriate" compensation in the Resolution on Permanent Sovereignty adopted by the U.N. General Assembly of 1962 (Res. 1803—XVII), or the formula of "reasonably adequate and reasonably prompt" compensation. See, further, W. Friedmann, *A.S.I.L. Proceedings*, 1963, pp. 127–128, Para. 187 of the *Restatement of the Law, Second—Foreign Relations Law of the United States* (1965), p. 563, and S. D. Metzger, *Law of International Trade*, Vol. I (1966), p. 112 *et seq.*

See also below, pp. 10 and 65 *et seq.*

22 Introduced into Oppenheim's *International Law*, Vol. I, Paragraph 155d in the 5th ed. (1937—ed. H. Lauterpacht). See, however, R. L. Bindschedler, *Verstaatlichungsmassnahmen und Entschädigungspflicht nach Völkerrecht* (1950), p. 17 *et seq.*

23 See, further, *Fundamental Principles*, p. 214 *et seq.*, and 10 C.L.P. (1957), p. 264 *et seq.*, and also A. Larson and Others, *Sovereignty within the Law* (1965), p. 332 *et seq.*

not of any change in the governing rule of international customary law by desuetude.[24]

The Soviet Union can be cited as the crown witness to contradict any suggestion of a " new " rule of international law which is supposed to apply to large-scale nationalisation. Even in the " heroic " phase—in Trotsky's terminology—of the October Revolution of 1917, the Soviet Union did not base its arguments exclusively on the " revolutionary-legal conceptions of the Russian people." In rejecting the claims of Russia's former allies for the repayment of loans made to Czarist Russia and compensation for the expropriation of foreign-owned property, the Soviet Government relied at least as much on more traditional justifications for its refusal. One was set-off claims for the damages suffered by the Soviet Union from the armed interventions staged by the Allied Powers in Russia. Another was the incompatibility with the public policy (*ordre publique* or *jus cogens*) of the Soviet Union of the loans made for purposes of maintaining the Czarist regime and encouraging Russian militarism. Similarly, in its subsequent treaty practice, the Soviet Union itself was hardly inhibited in accepting exacting clauses for the protection of foreign property.[25]

(2) *The Impact of New States.* When a new State is recognised as a subject of international law, this is done on an assumption made by the recognising State and for a purpose. The assumption is that the new subject of international law takes the rules of general international customary law existing at the time as it finds them. The purpose of recognition is to enable the parties concerned to conduct their relations in accordance with the rules of international customary law and consensual engagements, founded on these rules. Thus, views subsequently expressed by newly recognised States on their non-acceptance of particular rules of international law are legally relevant only in the context of the assertion of a general change in the formerly prevailing *convictio juris*. Otherwise,

24 See, further, Vol. I. p. 537 *et seq.*, and, for a different emphasis, for instance, C. W. Jenks, *The Common Law of Mankind* (1958), p. 29, and B. V. A. Röling, *International Law in an Expanded World* (1960), p. 73 *et seq.*

In this context, the treaties, concluded between Communist States and containing compensation clauses, are of particular interest. See, further, A. Drucker, 10 I.C.L.Q. (1961), p. 238 *et seq.*

25 See, further, J. Degras, *Soviet Documents on Foreign Policy*, Vol. I (1951), pp. 98, 124, 130, 138, 191–193, 220–221 (Decree of the Council of People's Commissars on the General and Legal Conditions for Concessions, November 23, 1920), pp. 313–314, 425, 449, 451 and 455–456; Article XI of the Trade Agreement of March 16, 1921, between Great Britain and the Soviet Union (L. Shapiro (ed.), *Soviet Treaty Series*, Vol. I (1950), p. 104); Article VI of the Treaty of Commerce and Navigation of February 7, 1924, between Italy and the Soviet Union (*ibid.*, p. 228); Article VIII of the Agreement of October 12, 1925, between Germany and the Soviet Union concerning Conditions of Residence and Business and Legal Protection in General (*ibid*, p. 1925) and addition to Article VIII in the Final Protocol of the same date (*ibid.*, p. 300).

In the case of the nationalisation of the Petsamo Nickel Mines, the Soviet Union recognised the principle of " full and final " compensation (Protocol of October 8, 1944, between Canada and the United Kingdom and the Soviet Union, Cmd. 6586 (1945), p. 11, as modified by the Protocol of September 29, 1947, U.N.T.S., Vol. 45, p. 125).

See also above, note 24.

such pronouncements merely serve warning of the dubious law-abidingness of the States concerned.[26]

Actually, the written constitutions of new States abound as much as those of old States with clauses affirming the protection of private and public property, and the growing number of statutes on the protection and encouragement of foreign investments are cast in a similar vein. Thus, in the last resort, the governing rules of international customary law could also be formulated in terms of a general principle of law recognised by civilised nations.[27]

(3) *Full or Partial Compensation*? It has been suggested that as expropriation in the public interest is lawful, insistence on full compensation in this case would blur the border line between lawful and tortious acts under international law. Actually, in strict law, if not necessarily in practice, an essential difference exists between the rules of international law governing the two situations. In the case of expropriation, the duty is one of compensation. In that of international torts, the primary duty is restoration of the *status quo* prior to the commission of the international tort.[28]

The difference between the terms " full " and " adequate " compensation is merely one between synonyms. A claimant is likely to consider full compensation in accordance with his own petition to be adequate. Conversely, compensation considered adequate by an impartial third party, but falling short of a claimant's exaggerated expectations is not necessarily less than full compensation. If, in this book, the term " full " compensation is preferred to that of " adequate " compensation, it is to a purpose. This formulation appears to bring out more precisely the actual rule on the question of damages.[29]

Such discrepancies as exist in judicial practice are the inevitable result of the exercise of an essentially equitable jurisdiction in accordance with a rule as relative as that of the minimum standard.

The combined effect of the presumptions in favour of the good faith and law-abidingness of all subjects of international law is likely to be

[26] See, further, *Inductive Approach*, p. 175 *et seq.*, and, for a different emphasis, for instance, W. Friedmann, *The Changing Structure of International Law* (1964), p. 317 *et seq.*

[27] See, further, A. J. Peaslee, *Constitutions of Nations* (4 vols.—1966), and below, p. 188.

[28] See, further, Vol. I, p. 653 *et seq.*, and D. P. O'Connell, *International Law*, Vol. II (1965), p. 861 *et seq.*

[29] For use of this terminology by the Soviet Union, see above, p. 9, note 25, and below, p. 98.

See, further, Bin Cheng, 44 *Grotius Society Transactions* (1958–59), p. 294; K.-H. Boeckstiegel, *Die allgemeinen Grundsätze des Völkerrechts über Eigentumsentziehung* (1963), pp. 83–84, and *loc. cit.* in note 7 above.

The term " full " compensation is also employed in the Resolution on Nationalisation adopted at the New York Conference of the International Law Association (*Report of the 48th Conference*, 1948, p. XI). Similarly, in A. Verdross, *Völkerrecht* (1964), p. 366, and the American Law Institute, *Restatement of the Law, Second, Foreign Relations of the United States* (1965), pp. 563–565, " adequate " and " full " compensation are used as synonyms. See also Whiteman, *Digest*, Vol. 8 (1967), p. 1143 *et seq.*

that international judicial institutions tend to confirm, rather than contest, the assertion of a State that it has resorted to expropriation in the public interest.

Similarly, what amounts to "full," "prompt" and "effective" compensation is a matter of judgment. According to international judicial practice, *full* compensation is the market value of the expropriated property. Yet, anybody who has any practical experience with the valuation of any property knows how widely even experts may differ on the market value of any such property. If the property involved is complex and liable to suffer in value through technological changes or, because of the absence of other comparable properties, the market value of a property is rather hypothetical, the subjective factors involved in any such valuation multiply.

Moreover, in equity, *prompt* compensation does not necessarily mean immediate compensation. It means compensation after a reasonable interval of discussions on all the relevant aspects of the expropriation, including the market value of the property concerned.

Finally, what is *effective* compensation depends very much on the uses the claimant desires to make of the compensation granted. According to his varying circumstances, compensation in the local currency, or only in a transferable form, may constitute effective compensation.

If these aspects of the matter are sufficiently taken into account, the limited practical significance of the theoretical arguments in favour of any of the various formulations advanced becomes apparent. Yet, even so, it is helpful to know what, by international law, is the most accurately defined starting point of any discussion between parties or judicial decision-making in concrete cases.

2—Objects of the Book

The real difficulties do not appear to lie in ascertaining the relevant rules of international law on the protection of foreign investments. As with other rules of international law in unorganised or partly organised international society, these difficulties arise from the lack of provision for the, if necessary, compulsory ascertainment and analysis of the legally relevant facts by an impartial authority and the enforcement of these rules through legally controlled processes.

Thus, the object of this book is threefold:

(1) to explore how these difficulties have been met in British practice; for, in more ways than one, this experience may claim to be of general interest [30];

(2) to analyse and evaluate the contribution made by multilateral efforts of recent years to the more effective application and enforcement of these rules;

[30] See below, p. 21.

(3) to respond, from the angle of International Economic Law, to the call sent out by the United Nations Conference on Trade and Development to study the various aspects of foreign private investment, with particular reference to developing countries.[31]

3—Complexities, Methods and Assumptions

Metalegal factors make the subject of the protection of foreign investments by international law more sensitive and controversial than its purely legal aspects would suggest. Some of these issues touch on the emotive aspects of the very object to be protected: property. They are intensified by the foreign character of the property involved and the sheer scale of such investments. They are further accentuated by the close links between international economics and the major issues of contemporary world politics: the deep divisions in contemporary world society and the ideological complexities of phenomena such as decolonisation, neo-colonialism and neo-imperialism.[32]

Some of these statements require further elaboration:

(a) Law and Property

In any mature legal system, the law of property counts among the most technical branches of the law. It needs the change of but one word, and a more formidable subject emerges: law *and* property. Now, we no longer think of the writers of standard textbooks on personal or real property, but of revolutionaries in the field of property relations: William the Conqueror, Henry VIII, Pizarro, Cortez, Lenin, Stalin, Mao Tse-tung and, perhaps, even tragicomic figures such as Hitler, Musaddiq and Sukarno.

Behind the technicalities of the more sophisticated systems of property law lie, shrewdly hidden, the fundamental political, social and economic decisions on which these legal rules are based. Once they are laid bare, we have uncovered one of the deepest roots of this law. It then becomes easier to understand why a subject that, on the surface, is merely technical is inextricably bound up with the most crucial decisions any social group has to make.

[31] Section E, Paragraph 10 of the Recommendation of UNCTAD on Promotion of Private Foreign Investment in Developing Countries, June 15, 1964 (Annex IV. 12 to Final Act of UNCTAD).

See also the Resolution of the United Nations General Assembly 1710 (XVI), calling upon member States to " adopt measures which will stimulate the flow of private investment capital for the economic development of the developing countries on terms that are satisfactory both to the capital-exporting countries and the capital-importing countries "; Resolution 33 (II), adopted by the Second UNCTAD Conference, on Increasing the Flow of Private Capital to Developing Countries (TD/II/RES/33, March 29, 1968), and the Charter of Algiers (October 24, 1967), adopted at a ministerial meeting of 77 Developing Countries, 7 I.L.M. (1968), p. 177, at p. 191; and below, p. 200, note 61.

On terminology, see below, p. 15.

[32] See, further, *Power Politics*, p. 488 *et seq.*

All the more do these considerations apply if we analyse these problems not in the shelter of highly integrated communities, but in the turbulent environment of world society. Even in a gentlemanly age, Palmerston's vigorous—or impetuous—action in the *Don Pacifico* case (1850) [33] raised tempers to a remarkable degree. Similarly, the heart-searching inter-British debate in the Twenties on the rules of international law applicable to the protection of property abroad was exceptionally animated.[34]

(b) The Size of the Issue

The world total investments abroad at the end of 1966 were estimated at $90 billion, and the value of private British long-term investments overseas at £9·6 billion.[35]

In 1967, the total earnings from these British overseas investments were thought to be £438 million and, during the same year, a further £267 million were privately invested overseas.[36]

Accumulated direct foreign investments by capital-exporters in less developed countries [37] were estimated to have amounted to $30 billion at the end of 1966 [38] and, between 1964 and 1966, the annual private capital export from members of the Development Assistance Committee (D.A.C.) of the Organisation for Economic Co-operation and Development to developing countries [39] averaged $3·5 billion, of which $2 billion were private investment. Annual governmental capital exports during the same period amounted to $6·1 billion.[40]

33 39 B.F.S.P. (1849–1850), p. 410 *et seq.*
Actually, Palmerston frequently exercised a restraining influence. See, for instance, the *Wallis Case* (28 *ibid.* (1839–1840), p. 966) or Palmerston's Circular to British Representatives in Foreign States, respecting Debts due by Foreign States to British Subjects, January, 1848 (42 *ibid.* (1852–1853), pp. 385–386).

34 A. P. Fachiri and John Fischer Williams, 6 B.Y.I.L. (1925), p. 159 *et seq.*; 9 *ibid.* (1928), p. 1 *et seq.*, and 10 *ibid.* (1929), p. 32 *et seq.*
See also the concluding remarks of the Rapporteur at the Siena Session of the *Institut de Droit International* (*loc. cit.* in note 3 above, p. 322): "*Les débats . . . ont révélé que plusieurs membres sont influencés dans leur votes et dans leur interventions par des considérations d'espèces*"; G. Brehme's comments as *tertius gaudens* on the Verdross-Mann controversy, *loc. cit.* above, p. 5, note 8, p. 233, and below, p. 14, note 44.

35 O.E.C.D., *Background Paper* on Private Investment in Less Developed Countries, May 6, 1968 (Press/A (68) 23, p. 2) and *An Inventory of U.K. External Assets and Liabilities: end-1966* (*Bank of England Quarterly Bulletin*, September 1967, p. 263). Actually, at the end of 1966, U.K. private long-term overseas liabilities were £4·2 billion, giving an excess of assets over liabilities of £5·4 billion (*ibid.* p. 267).
See also A. R. Conan (formerly Assistant Secretary of the Commonwealth Economic Committee), *Britain as Creditor, The Listener*, December 28, 1967, p. 837, British National Export Council, *Britain's Invisible Earnings* (1967), and the Written Answer by the Financial Secretary to the Treasury, H.C.Deb., Vol. 747, col. 131 (June 5, 1967).
1 billion, as used in this book, equals 1,000 million.

36 M. Corina, *The Times* (London), July 19, 1968.

37 O.E.C.D. terminology (*loc. cit.* above in note 35, p. 2). See also below, p. 15.

38 O.E.C.D. *Background Paper*, *loc. cit.* above in note 35, p. 2.

39 See *ibid.*, p. 2.

40 *Ibid.*, pp. 1–2, and U.N. Doc. on *International Flow of Long-Term Capital and Official Donations* (E/4170/Add. 2, Table 2, p. 3).

Roughly half of all present private foreign investments in less developed countries [41] is concentrated in the oil industry (Near and Middle East, North Africa, Venezuela and the Netherlands Antilles) and mineral-extracting industries (Latin America, Central Africa and Malaysia).[42]

In order to view these figures in a commensurate perspective, it should be mentioned that annual new investments in the United States of America alone were in 1965 nearly $100 billion, and that half of this amount was spent on new plant and equipment.[43]

(c) Emotive Overtones

The quantitative tests available for assessing the vested interests involved should suffice to put any disinterested student on his guard. If further evidence of the dangers and temptations besetting him in this field were required, they are furnished by splendid specimens of special pleading, emotive language and a touching, but self-neutralising reliance on conservative, reformist and revolutionary variants of natural law. In this atmosphere, international lawyers who employ such loaded terminologies should not be expected to refer to those holding different views when they speak or write of forward-looking, progressive or constructive views on these topics. These epithets are strictly reserved to those of the same hue, be it blue, pink or red.[44]

(d) The Methods Applied

In these circumstances, it is essential that the reader should not only be able to verify for himself any controversial statement, but also its methodological basis.

As in previous writings, the methods adopted in this book are those of an inductive, inter-disciplinary and relativist treatment of the subject.

It is *inductive* in that the applicable rules of international law are determined by reference to the hierarchy of law-creating processes, law-determining agencies and elements of such agencies laid down or implied in Article 38 of the Statute of the International Court of Justice, and legal principles are treated as mere abstractions, primarily for purposes of teaching and classification, from the operative rules of international law.[45]

It is *inter-disciplinary* in that whenever the complexity of a phenomenon under investigation makes it necessary, free use is made of the assistance

[41] O.E.C.D. *Background Paper*, *loc. cit.* in note 35 above, p. 4.

[42] *Ibid.*, p. 2.

[43] J. J. Kaplan, *The Challenge of Foreign Aid* (1967), p. 178.

[44] On the " partisan setting " of the problem, see R. S. Miller in R. S. Miller and R. J. Stanger (eds.), *Essays on Expropriation* (1967), p. V *et seq.* See also above, p. 13, note 34.

On the iconological significance of the symptoms discussed, see 19 C.L.P. (1967), p. 192 *et seq.*

[45] See, further, *Inductive Approach*, p. 19 *et seq.*

to be derived from other related disciplines of international studies, in particular that of International Relations.[46]

It is *relativist* in that the draft conventions to be analysed in Part Two are subject to transcendental and immanent forms of criticism, characteristic of another related discipline: that of International Legislation.[47]

(e) Major Assumptions

Three major assumptions are made in this book:

(1) The exposition of any rules of *lex lata* should remain unaffected by subjective evaluation—positive or negative—of new, emerging, developing, less developed or underdeveloped nations.[48]

(2) So long as views held on political or moral grounds on this topic are kept in a watertight compartment of their own, their disclosure helps rather than hinders a detached legal analysis. My own personal view happens to be that, even on grounds of enlightened self-interest, the affluent nations would be well advised to treat the issue of assistance to the world's poor South *as if*, by generous help, the problem were soluble.[49]

(3) Double-talk in this emotion-laden field is even more dangerous than in others. Thus, when what is meant is trade, it is inadvisable to speak of aid and *vice versa.* Even more so, utter frankness to the point of stating the obvious (to some, but not necessarily to others) is to be commended in the drafting of any conventions to which capital-exporting *and* capital-importing States are intended to be parties.[50]

If, in this frame of mind, international lawyers face the breeze of change coming up from the poor South, they will at least avoid being reduced to mere straws if ever this wind should rise.

4—Terminology

A few key-words require explanation and definition:

(a) Capital-exporting and Capital-importing Countries

Some of the terms employed for purposes of distinction between " have " and " have-not " States suffer from subjective and question-begging elements.

Thus, the distinction between advanced and backward countries appears to rest on inarticulate technological tests or undisclosed criteria relating

46 See, further, *Inductive Approach*, p. 56 *et seq.*

47 *Ibid.*, p. 65 *et seq.*, and *Power Politics*, p. 524 *et seq.*

48 See, further, below, pp. 16 and 185 *et seq.*

49 To enable poor States to achieve the rate of economic growth postulated in relevant U.N. resolutions, these countries would need additional annual aid on a scale which is estimated at amounts varying between $5 billion and 20 billion. See, further, Kaplan, *loc. cit.* above, p. 14, note 43, p. 159.

According to the Soviet Academician A. Sakharov, to help the poor countries to raise their standards of living effectively would require a 15-year tax on wealthy countries, equal to 20 per cent. of their national income (*The Times* (London), July 22, 1968).

50 See below, pp. 110, 143, and 155 *et seq.*

to the level of civilisation (further query: which ?) particular countries have attained.[51]

Similarly, the categories of undeveloped, underdeveloped, lessdeveloped, developed and, perhaps, overdeveloped countries give the impression of being based on questionable assumptions of an " ideal " balance between agriculture and industry and an unstated optimal ratio between man-power and machine-power.

For some purposes, the distinction between rich, poor and very poor countries provides an adequate classification. However relative the underlying standard is, at least it is rationally verifiable.

In the context of foreign investments, probably the most useful distinction is that between *capital-exporting* and *capital-importing* countries. Admittedly, one and the same State may fall into both categories. Yet, in most cases, one or the other characteristic predominates.[52]

(b) Decolonisation, Neo-colonialism and Neo-imperialism

Subject to suitable decontamination of their ideological associations, the terms *decolonisation, neo-colonialism* and *neo-imperialism* have their uses.

Decolonisation summarises the process by which salt-water colonialism is terminated.

Salt-water colonisation must be distinguished from overland colonisation of contiguous areas. Both have in common that the colonising Power has acquired political control of territories which are inhabited by ethnically distinct populations. Yet, owing to the tactical needs of relying in their anti-colonialist campaigns, in and outside the United Nations, on the support of the Soviet Union, in the post-1945 parlance of the " third " world the term is limited to salt-water colonialism. Nor, and for similarly tactical reasons, does it extend to countries whose indigenous populations—that is, earlier immigrants—have been exterminated or reduced to parasitic existence in tribal reservations.

If limited to forms of direct domination, the term *neo-colonialism* is helpful. It then denotes the reduction to a state of subjection of ethnic minorities in former colonies which, since 1945, have become independent States, mostly also sovereign and equal members of the United Nations and, as a rule, resolute opponents of the application of the principle of national self-determination in favour of their own ethnic minorities.

By way of contrast, the term *neo-imperialism* can be employed to describe those indirect forms of political, economic and military control

[51] See, further, *The Frontiers*, p. 65 *et seq*.

[52] A useful by-product of the application of this test is that it shakes preconceived notions on the predestined places of particular countries in the order of things. While, from this point of view, some of the Arab oil-producing countries fall into the same category as the major Western Powers, other States usually associated with the latter, such as Australia, Canada or New Zealand, are on the other side of this particular divide.

On U.N. terminology in this field, see Ü. Kirdar, *The Structure of United Nations Aid to Underdeveloped Countries* (1966), p. 1 *et seq*.

which, in our contemporary system of world power politics in disguise, stronger States tend to exercise over weaker fellow-members of the United Nations.[53]

(c) Investments and Property

The terms *investments* and *property* are treated as synonyms and cover all types of interests and rights in property.

Thus, unless otherwise stated, *foreign investments* are intended to include proprietary and portfolio investments abroad, as well as medium- and long-term credits or loans for the import of equipment or services into another country. In accordance with a widely accepted current usage, medium-term credits are considered to extend from two to five years,[54] and long-term credits are those granted for a longer period.

Such a liberal formulation of property and investments corresponds to the general practice of international law. More formally, property or investments in international law can be defined as including all rights and interests in anything owned or possessed, whether movable or immovable, tangible or intangible.[55]

(d) Expropriation and Confiscation

In any legal systems in which a line can be drawn between legal and illegal forms of interference by the State with property rights, it is advisable to limit the term *expropriation* to lawful forms of such interference.

Thus, *expropriation* in international law signifies lawful forms of interference with foreign property rights by a territorial sovereign or any of its subordinate organs in accordance with international law.[56]

By way of contrast, the term *confiscation* is limited to any form of such interference amounting to an international tort.

[53] See, further, *Power Politics*, p. 491 *et seq.*

[54] For different definitions in the context of particular agreements see, for instance, Article I of the Loan Agreement of September 15, 1966, between Argentina and the United Kingdom, Cmnd. 3215 (1967), p. 3, and Article 2 of the Agreement of February 27, 1967, between Ghana and the United Kingdom, Cmnd. 3247 (1967), p. 3.

[55] See, for instance, B. A. Wortley, *Expropriation in International Law* (1959), p. 8 *et seq.*; G. White, *Nationalisation of Foreign Property* (1961), pp. 266–267, and Katzarov, *loc. cit.* in note 19 above, p. 102 *et seq.*

[56] See above, p. 4.

PART ONE

THE PROTECTION OF INVESTMENTS ABROAD IN THE MIRROR OF BRITISH PRACTICE

CHAPTER 2

THE EVOLUTION AND SCOPE OF THE GOVERNING RULES

BRITISH practice concerning the protection of investments abroad—like on most other topics of international law [1]—has unique characteristics. Four of these are directly relevant:

(1) Since the time of the Norman Conquest, England—since 1707, Great Britain and, since 1932, the United Kingdom—can claim an unparalleled continuity in her practice of international law.

(2) Great Britain led the industrial revolutions of the eighteenth and nineteenth centuries and, as the foremost colonial and maritime Power, was in an exceptionally favourable position to gain wide acceptance for her views of internationally acceptable conduct.[2]

(3) Beginning with the decolonisation of her American empire at the end of the eighteenth century and the "old" Dominions in the early decades of this century, Great Britain was the first object of contemporary anti-colonialism and, subsequently, became the chief active agent in a process of voluntary withdrawal from her colonial and imperial roles.

(4) As the cradle of Anglo-American law and in its position on the Atlantic fringe of Western Europe, the United Kingdom continues to form a bridge between the legal systems of the transatlantic and Continental capital-exporting States as well as between the Anglo-American legal systems and those of a considerable number of new independent States.[3]

1—THE EVOLUTION OF THE GOVERNING RULES

Looking at the governing rules in historical perspective, a distinction must first be made between the protection of foreign property in times of peace and war. The evolution of the rules on enemy and neutral property in land warfare is essentially the product of compromises between two chief formative factors: the necessities of war and the standard of civilisation.[4]

[1] See, further, *The Frontiers*, p. 85 *et seq.*

[2] See B.D.I.L.; *The Frontiers*, p. 130 *et seq.*, and *Most-Favoured-Nation Standard*, p. 96 *et seq.*

[3] See, for instance, O. W. Holmes, *The Common Law* (1881); R. Pound, *The Spirit of the Common Law* (1921); Frederick Pollock, *The Expansion of the Common Law* (1904); R. H. Graveson, *The Restless Spirit of English Law* in G. W. Keeton and G. Schwarzenberger (eds.), *Jeremy Bentham and the Law* (1948), p. 101 *et seq.*; F. H. Lawson, *The Rational Strength of English Law* (1951); W. W. Buckland and Sir Arnold McNair (ed. F. H. Lawson), *Roman Law and Common Law* (1952); A. L. Goodhart, *English Law and the Moral Law* (1953), and L. A. Sheridan, 18 C.L.P. (1965), p. 61 *et seq.*

[4] See, further, Vol. II, pp. 9 and 582 *et seq.*

In sea warfare, the applicable rules are further complicated by the simultaneous use of the high seas by belligerents and neutrals.[5]

The international law applicable to property in a state of war contains so many rules of its own that it can safely be excluded from this survey. It is, however, indirectly relevant in that it establishes an absolute minimum standard. In no circumstances may the treatment of foreign nationals in times of peace or *status mixtus* between peace and war [6] fall below that accorded to enemy property.

Secondly, a distinction must be made between the evolution of the rules on State property and private property. British practice has given the lead in establishing the rule that, subject to minor reservations regarding immovable State property, the property of a sovereign State situated abroad is immune from the jurisdiction of the territorial State.[7] So far, British practice does not show any signs—beyond isolated judicial *obiter dicta* [8]—of yielding to pressures as they have been exerted in other countries [9] to whittle down this immunity or assert an unbridled discretionary power of the local sovereign over foreign State property.[10]

In contrast, the growth of the rules of international customary law on the protection of private property abroad was more complicated. It passed through three clearly discernible stages.

Initially, foreigners had to rely on such precarious protection as was granted to them and their property under safe-conducts or the municipal law of the State of residence.[11]

Gradually and pragmatically, international law in this field was elaborated in a multitude of treaties of commerce, navigation and establishment. These treaties apart, international law lacked any settled principles for the protection of private property abroad.[12]

During the nineteenth century, some of these optional treaty standards hardened into rules of international customary law or came to be considered as general principles of law recognised by civilised nations. The law as it had crystallised during this formative period has been outlined in the previous Chapter.[13]

This exposition requires to be supplemented in three respects:

(1) Compliance with the minimum standard of international law demands that the organisation of a State must correspond to reasonably defined minimum requirements of the Rule of Law in the Anglo-Saxon

[5] See, further, Vol. II, pp. 361 and 592 *et seq.*
[6] See *ibid.*, p. 38 *et seq.*
[7] See further, *Principles of I.E.L.*, pp. 35 and 92–93, and above, p. 3, note 1.
[8] See especially, *The Cristina* [1938] A.C. 485, and, further, *loc. cit.* above, note 7.
[9] See above, p. 3, note 1.
[10] For the evidence regarding early English practice, see *The Frontiers*, p. 123 *et seq.* On corresponding Scots and Continental practice, most of inductively verifiable research work yet waits to be done.
[11] See, further, *Most-Favoured-Nation Standard*, p. 96 *et seq.*
[12] See, further, *The Frontiers*, p. 130 *et seq.*
[13] See above, p. 3 *et seq.*

sense or in the meaning of the Continental *Rechtsstaat*. In particular, States must provide for an independent judiciary.[14]

(2) In circumstances in which the property is required for public purposes, the owner has a right to expect that his full, prompt and effective compensation will be established in judicial or quasi-judicial proceedings. Unless he has waived this right and consented to a settlement of the compensation by means of free negotiation, an expropriation which does not comply with these requirements amounts to illegal confiscation and is an international tort.[15]

(3) Even in the case of an illegal interference with property rights, a foreigner has first to exhaust all available local remedies. If he has done so or there has been a delay or denial of justice, it is for the home State to decide whether it desires to make the case of its national its own and take up the claim with the tortfeasor State on the international level.[16]

During the nineteenth and early twentieth centuries, these principles came to be generally accepted. Only in the case of new States and States with a bad record or on the fringes of the Western world was it still thought necessary to embody these standards expressly in treaties of commerce, establishment and navigation. As the leading commercial nation, Great Britain took the lead in this work of consolidating the minimum standards of international law. Through the automatism existing in any system of interlocking most-favoured-nation treaties, the benefits thus obtained for British merchants were liberally generalised, and this network of, on the whole, declaratory treaties gave even greater precision to the minimum standard of international law on the protection of property abroad.[17]

The law embodied in the minimum standard rested on three metalegal assumptions which, until 1914, were substantially correct:

(1) The State whose jurisdiction foreigners were meant to accept was the liberal State of the nineteenth century, the guardian of a capitalist economy and free enterprise. It could be trusted to exercise sparingly its indirect powers of interfering with private property such as, for instance, in the field of taxation or, at least, to limit excessive favouritism of its executive organs in favour of its own nationals.

(2) By common consent, the public purposes for which property might be lawfully expropriated were restrictively construed. If expropriation was

14 See B.D.I.L. (First Phase), Vol. 6, p. 247 *et seq.*; B.I.L.C., Vol. 5, p. 20 *et seq.*, and, further, *The Frontiers*, p. 130 *et seq.*; Vol. I, p. 200 *et seq.*, and *Principles of I.E.L.*, pp. 66 and 94 *et seq.*

For an outline of the history of expropriation in Western municipal law, see F. A. Mann, 75 L.Q.R. (1959), p. 188 *et seq.*, and, on eminent domain in Anglo-American law, E. D. Brown, 18 C.L.P. (1965), p. 169 *et seq.*

15 See above, p. 4 *et seq.*

16 See Vol. I, p. 562 *et seq.*

17 See, further, *The Frontiers*, p. 130 *et seq.*; *Most-Favoured-Nation Standard*, p. 96 *et seq.*, and, on the model treaty of 1825 between Great Britain and the United Provinces of Rio de la Plata (subsequently Argentina), below, p. 91, note 6.

unavoidable, liberal compensation was granted, and this was freely convertible and transferable.

(3) The British Navy maintained *Pax Britannica* and ensured that representations made by British envoys abroad received speedy and proper attention. Even beyond the reach of the British Navy, the key position of the City of London in international commerce ensured that foreign governments would not lightly tamper with the sacrosanctity of British investments abroad.

In the post-1919 period every one of these assumptions became increasingly problematic:

(1) State activities everywhere expanded to a marked extent, and the emphasis shifted sharply from the rights of the owners of private property to their social duties towards the community. Experiments ranged from mild but new forms of public and mixed enterprise *via* moderate programmes for the nationalisation of key industries and land reform to the more extreme measures taken by the Communist regime then emerging in Russia. Even governments which were emphatic in their protests against illegal interference with the property rights of their nationals abroad, exercised their sovereign right of taxation with growing enthusiasm in order to finance the expansion of their own State machineries.

(2) The public purposes for which expropriation came to be regarded as being legitimate correspondingly widened, and the tests of compensation became less favourable to private owners even in States which considered themselves to be standard-bearers of private enterprise. Moreover, policies of currency devaluation, including the abrogation of gold clauses, the establishment of exchange control and concomitant restrictions on the free transfer of capital abroad became common form.

(3) As a result of the First World War, the position of Great Britain and the City of London underwent significant changes. Great Britain had ceased to be the world's biggest banker and creditor, but had contracted huge political and private debts towards the United States. Yet, as the United States and Wall Street stepped into the shoes of Great Britain and the City of London, this more than balanced the change in Great Britain's international position.

It would be mistaken to assume that these structural changes meant the end of the minimum standard of international law for the protection of private property abroad. Most of the written constitutions of the post-1919 period attest to, at least, the lip-service States continued to pay to the principle of the sanctity of private property. Even the Soviet Union had to work its passage home into the nexus of international trade by accepting in a series of treaties stringent formulations of the rights of new investors in that country.[18]

[18] See above, p. 9, and, further, R. M. Slusser and J. F. Triska, *A Calendar of Soviet Treaties 1917–1957* (1959).

Moreover, the Permanent Court of International Justice did its best to stigmatise the measures of liquidation of enemy property under the Peace Treaties of 1919 as exceptions from the traditional rules of international customary law and to reaffirm the minimum standard of international law on the protection of private property abroad. In particular, the Court made it clear beyond doubt that, once the international standard had been violated, it was irrelevant if the State concerned applied the same treatment to its own nationals. Non-discrimination was not to be regarded as a justification for the breach of the minimum standard of international law.[19]

Nevertheless, the growing recognition of the need for a vast increase in State activities and extensive State control of economic life, and of the overriding right of States to limit the freedom of nationals and foreigners alike by means of unilateral exchange regulations, indicated a profound change in outlook. It found vivid expression in inconclusive debates on the subject in the League of Nations,[20] the division of expert opinion on issues such as the legality of the Rumanian land reform [21] and the deadlock between the United Kingdom and the United States, on the one hand, and Mexico, on the other, over the nationalisation of the British- and United States-owned Mexican oil companies.

The position taken in this dispute by both Anglo-Saxon Powers may be summed up in the words of one of the Notes of the United Kingdom Government to that of Mexico: "His Majesty's Government in the United Kingdom do not question the general right of a Government to expropriate in the public interest and on payment of adequate compensation; but this principle does not serve to justify expropriations essentially arbitrary in character." [22]

Even so, a defeatist tendency became noticeable to accept as inevitable a relaxation of the standards previously maintained and to exchange the minimum standard in favour of those of national or equitable treatment.

In the post-1945 period, the classical standard of the protection of property abroad was exposed to further erosion. Five major factors deserve to be singled out:

(1) During the Stalinist period, disrespect by the Soviet Union and its East-European allies for most of the canons of traditional international law was at a premium.[23]

19 See above, p. 5, and, further, Vol. I, pp. 203, 563 and 630, and A. H. Roth, *The Minimum Standard of International Law applied to Aliens* (1949), p. 81 *et seq.*

20 See, for instance, the Report of the Economic Committee to the League Council (C 309 (I) M. 114, 1925. (II)) or the Acts of the League of Nations Conference for the Codification of International Law, Vol. IV (1930, V. 17), p. 36 *et seq.*

21 See above, p. 13, note 34, F. Deák, *The Hungarian-Rumanian Land Dispute* (1928); *La réforme agraire roumaine en Transylvanie devant la justice internationale et le Conseil de la S.N.* (1928—2 vols.), and S. Friedman, *loc. cit.* above, p. 7, note 19, pp. 82–83.

22 Note of April 8, 1938, Cmd. 5758 (1938), p. 2.
See also below, p. 40 *et seq.*

23 See, further, *The Frontiers*, p. 146 *et seq.*, and Vol. I, pp. 450–451 and 523–524.

(2) Reparation for and restitution of property looted by the Nazis and their hangers-on in other parts of Europe were, at the most, symbolical.[24] Successor governments of the totalitarian aggressors were treated lightly as potential allies in the realignment of the Western Powers and the Soviet Union against each other. Moreover, to prevent the defeated countries under the control of the Western Allies from turning Communist, the United States of America and the United Kingdom poured huge amounts of capital into these former enemy countries. It was, therefore, considered pointless to deprive these countries again of a large portion of this assistance by commensurate payments of reparation and more than partial satisfaction of restitution claims.[25]

(3) Waves of anti-foreign nationalism swept the world's poor countries and, under the banners of anti-colonialism and anti-imperialism,[26] found easy targets in foreign investments.[27]

(4) Countries such as the United Kingdom, which were involved in processes of relinquishing their imperial and colonial responsibilities, were divided in their own minds on the best ways of defending their foreign assets and thus lacked the necessary sureness of touch.

(5) The position was further complicated by the system of power politics in disguise in which, in the post-1945 climate, former Great Powers, such as the United Kingdom and France, had to operate. Middle Powers of this type were, and are, conditioned by the supreme role played in this international system by the two super-Powers[28] and further handicapped by their obligations under the Charter of the United Nations.

In the case of breaches by member States of international law other than their obligations not to use force for purposes of armed attack, the member State which is the victim of such lawlessness may not retaliate with military reprisals.[29] At the same time, the collective system of the United Nations is so lop-sided that no automatic adjudication of the issue on the basis of international law or even mere equity is assured. The potentialities of this situation were, and are, not lost on the hardly diminishing number of small-Power law-breakers.[30]

2—The Scope of Protection

Both the personal and functional scope of the protection of British property abroad call for attention.

24 See, further, Vol. II, pp. 767 *et seq.* and 854.
25 See, further, *Power Politics*, p. 307 *et seq.*
26 See above, p. 16 *et seq.*
27 See below, p. 65 *et seq.*
28 See, further, *Power Politics*, p. 249 *et seq.*, 19 Y.B.W.A. (1965), p. 223 *et seq.*, and 21 *ibid.* (1967), p. 179 *et seq.*
29 See, further, Vol. II (1968), p. 50 *et seq.*
30 See below, pp. 65 *et seq.*, and 186.

(a) Personal Scope

Under international customary law, the personal scope of the protection of British property extends to the protection of the property of citizens of the United Kingdom and Colonies, and Rhodesia; other British subjects except citizens of any other member State of the Commonwealth; British-protected persons; companies incorporated under the laws of the United Kingdom or in any territory for the international relations of which the government in the United Kingdom is responsible [31] and, in extreme cases of an alleged international tort, on grounds of equity, also companies incorporated under the law of the alleged tortfeasor, provided that British shareholders in any of the categories enumerated above hold a controlling interest in such companies.[32]

By and large, this delimitation of the personal scope of British property has been found adequate in British practice.[33] When the need has arisen, it has been limited or enlarged on a basis of consent.

Thus, to allow for flexibility regarding internally autonomous British territories, a special device has been evolved. For instance, in the Treaty of Commerce, Establishment and Navigation of November 14, 1962, between Japan and the United Kingdom, the term " British nationals " is restricted to British nationals of those dependent British territories to which,

31 See, further, B.D.I.L. (First Phase) Vol. 5; B.I.L.C., Vol. 4; C. Parry, *Nationality and Citizenship Laws of The Commonwealth and of the Republic of Ireland* (1957 and 1960), and Vol. I, pp. 354 and 589 *et seq.*

32 On the position of British-owned foreign companies—in the concrete case, the majority of shareholders were British subjects—see the Note of April 20, 1938, of the Government of the United Kingdom to the Mexican Government (Cmd. 5758—1938, p. 7 *et seq.*) in contrast to the earlier Note of July 5, 1928, of the United Kingdom Government to that of the United States in the *Romano-Americana Company Case* (5 *Hackworth Digest*, p. 842 *et seq.*).

See, further, Vol. I, pp. 390–391 and 406 *et seq.*; Judge Wellington Koo's Sep. Op. in the *Barcelona Traction* case (*Preliminary Objections*), *I.C.J. Reports 1964*, p. 51, at p. 53 *et seq.*; Eric Beckett, 17 *Grotius Transactions* (1931), p. 175 *et seq.*; J. Mervyn Jones, 26 B.Y.I.L. (1949), p. 225 *et seq.*; Bindschedler, *loc. cit.* above, p. 8, note 22, p. 45 *et seq.*; H. J. Clay, 45 *Georgetown Law Journal* (1956), p. 1 *et seq.*; C. Parry, *loc. cit.* in note 31 above (1957), pp. 141–142; P. de Visscher, Hague *Recueil*, Vol. 102 (1961), p. 463 *et seq.*; J.-P. de Hochepied, *La protection diplomatique des sociétés et des actionnaires* (1965), pp. 83 and 173 *et seq.*; Sir Francis Vallat, *International Law and the Practitioner* (1966), pp. 28–29, and C. Joseph, *Diplomatic Protection and Nationality. The Commonwealth of Nations* (1968), p. 198 *et seq.*

On United Kingdom practice regarding eligible claimants under the Foreign Compensation Act 1950, see Lillich (1967), p. 24 *et seq.*

33 See B.D.I.L. (First Phase), Vol. 5, p. 507 *et seq.*, and, further, *Most-Favoured-Nation Standard*, p. 107.

For recent illustrations see, for instance, Article 4 (1) (a) of the Agreement of November 11, 1954, between Poland and the United Kingdom regarding the Settlement of Financial Matters, Cmd. 9343 (1954), p. 3; Article 3 (1) of the Agreement of September 22, 1955, between Bulgaria and the United Kingdom regarding the Settlement of Financial Matters, Cmd. 9625 (1955), p. 3, and Annex A (3) to the Agreement of February 28, 1959, between the United Arab Republic and the United Kingdom concerning Financial and Commercial Relations and British Property in Egypt, Cmnd. 723 (1959), pp. 7–8.

in accordance with the Treaty, the application of its provisions is actually extended.[34]

In the Exchange of Notes of October 1, 1953, between Brazil and the United Kingdom for the Settlement of Brazilian Commercial Arrears with the United Kingdom, the term "United Kingdom creditor" has an exceptionally wide meaning. It covers any person or corporation *resident* in the United Kingdom or a territory for the international relations of which the United Kingdom is responsible.[35]

Similarly, in the Financial Agreement of February 28, 1959, between Egypt and the United Kingdom, British property is liberally defined. It is "deemed to include shares, of which United Kingdom nationals are the owners, in corporations or associations incorporated or constituted under the laws in force in the United Arab Republic even though the documentary evidence of title to those shares is held outside the United Arab Republic."[36]

In the Exchange of Notes of December 1, 1966, between Indonesia and the United Kingdom on the losses incurred by the Government of the United Kingdom and by British nationals as a result of the Indonesian disturbances of 1963, United Kingdom nationals are defined as including physical persons, corporations and unincorporated associations.[37]

(b) Functional Scope

Corresponding to the position in international customary law,[38] the functional scope of British property is widely defined in British treaty practice.

[34] Article 2 (2), Cmnd. 2085 (1963), pp. 3–4.
See also Article 1 (2) of the Treaty of Friendship, Commerce and Navigation of December 20, 1951, between the Sultan of Muscat and Oman, Cmd. 8633 (1952), p. 2, and Article 2 (2) of the (unratified) Treaty of Commerce, Establishment and Navigation of March 11, 1959, between Iran and the United Kingdom, Cmnd. 698 (1959), p. 6.

[35] Cmd. 8978 (1953), p. 3.

[36] Annex A (2), Cmnd. 723 (1959), p. 7.
See also Number 2 (e) and (f) of the Exchange of Notes of August 7, 1962 (Cmnd. 1820 (1962), pp. 20–21), and Article 6 (3) of the Foreign Compensation (Egypt—Determination and Registration of Claims) Order 1962 (S.I. 1962, No. 2187 or *Contemporary Practice* 1962 (II), p. 194 *et seq.*).

[37] Article 2, Cmnd. 3277 (1967), p. 2.
Under Paragraph 3 of Article 7 of the unratified Treaty of Commerce, Establishment and Navigation of March 11, 1959, between Iran and the United Kingdom, the term "companies" has been extended so as to include the members of Lloyd's (Cmnd. 698 (1959), p. 8), who, as individual members of Lloyd's, co-operate in informal syndicates without legal personality. See, further, Scrutton L.J. in *Rozanes* v. *Bowen* (1928) 31 Ll.L.R. 231 (C.A.), and D. E. W. Gibb, *Lloyd's of London* (1957), p. 139 *et seq.*
Similarly, in the Agreement of July 29, 1963, between Cameroon and the United Kingdom on Commercial and Economic Co-operation, "concerns" and "associations" have been added to nationals and companies as beneficiaries of the protection of investments (Article 3—Cmnd. 2133—1963, p. 3).
If the United Kingdom acts not only in its own right, but also on behalf of other members of the Commonwealth, these are included in the definition of British nationals. See, for instance, Article IV of the Nationalisation Agreement of December 23, 1948, between the United Kingdom and Yugoslavia, Cmd. 7600 (1949), p. 3. See also below, p. 56.

[38] See above, p. 17.

Thus, in the Agreement of November 11, 1954, between Poland and the United Kingdom regarding the Settlement of Financial Matters, British property affected by measures of nationalisation, expropriation and other similar measures includes property, rights and interests "owned directly or indirectly, in whole or in part, and whether legally or beneficially by British nationals, to the extent to which they were so owned." [39]

In the Agreement of February 28, 1959, between the United Arab Republic and the United Kingdom concerning Financial and Commercial Relations and British Property in Egypt, the term "British property" covers "all movable or immovable property whether tangible or intangible, and includes rights to receive payment (whether contractual or not), other contractual rights, copyright, patents, trade marks and other forms of industrial property, as well as rights or interests of any kind in property, including shares in Egyptian companies." [40]

Under the Treaty of Commerce, Establishment and Navigation of November 14, 1962, between Japan and the United Kingdom, the protected property of nationals and companies of one Contracting Party in any territory of the other extends to "property, rights and interests," including beneficial interests in the property, rights and interests of any company of the other Contracting Party.[41]

[39] Article 4 (1) (b), Cmd. 9343 (1954), p. 3.
See also below, p. 41 *et seq.*

[40] Annex A (1) and (2), Cmnd. 723 (1959), p. 7.
See also above, p. 17, and below, p. 54 *et seq.*

[41] Article 14, Cmnd. 2085 (1963), p. 9.
See also below, p. 35.

CHAPTER 3

POST-1945 BRITISH TREATY PRACTICE: I—PEACE TREATIES AND GENERAL ECONOMIC TREATIES

SEVEN types of treaties represent British practice since the Second World War in the field of the protection of foreign investments: the post-1945 peace settlements and equivalent treaties; general economic treaties and treaties of commerce; nationalisation agreements; devolution agreements; rescue agreements; agreements liquidating a *status mixtus* and, finally, relevant regional and sectional treaties.

1—THE PEACE SETTLEMENTS

The post-1945 peace settlements [1] and equivalent treaties with Austria [2] and the Federal Republic of Germany [3] contain detailed clauses relating to Allied private property and to property of the nationals of the defeated States abroad.

Systematically, these provisions raise an intriguing problem. Under international customary law, confiscation, as distinct from expropriation in compliance with the minimum standard of international law, is an international tort. Thus it entails, primarily, restitution of the *status quo* before the commission of the tortious act and not merely full, prompt and effective compensation.[4] *A fortiori* a tortious character attaches to the waging of wars of aggression, under the law of the Kellogg Pact and the United Nations.[5] Thus, the primary duty of the defeated enemy States

[1] The Peace Treaties of February 10, 1947, with Italy (Cmd. 7481—1948), Bulgaria (Cmd. 7483—1948), Finland (Cmd. 7484—1948), Hungary (Cmd. 7485—1948) and Rumania (Cmd. 7486—1948), and the Peace Treaty of September 8, 1951, with Japan (Cmd. 8601—1952).

[2] State Treaty of May 15, 1955 (Cmnd. 214—1957) and Exchange of Notes of May 8/15, 1959, between Austria and the United Kingdom regarding certain claims in connection with Article 26 of the State Treaty of 1955 (Cmnd. 784—1959).

[3] Exchange of Notes of March 6, 1951, between the Allied High Commission for Germany and the Federal Republic of Germany (Cmd. 8368—1951); Protocol on the Termination of the Occupation Régime in the Federal Republic of Germany, October 23, 1954 (Cmnd. 658—1959), Convention on the Settlement of Matters arising out of the War and the Occupation, May 26, 1952, and October 23, 1954 (Cmnd. 656—1959), and Agreement of June 9, 1964, between the Federal Republic of Germany and the United Kingdom concerning Compensation for United Kingdom Nationals who were Victims of National-Socialist Measures of Persecution (Cmnd. 2445—1964).

See also H. Mosler and K. Doehring, *Die Beendigung des Kriegszustands mit Deutschland nach dem zweiten Weltkrieg* (1963); 1 *Contemporary Practice*, 5 I.C.L.Q. (1956), p. 425, and B.P.I.L. 1964 (II), p. 120.

[4] See also above, pp. 17 and 23.

For the *ex gratia* payment made by the United Kingdom to the Republic of San Marino for damage caused by the bombing of territory of the Republic by British aircraft, see the Exchange of Notes of July 17/22, 1961, between the Republic of San Marino and the United Kingdom, Cmnd. 1571 (1961).

[5] See, further, Vol. II, p. 758 *et seq.*

consisted in making, as far as possible, restitution and, otherwise, full reparation for the economic consequences of their criminal and tortious acts.

In the Agreement of January 1, 1946, with Thailand for the Termination of the State of War, India and the United Kingdom firmly maintained this position.[6] At the Paris Peace Conference of 1946, the United Kingdom Delegation made the same point but had to give way to the combined pressure of the United States and the Soviet Union.[7]

The actual settlement was based on the rule of compensation at two-thirds of the value for lost or damaged property of Allied nationals. If any of the defeated States were to grant more favourable treatment to its own nationals, the standard of national treatment was to apply also in favour of Allied nationals. While the compensation was freely usable in the debtor State concerned and exempt from special charges, it was subject to the foreign exchange regulations of the debtor State.[8]

The lenient attitude taken towards Italy and the four satellites of the European Axis was explained in the Peace Treaties of 1947 by the early withdrawal of some of these States from the German side and by their active contributions to the victory of the Allies. In fact, other considerations were more decisive. The United States shouldered the major burden of financing Italian recovery. They, therefore, desired as lenient a settlement for Italy as could be obtained. The Soviet Union was equally protective over the ex-satellites of the Axis except Finland, and either side could secure lenient treatment for its *protégés* only by granting the same concessions to the other's satellites. Thus, the United States stood out successfully for a compromise at the level of two-thirds against both the position taken by the Soviet Union in favour of compensation at the rate of one-third and the British claim for full compensation.[9]

In the Peace Treaty of San Francisco with Japan, in which the Soviet Union did not participate, the principles of restitution and compensation were safeguarded to a greater extent. Japan was not to grant less favourable terms than those contained in the draft Allied Powers Property Compensation Law, approved by the Japanese Cabinet on July 13, 1951. This provided for full compensation, but payments were subject to Japanese foreign exchange legislation.[10]

[6] Article 3 (Cmd. 8140—1951).
See, however, the Exchange of Notes of May 4, 1950 (Cmd. 8140—1951), November 8, 1950/January 3, 1951 (Cmd. 8163—1951) and January 14, 1954 (Cmd. 9090—1954).

[7] See United States Department of State, *Paris Peace Conference 1946*, pp. 115, 476, 531, 666, 852, 1029 and 1230–1231.

[8] See, for instance, Article 78 (4) (c) of the Peace Treaty with Italy, Cmd. 7481 (1948), p. 40, and, further, the Memorandum of Understanding of March 29, 1957, between Italy and the United Kingdom regarding Claims by British Nationals under Article 78 of the Peace Treaty with Italy (Cmnd. 241—1957).

[9] See, further, Vol. II, p. 767 *et seq.*

[10] For footnote, see p. 32.

Actually, the further the peace-makers moved into the era of the Cold War,[11] the better fared the objects of the settlements yet to be made.[12] Correspondingly, the significance of these arrangements from the point of view of legal principle diminished.

Even so, all these agreements are indicative of a trend under the thin cover of consensual undertakings,[13] to shed remaining nineteenth-century inhibitions against interfering, otherwise than absolutely necessary, with the private property of even defeated enemies.

2—General Economic Treaties

In British treaties of commerce and navigation of the pre-1914 period, especially in relation to capital-importing States, considerable care was taken to declare the law on the protection of foreign investments.[14] In the post-1945 period, the United States of America pursued a vigorous policy on similar lines [15] and a number of Continental States, especially France and, more recently, the Federal Republic of Germany and Switzerland followed suit.[16]

Compared with these efforts, recent British treaty practice is rather meagre. In the Exchange of Notes of September 21, 1946, between the Governments of Brazil and the United Kingdom, the position of foreign enterprises in Brazil is described in a studiously circuitous and non-committal manner: "The Brazilian Foreign Minister stated that the new Constitution offers full guarantees to foreign capital, the entry of which into Brazil is welcomed. The development of mineral and petroleum resources in Brazil is regulated by Government concessions which can be granted to individuals of Brazilian nationality or to juridical entities organised and established in Brazil in accordance with local law. The Constitution places no obstacles in the way of participation by foreign capital in such juridical entities. The Brazilian Foreign Minister added that, in his opinion, this principle will be maintained in future legislation

10 Article 15 of the Peace Treaty with Japan, Cmd. 8601 (1952), p. 9. See also the Agreement of June 12, 1952, for the Settlement of Disputes arising under Article 15 (a) of the Peace Treaty between the Allied Powers and Japan (Cmd. 8675—1952); the Allied Powers Property Compensation Law (Japanese Law No. 264 of 1951—14 *U.N. Reports of International Arbitral Awards*, p. 455 *et seq.*); the Arrangement of October 7, 1960, between Japan and the United Kingdom regarding the Settlement of Certain British Claims (Cmnd. 1229—1960) and, further, Vol. II, p. 767 *et seq.*

11 See above, pp. 25 and 26.

12 See, further, Vol. II, p. 767 *et seq.*

13 For the liquidation of enemy property under the post-1945 settlements, see, further, *ibid.*, p. 88 *et seq.*

14 See above, p. 23.

15 See, for instance, R. R. Wilson, *United States Commercial Treaties and International Law* (1960), p. 116 *et seq.*; M. Domke, 105 *University of Pennsylvania L.R.* (1957), p. 1033 *et seq.*; H. Walker, 5 *A.J.C.L.* (1956), p. 229 *et seq.*, and 42 *Minnesota L.R.* (1958), p. 805 *et seq.*; S. D. Metzger, 50 *Virginia L.R.* (1964), p. 594 *et seq.*, and R. Preiswerk, *La Protection des investissements privés dans les traités bilatéraux* (1963), p. 100 *et seq.*

16 See Preiswerk, *loc. cit.* in note 15 above, p. 178 *et seq.*, and 3 *Revue Belge de Droit International* (1967), p. 173 *et seq.*

For comparative figures, see *O.E.C.D. Press Release*, May 6, 1968, p. 4.

regarding petroleum. He gave an assurance that President Dutra heartily desires the co-operation of foreign enterprise in Brazil and wishes to assure to it all necessary guarantees consistent with the new Constitution. His Majesty's Government welcomed this declaration." [17]

In the Treaty of Peace and Friendship of October 30, 1950, with Nepal, at least a reference is made to the minimum standards of international law. They are described as the "generally recognised requirements of international law and practice" regarding the treatment of each other's nationals.[18]

Similarly, such protection as is granted to British property under the Treaty of Friendship, Commerce and Navigation of December 20, 1951, with Muscat and Oman, is, at most, indirect. The nationals of each Contracting Party enjoy the benefits of national and most-favoured-nation treatment in all matters affecting commerce, shipping and the exercise of trade.[19] It is further stipulated in favour of British nationals that they may hire, acquire and dispose of property of any description "in any legal manner," but subject to two qualifications. In relation to movable property, they are entitled to the combined benefits of the national and most-favoured-nation standards,[20] yet, in relation to immovable property, merely to the application of the most-favoured-nation standard.[21]

The right to discriminate in Muscat and Oman in favour of the Sultan's subjects and against British nationals—compared with the right of nationals of the Sultan who are free to invest also in immovable property in the United Kingdom—explains the non-reciprocal formulation of the relevant Article of the Treaty.

It is more significant that the continued operation of the minimum standard is merely implied. That this is the position, and no argument *a contrario* applies, follows from the interpretation of this Treaty in accordance with the typical intention of parties to general economic treaties. It is, with the assistance of the optional standards of International Economic Law, to secure additional advantages to the nationals of contracting parties, but not to deprive them of benefits due to them in any case under international customary law.[22]

17 Cmd. 6952 (1946), p. 4.
On subsequent Brazilian legislation, limiting the repatriation of capital invested in Brazil and profits earned there, see 1 I.L.M. (1962), p. 306; 3 I.L.M. (1964), pp. 236 and 1053, and 4 I.L.A. (1965), p. 405.
See also the Exchange of Notes of October 17, 1947, between the Governments of Burma and the United Kingdom, referred to in Article 8 of the Treaty of the same date, recognising Burmese independence (Cmd. 7360—1948).

18 Article 5, Cmd. 8271 (1950), p. 4.

19 Article 3 (1), Cmd. 8633 (1952), p. 3.

20 Article 5 (*ibid.*, p. 4).

21 Article 5 (*ibid.*, p. 4).
See also Section 14 of the United Kingdom Memorandum, submitted in 1965 to the United Nations, on the relations between the United Kingdom and the Sultanate of Muscat and Oman, B.P.I.L. 1965 (II), p. 114.

22 See *Principles of I.E.L.*, pp. 78–80.

Although the Treaty of Commerce, Establishment and Navigation of March 11, 1959, between Iran and the United Kingdom has remained unratified, the property clause of this Treaty may claim especial interest. It was drafted against the background of the Iranian Nationalisation Law of 1951 and the settlement of the Anglo-Iranian Dispute.[23] Moreover, it influenced the formulation of corresponding clauses in the subsequent Treaty of Commerce, Establishment and Navigation with Japan.[24]

Under the Treaty between Iran and the United Kingdom, the nationals and companies of the one Contracting Party shall enjoy in any territory of the other " constant and complete protection and security for their persons and property." [25] Each Contracting Party shall " at all times accord fair and equitable treatment " [26] to nationals and companies of the other, and to their property and enterprises; shall refrain from " applying unreasonable or discriminatory measures that would impair their rights and interests " [27] and shall ensure that their contractual rights are afforded effective means of enforcement in conformity with the applicable laws.[28]

The nationals and companies of the Contracting Parties are protected against discriminatory taxation [29] and, on the footing of national and most-favoured-nation treatment, are granted the rights of acquisition, enjoyment and disposal of movable and immovable property or any interest therein.[30] On the same basis, they may also remove their movable property and the proceeds of the sale of any property or of any interest therein.[31] The Contracting Parties remain free to restrict the acquisition, ownership or disposal of ships entitled to fly their national flags.[32]

The national and most-favoured-nation standards also apply to the continued control and management of companies which, under the law of the Contracting Party concerned and in accordance with the most-favoured-nation standard, nationals of the other Contracting Party have been permitted to form.[33]

Regarding " measures of requisition, civil or military, or of disposal, limitation, restriction or expropriation affecting their property, rights and interests, or affecting the property, rights and interests of any company " of one Contracting Party " in which they own interests," the nationals and companies of the other Contracting Party shall receive equitable treatment.

[23] See below, p. 66 *et seq.*
[24] See below, p. 35.
[25] See also below, pp. 115 and 156 *et seq.*
[26] See below, pp. 112 and 158 *et seq.*
[27] See below, pp. 120 and 163.
[28] Article 8, Cmnd. 698 (1959), p. 8.
[29] Article 10 (*ibid.*, p. 9).
[30] Article 12 (1) and (2) (*ibid.*, p. 10).
These provisions do not apply to the conditions of registration of aircraft in the national registers of the Contracting Parties (Article 12 (4)—*ibid.*, p. 11).
[31] Article 12 (3) (*ibid.*, pp. 10–11).
[32] Article 12 (5) (*ibid.*, p. 11).
[33] Article 14 (*ibid.*, p. 11).

In any case, if any such measure is applied to their property, they are entitled to "prompt, adequate and effective compensation."[34]

Unless the Contracting Parties otherwise agree, any dispute between them on the interpretation or application of the Treaty is to be submitted to the International Court of Justice.[35]

Perhaps the most remarkable feature of this undaunted attempt at reaffirming, in Musaddiq's shadow, the pertinent rules of international customary law is the fact that, for nearly a decade, the Treaty has remained unratified.[36]

Japan is in a different category from Iran. She is both a major capital-importing State and a capital-exporting State of some magnitude.[37] Moreover, Japan is a fellow-member of the rich men's club, the Organisation for Economic Co-operation and Development, and a co-sponsor of the O.E.C.D. Draft Convention of 1967 on the Protection of Foreign Property.[38] In the analysis of the Treaty of Commerce, Establishment and Navigation of November 14, 1962, between Japan and the United Kingdom, it is advisable to keep these aspects of the matter in mind.

The clause on constant and complete protection for the persons and property of nationals of the other Contracting Party is identical with that of the Iranian Treaty.[39] Regarding the treatment of companies, however, the references to the standard of equitable treatment and the formation of companies have been deleted, and questions of their operation are regulated on the basis of the most-favoured-nation standard.[40] The taxation clauses correspond substantially to the Iranian model treaty.[41]

An additional clause has been introduced regarding the import of capital and technology on a most-favoured-nation basis[42] but the—in this context—crucial clause on the protection of property is reproduced in almost identical terms.[43]

It remains to discuss an agreement *sui generis* among recent British treaties in this field: the Agreement of July 29, 1963, on Commercial and Economic Co-operation between Cameroon and the United Kingdom.

34 Article 15 (*ibid.*, p. 12).
35 Article 32 (*ibid.*, p. 20).
36 Various explanations for this state of affairs have been offered. Yet, all of them leave matters in a state of conjecture.
37 See, for instance, I. H. Nish, 21 Y.B.W.A. (1967), p. 71 *et seq.*; E. Solomon in J. G. Starke (ed.), *The Protection and Encouragement of Foreign Investment* (1966), pp. 143 and 196–198, and *The Times* (London), August 6, 1968.
On the background of the Treaty, see the Statement by the Government of the United Kingdom (Cmnd. 1875—1962) and H. H. Almond, 13 I.C.L.Q. (1964), p. 925 *et seq.*
38 See below, p. 155 *et seq.*
39 Article 7 (1), Cmnd. 2085 (1963), p. 6. See above, p. 34, and below, pp. 112 and 156 *et seq.*
40 Article 6 (1), Cmnd. 2085 (1963), p. 5.
41 Article 8 (*ibid.*, p. 7). See above, p. 34.
42 Article 13, Cmnd. 2085 (1963), p. 9.
On the Decision of June 6, 1967, by the Japanese Cabinet to liberalise the treatment of inward investments, see 6 I.L.M. (1967), p. 1164.
43 Article 14 (*ibid.*, pp. 9–10).

The protection of investments under the Treaty is based on the combined application of the standard of equitable treatment and the minimum standard.

In principle, fair and equitable treatment[44] of "investments, real property, rights and interests owned by, or held indirectly by, nationals, concerns, associations or companies of the other country" is to be granted, but subject to an important qualification: "within the framework of national legislation" in force on the date of signature of the Agreement.[45]

The expropriation clause deserves to be quoted in full:

"Nationals, concerns, companies and associations of one country shall only be subjected to expropriation in the other on the grounds of public interest. If one of the Contracting Governments expropriates or nationalises or takes any other confiscatory measures against the property, rights or interests of the nationals, concerns, associations or companies of the other country it shall, in accordance with international law, make provision for the payment of adequate and effective compensation. Such compensation shall be paid without undue delay to those entitled to it. Measures of expropriation, nationalisation or confiscation shall not be discriminatory or contrary to a specific undertaking."[46]

Commendably, public interest is mentioned as one of the prerequisites of lawful expropriation.[47] Similarly, the restatement of the requirements of the classical standard of full or adequate, prompt and effective compensation is unexceptionable.[48] The same is true of the exclusion of lawful expropriation contrary to specific undertakings,[49] and it is even arguable that the formulation of the non-discrimination clause without distinction between lawful and unlawful forms of discrimination goes further than the requirements of the minimum standard.[50]

What is odd is the equation of lawful forms of expropriation and nationalisation with "other confiscatory measures" (*toute autre mesure en vue de leur confiscation* in the equally authoritative French text) and of measures of expropriation and nationalisation with confiscation (*mesures d'expropriation, de nationalisation ou de confiscation*).

This formulation is completely alien to British practice and involves an equation which is about the last thing one would expect any capital-exporting agency to accept. Thus it is helpful to compare this Treaty with two other bilateral investment conventions concluded with Cameroon by two other capital-exporting countries prior to the United Kingdom Agreement: the Treaty of June 29, 1962, between the Federal Republic

44 See below, pp. 114 and 156 *et seq.*

45 Article V (1), Cmnd. 2133 (1963), p. 3.

46 Article V (2) (*ibid.*, p. 3).

47 See below, pp. 118 and 162.

48 In the French text: "*au paiement d'une indemnité réelle et suffisante*" (*ibid.*, p. 7). See also above, pp. 4 and 10, and below, pp. 117 and 162 *et seq.*

49 See below, pp. 121 and 160 *et seq.*

50 See above, p. 4, and below, pp. 120 and 163 *et seq.*

of Germany and Cameroon[51] and that of January 28, 1963, between between Switzerland and Cameroon.[52]

For what it is worth the German Treaty is an investor's dream come true. In addition to the other conditions of lawful expropriation, it is expressly provided that compensation shall not only be paid but also fixed without delay; that it must be effectively realisable and freely transferable. Moreover, opportunity must be given to verify the legality of any expropriation and the amount of compensation by ordinary judicial processes.

In an accompanying Protocol, expropriation is defined as including the transfer of an investment to public ownership, the subjection of an investment to public control and similar interventions by public authorities, and the taking away or restricting by sovereign measure and to an extent equivalent to expropriation of any asset or right which itself or together with other assets or rights constitutes an investment.

If the investments of nationals or companies of either Contracting Party should suffer damage through armed conflicts, revolution or revolt in the territory of the other Contracting Party, such nationals or companies are to receive national treatment regarding restitution or compensation and most-favoured-nation treatment regarding the transfer of payments under the Treaty. The full protection and security granted to investments of nationals of the other Contracting Party also applies to returns from such investments.

In a further Article, the Contracting Parties guarantee to nationals or companies of the other Contracting Party the transfer of the capital, the returns from it and, in the case of the liquidation of any enterprise, the proceeds of the liquidation.

If, regarding matters governed by the Treaty, a Contracting Party has given guarantees to any of its nationals or companies under a national guarantee (or insurance) scheme and made payments under it, the other Contracting Party shall recognise the subrogation of the first-mentioned Contracting Party to all such rights and interests, and the same rules, as regarding the transfer of investments or returns from investments, apply to the transfer of payments to be made by virtue of subrogation.

Detailed provisions are made regarding the rates of exchange for the transfer of payments under the Treaty and for transfers without delay which on no account may exceed two months.

Investments are comprehensively defined. They cover every kind of asset: movable and immovable property and other property rights; shares or other interests in companies; titles to money or to any acts of economic value; copyrights, industrial property rights, technical processes, trade names and goodwill, and business concessions under public law, including concessions to search for, extract or exploit mineral resources. Alterations

51 *Bundesgesetzblatt* 1963 (II), 992.
52 FF 1963 (I), p. 1409.

in the form of the investment of assets do not affect their classification as an investment.

As in the two other treaties mentioned above, disputes regarding the interpretation and application of the Treaty which cannot be settled by negotiation are to be submitted to an arbitral tribunal consisting of three members. Two are appointed by the Parties and the third is selected by agreement between the Parties or, in the absence of such agreement, by the President, Vice-President or next senior member of the International Court of Justice (in descending order).

The provisions of the Treaty remain in force also in the event of a conflict between the Contracting Parties, but without prejudice to the right of taking such temporary measures as are permitted under the general rules of international law. Such measures must be repealed not later than on the date of the actual termination of the conflict, irrespective of whether diplomatic relations have been re-established.

While the treaties subsequently concluded with Switzerland and the United Kingdom are on an annual basis, with subsequent indefinite duration and three months' notice, that with Germany is concluded for a period of ten years and, later, may be terminated only with one year's notice.[53]

The United Kingdom Treaty is modelled on the simpler but, from the investor's point of view, less attractive Swiss Treaty. Yet, in the expropriation clause of the Swiss Treaty, no word of confiscation is to be found. The relevant acts are described as " *toutes autres mesures de dépossession* " and " *les mesures d'expropriation, de nationalisation ou de dépossession.*"[54] Thus, it remains a mystery why the United Kingdom should have agreed to so inadvisable a formulation of the expropriation clause.

Whatever the explanation may be, remedies for the correction of this *faux pas* exist. In the Treaty, provision is made for a Mixed Commission to supervise the operation of the Agreement and its implementation.[55] Moreover, after one year, either side may denounce the Agreement, with three months' notice. With this right in the background, it should prove possible to achieve an agreed rewording of the obnoxious term " confiscation " so as to bring the text at least in line with the Swiss model clause.

In view of the arbitration clause in the Treaty concerning investment disputes,[56] it is desirable to clarify this point before any actual dispute arises. Moreover, there was a time when the prestige of British draftsmanship in the field of economic agreements was such that other States freely copied the texts of British treaties. If this practice is to continue, it means living up to this reputation, and only the best is good enough.

[53] *Bundesgesetzblatt* 1963, Part II, p. 992 *et seq.*
[54] Article 7 (*loc. cit.* in note 52 above, pp. 3–4).
[55] Article IX, Cmnd. 2133 (1963), p. 4.
[56] Article VI (*ibid.*, p. 3).

For an interest-free loan granted by the United Kingdom to Cameroon, see the Agreement of June 16, 1967, Cmnd. 3416 (1967).

In evaluating British treaty practice on the protection of foreign investments since the Second World War, it is only fair to emphasise the lesser importance of the traditional type of treaty of commerce since the rise of GATT with its system of combined bilateral and multilateral trade bargaining at the Sessions of the Contracting Parties. Yet, compared with the record in these fields of the United States and the leading capital-exporting countries on the Continent,[57] this change in emphasis from bilateral to multilateral trade agreements does not fully explain the paucity of bilateral economic and investment treaties. Four major factors appear to account for this state of affairs:

(1) In an international society giving birth to new States at a remarkable production rate, any but the most lavishly staffed governments are hesitant to involve their limited manpower, qualified for the task, in possibly long-drawn-out negotiations on bilateral treaties of this type.[58]

(2) Experience since 1945 with small-Power law-breakers [59] appears to have further dampened enthusiasm, on a bilateral footing, to strengthen legal ties which, unless sustained by the continuing self-interest of the other Contracting Party concerned, appear to mean less to some of the newer breeds of State than to their Western counterparts.

(3) Post-imperial and post-colonial guilt complexes, for which, in relation to devolution agreements,[60] even more articulate evidence exists, have probably further contributed in the United Kingdom to a largely negative attitude to bilateral treaties of this type. In particular, this applies to the relations with new members of the Commonwealth of Nations.

(4) Belief in the superiority of more recent multilateral approaches to the issue of the protection of property abroad may have been a further reason for the poverty of the land traversed.[61] In any case, this ideology provides a " progressive " façade and assists in covering up more pragmatic considerations.

[57] See above, p. 32.

[58] On the position in the United Kingdom, see, further, C. Parry in H. C. L. Merillat (ed.), *Legal Advisers and Foreign Affairs* (1964), p. 101 *et seq.*, especially pp. 128, 130 and 141 *et seq.*

[59] See above, p. 26, and below, pp. 57 and 65 *et seq.*

[60] See below, p. 48 *et seq.*

[61] See below, p. 109 *et seq.*

CHAPTER 4

POST-1945 BRITISH TREATY PRACTICE: II—NATIONALISATION AGREEMENTS

A NUMBER of nationalisation agreements concluded with Latin American States, East and South-East European Communist States, France and the Soviet Union call for consideration.

1—THE LATIN AMERICAN TREATIES

The three treaties concluded in 1947 and 1948 with Argentina,[1] Mexico[2] and Uruguay[3] are confirmatory of agreements reached between the governments concerned and the shareholders of the companies taken over or to be taken over at the time when the agreements were concluded. In fact, each of these agreements merely put on a contractual basis unilateral action taken by Mexico, threatened by Argentina and more discreetly hinted at by Uruguay.[4]

Strictly speaking, only the Anglo-Mexican Agreement was concerned with an act of expropriation. In connection with the settlement of the claims arising from the Mexican expropriations of British property in 1938, the two parties made an important reservation: "Nothing contained in this Note shall be regarded as a precedent or be invoked by either of the two Governments in the settlement between them of any future difficulty, conflict, controversy or arbitration. The present provisions shall be considered as singular and exceptional, appropriate solely to this case, and motivated by the character of the problem itself."[5] Mexico agreed that the compensation should be "just and equitable."[6]

According to private British estimates, the compensation amounted to about one-third of the real value of the oil properties. In the case of

[1] Cmd. 7405 (1948).
[2] Cmd. 7275 (1947).
[3] Cmd. 7629 (1949).
[4] See the Exchange of Notes contained in Cmd. 7340 (1948), pp. 6–7.

On the expropriation by Brazil in 1940 of the Port of Para Company, which affected French bondholders to a greater extent than United Kingdom nationals, see the Lord Privy Seal's reply in H.C.Deb., Vol. 679, col. 1 (Written Answers—June 17, 1963), or B.P.I.L. 1963 (II), p. 25.

[5] Point 19 of the Exchange of Notes of February 7, 1946 (Cmd. 6768—1946), p. 4.
[6] Point 3 (*ibid.*, p. 2) and Point 4 of the Correspondence of August 29, 1947 (Cmd. 7275—1947), p. 7. See also *ibid.*, p. 9.

Actually, the compensation paid was 35 per cent. higher than the nominal value of the stock, which was greatly undervalued.

See, further, S. Mendoza, *La doctrina Cárdenas* (1939); W. C. Gordon, *The Expropriation of Foreign-Owned Property in Mexico* (1941), p. 168 *et seq.*; J. L. Kunz, 17 N.Y.U.L.Q.R. (1940), p. 327 *et seq.*; J. S. Herzog, *La expropriacion del petroleo en Mexico* (1963); *Whiteman Digest*, Vol. 8, p. 1272, and the bibliography to Chap. 4, below, pp. 211–212.

the purchase agreements concluded between the British-owned railway companies and Argentina and Uruguay, respectively, the compensation was thought to represent about 60 per cent. of the capital value of these enterprises.

In all three cases, the Latin American governments concerned granted effective compensation. While Mexico paid the compensation in instalments payable at New York in United States currency, Argentina and Uruguay made available at the Bank of England in Pounds Sterling the full amount of their compensation payments.

2—Treaties with East and South-East European Communist States

In the majority of the nationalisation treaties concluded between the United Kingdom and its East and South-East European treaty partners, measures of nationalisation, expropriation and dispossession are lumped together with other restrictive measures of a similar kind taken against British-owned property.

In the Treaties with two of these Communist States—those with Bulgaria (1955) and Hungary (1956)—the measures of nationalisation, expropriation and other similar measures taken against British-owned property are limited to those arising out of structural changes in the economies of these countries. Yet, these Treaties are followed by the Rumanian Treaty of 1960 in which the various Rumanian measures covered by the duty of compensation are again described as in the treaties prior to those concluded with Bulgaria and Hungary.[7]

As explained in an earlier Chapter, so long as an expropriation takes place for public purposes and is accompanied by full or adequate, prompt and effective compensation, it is legal. It is irrelevant whether the object of the measure is a structural change in the economy of the country concerned.[8] If any one of these conditions of a lawful expropriation is not fulfilled, the illegality of such acts is not healed by their connection with any alleged structural change in the economy of the country concerned, nor does an otherwise legal expropriation become illegal because it does not form part of a nationalisation programme. International customary law merely distinguishes between lawful expropriation and illegal confiscation. It does not know of any third category concerned with differentiations on political, ideological or sociological grounds.

It does not appear that any of these treaties were intended to constitute departures from the rules of international customary law on this basic

7 Compare, for instance, Article 1 (d) of the Agreement of September 22, 1955, between Bulgaria and the United Kingdom (Cmd. 9625 (1955), p. 2) with Article (1) (b) of that of November 10, 1960, between Rumania and the United Kingdom (Cmnd. 1232 (1960), p. 3).

8 See above, p. 8 *et seq.* See also E. Lauterpacht, 6 I.C.L.Q. (1957), pp. 151–152.

distinction under international customary law. From the angle of compensation, however, the treaties discussed in this Section fall into two categories. While one of these treaties is based on the principle of individual compensation, the others incorporate that of global compensation.

The first type is represented by the Exchange of Notes of January 24, 1948, between Poland and the United Kingdom on Compensation for British Interests affected by the Polish Nationalisation Law of January 3, 1946.

In this Agreement provision was made for adequate and effective compensation for the individual British investors concerned.[9] The arrangement soon proved unworkable and, in 1949, it was agreed to contemplate replacing it by a global indemnity in Pounds Sterling.[10] This pattern was adopted in relation to all Communist regimes in Eastern and South-Eastern Europe except Albania. In this case, the United Kingdom found it impossible to recover even the indemnity awarded to it by the International Court of Justice in the *Corfu Channel* case (1951).[11]

The relevant agreements are those with Yugoslavia (1948 and 1949),[12] Czechoslovakia (1949),[13] Poland (1954),[14] Bulgaria (1955),[15] Hungary (1956)[16] and Rumania (1960).[17]

Under United Kingdom legislation, machinery for the adjudication of claims under these agreements and distribution of the compensation received by the United Kingdom has been established.[18] The Foreign Compensation Commission, a statutory commission of quasi-judicial character, operates exclusively within the framework of the United Kingdom Foreign Compensation Act 1950 and, in fact, merely on the basis of the applicable Orders in Council.

At most, its decisions—merely minuted for internal use and diligently examined in a recent monograph[19]—offer indirect evidence of United Kingdom practice on subordinate but practically important rules of

9 Point 3, Cmd. 7403 (1948), p. 3.

10 Article 13 of the Anglo-Polish Trade and Finance Agreement of January 14, 1949, Cmd. 7628 (1949), p. 6.

11 See, further, *The Frontiers*, p. 151.

12 Agreements of December 23, 1948, Cmd. 7600 (1949), and December 26, 1949, Cmd. 7875 (1950).

13 Agreement of September 28, 1949, Cmd. 7797 (1949).

14 Agreement of November 11, 1954, Cmd. 9343 (1954).

15 Agreement of September 22, 1955, Cmd. 9625 (1955).

16 Exchange of Notes of August 19, 1954, Cmd. 9263 (1954) and Agreement of June 27, 1956, Cmd. 9820 (1956).

17 Agreement of November 10, 1960, Cmnd. 1232 (1960).

18 Foreign Compensation Act, 1950 (14 Geo. 6, c. 12).

In British and United States practice, this type of national commission was first established at the beginning of the last century. See, further, Lillich (1962), p. 7, and (1967), p. 3.

See also E. Lauterpacht, 4 I.L.Q. (1951), p. 361 *et seq.*; A. Drucker, 49 A.J.I.L. (1955), p. 477 *et seq.*; N. H. Moller, 44 *Grotius Transactions* (1959), p. 223 *et seq.*, and Lillich (1967), p. 143 *et seq.*

19 Lillich (1967).

international law, such as dual and continuous nationality.[20] In contrast, the United States Foreign Claims Settlement Commission is charged expressly with applying the provisions of the relevant claims agreements and principles of international law, justice and equity.[21]

As in the United States of America, it is possible under the United Kingdom legislation of 1950 on foreign compensation for claims to be registered and adjudicated prior to the conclusion of a compensation agreement with the government of any " foreign " government.[22] Although the term " foreign " is not defined in the Foreign Compensation Act, it does not appear to include member States of the Commonwealth.[23] In any case, any such preregistration or preadjudication of claims against a particular State requires an enabling Order in Council.[24]

As is proved by British practice since 1954, presettlement registration, even if not followed by presettlement adjudication, makes it easier to obtain a rational picture of the upper ceiling of national claims and provides negotiators with more convincing arguments than those based in earlier negotiations on, at best, administrative verification of *ex parte* statements.[25]

It is difficult to evaluate these agreements from a quantitative point of view. Private and official estimates show considerable variations. Moreover, some of the lump-sum agreements include items other than nationalisation claims.[26]

According to official estimates, the Yugoslav settlement of £4½ million under the 1948 Agreement represents 50 per cent. of the value of the nationalised British property.[27] Yet, the claims submitted amounted to over £25 million and the *pro rata* payments made to claimants were merely 17·9 per cent. of the awards.[28]

Again, according to official estimates, the compensation of £8 million under the 1949 Agreement with Czechoslovakia represented one-third of the value of the British properties affected. Yet, the claims submitted

20 Claimants receive merely communications from the Commission's Registrar, indicating the amount of the awards and the portions of the claims allowed.

See, further, below, p. 112 *et seq.*; Moller, *loc. cit.* above, p. 42, note 18, p. 232, and, for illustrations of relevant questions of international law, Lillich (1967), pp. 9, 27 *et seq.* and 142.

On the reversal of decisions of the United Kingdom Foreign Claims Commission by subsequent Orders in Council, see Lillich, 17 C.L.P. (1964), p. 177, or (1967), pp. 140–141.

21 See, further, *Whiteman Digest*, Vol. 8, p. 949 *et seq.*; Lillich (1965), p. 172 *et seq.*; E. D. Re in *Domke Symposium*, p. 214 *et seq.*

22 Section 3, Foreign Compensation Act 1950.

On the Foreign Compensation Act 1962, see below, p. 56, note 51.

23 See also the interview reported in Lillich (1967), p. 4, n. 24.

24 *Loc. cit.* in note 22 above.

25 See, further, below, p. 54 *et seq.*; Drucker, *loc. cit.* above, p. 42, note 18, pp. 485–486; E. A. S. Brooks, 44 *Grotius Transactions* (1959), p. 187 *et seq.*

26 See, for instance, Article 1 of the Agreement of 1956 with Hungary (*loc. cit.* above, p. 42, note 16, p. 2), and Brooks, *loc. cit.* above, note 25, p. 193.

27 See, for instance, the statements by the Attorney-General in the House of Commons on May 8, 1950 (H.C.Deb., Vol. 475, col. 64) and the Lord Chancellor in the House of Lords on June 27, 1950 (H.L.Deb., Vol. 167, col. 1114).

28 Lillich (1965), p. 178.

amounted to £100 million, and the *pro rata* payments to owners fell below 9 per cent. of the awards.[29]

The Polish settlement of 1954 of £2½ million for nationalisation measures was probably less than one-quarter of the value of the British properties affected. In any case, the claimants received merely 20 per cent. of the amounts awarded to them.[30]

The Bulgarian payment of £400,000 under the 1955 Agreement included items other than compensation for nationalisation measures, and the claimants received 32·6 per cent. of their awards.[31]

The Agreements of 1956 with Hungary and of 1960 with Rumania involved payments to the United Kingdom of £4 million under the Hungarian Agreement[32] and of £1¼ million under the Rumanian Agreement.[33] Both amounts included claims other than those arising from the nationalisation of British property. The interim percentage of the *pro rata* payments received by claimants under the Hungarian and Rumanian Agreements is 24·4 per cent. and 32·5 per cent., respectively, of the awards.[34]

In any evaluation of these agreements, the complexity of the metalegal factors involved must be borne in mind. All the countries involved were liberated countries which had suffered fearfully from the totalitarian invaders. Thus, leniency towards them was part of a co-ordinated policy of European reconstruction. Moreover, all the countries concerned had fallen under the hegemonial control of the Soviet Union or, like Yugoslavia, were only just liberating themselves from this domination. Thus, for this reason alone, any heavy-handed policy towards any of these countries was out of the question.[35]

The results of such statesmanship for the investors concerned were necessarily disappointing. Yet, limited though the compensations agreed on were, in some cases even these meagre results were attained only by further indirect concessions for which the United Kingdom as such—that is, in the end, the British tax-payer—had to foot the bill. In this way alone was it possible to induce some of the Communist governments concerned

[29] Drucker, *loc. cit.* above, p. 42, note 18, p. 485, and Lillich (1965), p. 178.

[30] See *loc. cit.* above, p. 42, note 14, and Lillich (1967), p. 20.

[31] See *loc. cit.* above, p. 42, note 15, and Lillich (1967), p. 21.
The Bulgarian external Sterling bonded debt remains in default (Written Answer by the Secretary of State for Foreign Affairs, H.C.Deb., Vol. 751, cols. 32–33 (July 24, 1968). See also Council of Foreign Bondholders, 84th *Annual Report* (1967), p. 85 *et seq.*

[32] See *loc. cit.* above, p. 42, note 16.

[33] See *loc. cit.* above, p. 42, note 17.

[34] State of payments made by July, 1968.
The claims filed under the Hungarian Agreement amounted to just under £30 million, and under the Rumanian Agreement to about £4½ million (Lillich (1967), p. 22).
Estimates of the value of British properties in Bulgaria, Hungary and Rumania are not available.
On continuing negotiations with Hungary and Rumania, see H.C.Deb., Vol. 750, col. 168 (Written Answers—July 17, 1967) and Vol. 751, cols. 32–33 (Written Answers—July 24, 1967) and col. 365 (Written Answers—October 23, 1967).

[35] See above, p. 25 *et seq.*

to make the requisite amounts of compensation available in convertible form, if only in long-extended payments in instalments.

Thus, in the Agreement of 1949 with Yugoslavia, the terms and conditions of the payment of the major part of the Yugoslav debt were left to be settled, "during the negotiations for a long-term trade agreement." [36] Actually, the payment of the fifteen instalments extended from 1950 to 1957,[37] and the United Kingdom undertook, during the same period, to lend to Yugoslavia about twice the amount of the compensation to be paid by Yugoslavia.[38]

It must be left to case studies beyond the compass of this Chapter, and best undertaken by interdisciplinary teams of lawyers and economists, to analyse the extent to which, in effect, the United Kingdom and other capital-exporting States themselves paid for such partial compensation for nationalisation claims as their nationals received by generous agreements regarding commerce, debts and development aid.

If these settlements are judged by results, Communist States in positions comparable to those of the post-1945 East and South-East European States may claim to have found the answer to the nationalisation without tears (of theirs) of foreign-owned property. If they nationalise the property of nationals of capital-exporting States but, in principle, express their earnest desire to compensate the foreign nationals affected within the limits of what is possible but, otherwise, in strict compliance with international law, they have acquired powerful levers. They can point out with apparent justice that they should not be asked to convert larger amounts into foreign exchange than, within reason, they can make available for the purpose. They may further suggest that an increase in the level of trade would be a constructive way of allowing them to earn the foreign currencies required to comply with their international obligations. As a final touch, they may even hint to the major investors involved that if they adequately lobby their home governments on such mutually advantageous lines, they can expect at least some compensation for their lost properties.

As always, commensurate responses to these as to any other challenges exist. Yet, they may require greater toughness than, in the post-1945 period, the United Kingdom considered it advisable to display.[39]

36 Article I (a) of the Compensation Agreement of December 23, 1948, Cmd. 7600 (1949), p. 2.

37 Article I of the Agreement of December 26, 1949, on the Terms and Conditions of Payment, Cmd. 7875 (1950).

See also Paragraph 3 of the Preamble of the Compensation Treaty of 1949 with Czechoslovakia, Cmd. 7797 (1949), p. 2, and the Trade and Finance Agreement of September 28, 1949, between Czechoslovakia and the United Kingdom, Cmd. 7779 (1949); Article 3 of the Compensation Agreement of 1954 with Poland, Cmd. 9343 (1954), p. 3; Article 2 of the Compensation Agreement of 1955 with Bulgaria, Cmd. 9625 (1955), p. 2, and the corresponding Agreements with Hungary, Cmd. 9820 (1956), p. 3 and Rumania, Cmnd. 1232 (1960), pp. 3–4.

38 A. Drucker, 36 *Grotius Transactions* (1950), p. 102.

39 See, further, below, pp. 126, and 189 *et seq.*

Another aspect of these settlements also calls for attention. British nationals did not in all cases receive identical treatment. In one case, particular claims received individual and, as it appears, preferential treatment.[40] In another, the claims of some claimants were excluded from the settlement agreement, and these claimants were permitted to make their own arrangements with the other government concerned.[41]

It may be wondered whether such differential treatment was as beneficial for the small investors concerned as for the banking, insurance and oil interests singled out in this way. In any case, if such a possibility of differentiation exists, it increases the nationalisation hazards run by private investors abroad other than powerful national and transnational organisations.

3—The Anglo-French Agreement of 1951

Like Belgium, Canada and Switzerland, the United Kingdom accepted compensation to British interests in the French nationalised gas and electricity industries on the same footing as for French citizens. In the event of France subsequently granting more favourable treatment to claimants of any other nationality, a most-favoured-nation reservation was to come into operation. The basis of calculation were *Bourse* quotations on alternative dates in 1944 and 1945. Interest and redemption payments were to be in French francs, but were subject to an exchange guarantee based on the United States/French franc rate of exchange on April 8, 1946. The capital value of the compensation could be used or reinvested only in France.

In consideration for this settlement, and as in the case of the other global settlements, the Government of the United Kingdom undertook expressly " not to recognise, nor to bring before any tribunal, nor to support by diplomatic action," any claims which might be made by British nationals under the Nationalisation Law of April 8, 1946.[42]

According to private estimates, compensation in these cases amounted to 70 per cent. of the value of British holdings in these nationalised properties.

4—The Anglo-Russian Agreement of 1968

The Agreement of January 5, 1968, on the Settlement of Mutual Financial and Property Claims between the Soviet Union and the United Kingdom [43] is in a category of its own. It is the result of prolonged negotiations, begun in 1959 and culminating in a Joint Declaration of February 12, 1967.[44]

[40] See Article 1 (2) of the Compensation Agreement of 1954 with Poland, Cmd. 9343 (1954), p. 2, and the Exchange of Notes of November 11, 1954, *ibid.* p. 14.
[41] See Article 1 of the Compensation Agreement of 1960 with Rumania, Cmnd. 1232 (1960), p. 1, and the Schedule annexed, *ibid.*, p. 7.
[42] Cmd. 8224 (1951). See also Cmds. 8227 and 8358 (1951).
[43] Cmnd. 3517 (1968).
[44] Preamble, *ibid.*, p. 2.

By this Agreement, the previous *de facto* recognition by the United Kingdom of the incorporation of the Baltic States into the Soviet Union [45] has been transformed into *de jure* recognition. Similarly, this Treaty amounts to a *de jure* recognition of such other territorial changes made in the Western frontiers of the Soviet Union during the Second World War as the United Kingdom had not previously recognised.[46]

In relation to British property, rights and banking, commercial and financial interests, including those affected by nationalisation and other measures in any of these territories, the United Kingdom has undertaken not to pursue or support any claims arising after January 1, 1939.[47] Conversely, the Soviet Union will not pursue or support claims on behalf of its own nationals of these areas regarding assets situated in the United Kingdom, including the gold of the former central banks of the former Baltic States held in the Bank of England.[48] The Contracting Parties make themselves exclusively responsible for the settlement of any claims of their own nationals and the distribution to such nationals of the assets held in each country.[49]

Two further clauses of the Agreement deserve attention. The United Kingdom has undertaken to settle the unredeemed Notes issued by the Soviet Union to two named British joint stock companies, "irrespective of the nationality of such holders." [50] Moreover, from the assets in the United Kingdom mentioned above, the Government of the United Kingdom undertakes to make a payment of £500,000 to the Government of the Soviet Union for the payment of consumer goods of British manufacture above the current Five-Year Trade Agreement between the two countries.[51]

British pre-1939 claims excluded from the 1968 Agreement, and still outstanding, amount to approximately £860 million, of which £500 million are governmental and £360 million private.[52]

45 See *A/S Tallina Laevauhisus and Others* v. *Estonian Steamship Line and Another* (1946—England, Court of Appeal), 80 Ll.L.Rep. 99 or *Annual Digest* 1946, p. 12. See also The *Elise* (1949—Supreme Court of Canada), *ibid*. 1948, p. 176; the Foreign Compensation (Union of Soviet Socialist Republics) (Registration) Order 1959 (S.I. 1959 No. 1968); E. Lauterpacht, 10 I.C.L.Q. (1961), p. 559 *et seq*., and, generally, H. W. Baade in *Strupp-Schlochauer*, Vol. I, p. 146 *et seq*.

46 Thus, the signature of the Armistice Agreement of September 12, 1944, with Rumania, in which reference is made to the restoration of the State frontier between Rumania and the Soviet Union, established by the Agreement of June 8, 1940, between the two countries, constitutes an implied recognition of Russian sovereignty within these frontiers (Article 4—Cmd. 6585 (1945)). See also R. Langer, *Seizure of Territory* (1947), p. 254 *et seq*.

47 Article 1, Cmnd. 3517 (1968), p. 2.

48 Article 2, *ibid*., p. 2.

49 Article 3, *ibid*., p. 3.

50 Article 4, *ibid*., p. 3.

51 Article 5 (1), *ibid*., p. 3.

52 Written Answer by the Secretary of State for Foreign Affairs, H.C.Deb., Vol. 742, cols. 15–17 (February 27, 1967). See also H.C.Deb., Vol. 754, cols. 224–225 (Written Answers—November 20, 1967).

On both occasions, the Minister refused to divulge the Government's estimate of the value of the claims covered by the Agreement then still under negotiation.

It is also worth mentioning that, on signature, and Agreement came immediately into force (Article 7—*loc. cit.* above, p. 46, note 43, p. 4).

See also Council of Foreign Bondholders, *loc. cit.*, above, p. 44, note 31, p. 24 *et seq.*

CHAPTER 5

POST-1945 BRITISH TREATY PRACTICE: III—OTHER RELEVANT TREATIES

IT remains to discuss four other types of relevant agreements: devolution agreements; rescue agreements; agreements liquidating a *status mixtus* and a number of regional and sectional conventions.

1—DEVOLUTION AGREEMENTS

In connection with the grant of independence to former imperial and colonial dependencies, the United Kingdom concluded devolution or inheritance agreements with such of the new States as were willing to enter into such engagements.[1] Under these treaties, the United Kingdom attempted to transfer its rights and obligations affecting these territories to the new States concerned. In relation to other States, the effectiveness of such action depended on the express or tacit consent of such third parties.

It might be thought that these devolution agreements offered suitable opportunities for defining also such acquired rights of British nationals as would survive the transfer of sovereignty. Actually, little use was made of these agreements for this purpose. To have attempted to do so might have spoiled the psychological effect of the grant of independence.[2]

In any case, it was considered that the new States were bound under international customary law to respect acquired rights [3] and, in a number of cases, it was possible to protect, if more precariously, property rights by appropriate provisions in agreed draft constitutions.[4] Moreover, it was arguable that, on the international level, the proper place for provisions on the protection of property rights was in treaties of commerce and navigation.[5]

[1] Thus, for instance, the Exchange of Letters of June 20, 1966, between the Governments of The Gambia and the United Kingdom is described as relating to the "inheritance of international rights and obligations by the Government of The Gambia," Cmnd. 3076 (1966).

In contrast, Malawi, for instance, did not conclude such an agreement with the United Kingdom, but stated her position regarding relevant treaties in a communication to the Secretary-General of the United Nations, and the United Kingdom did likewise regarding the termination of her own obligations under such treaties, B.P.I.L. 1965 (II), p. 126.

[2] The first of these Agreements was concluded with Iraq in 1930, Cmd. 3797 (1931). See, further, D. P. O'Connell, *State Succession in Municipal Law and International Law* (1967), Vol. II, p. 360 *et seq.*

See also E. Lauterpacht, 7 I.C.L.Q. (1958), p. 523 *et seq.*; International Law Association, *The Effect of Independence on Treaties* (1965), p. 191 *et seq.*, and O'Connell, *loc. cit.* above, Vol. II, p. 358 *et seq.*

[3] See, further, above, p. 6; below, p. 114 *et seq.*, and Vol. I, pp. 171 and 204 *et seq.*

[4] See also above, p. 10, and K. Zemanek, Hague *Recueil*, Vol. 116 (1965), p. 284.

[5] On the weakness of this argument in the post-1945 climate, see above, p. 32 *et seq.*

An exception was made in relation to acquired rights of British officers and civil servants which, in a number of treaties,[6] were specifically protected.

(a) Burma

In only one of the post-1945 devolution treaties—that of October 17, 1947, with Burma—did other property rights receive any attention. In an accompanying exchange of notes, it was agreed that, pending the conclusion of a treaty of commerce and navigation,[7] the policy of State socialism contemplated by the Provisional Government of Burma had to be taken into consideration. Thus, if Burmese action involved the "expropriation or acquisition in whole or in part of existing United Kingdom interests in Burma," such a contingency should not be "left entirely unregulated."[8] In this eventuality, the owners concerned were to receive "equitable compensation."[9]

(b) Northern Rhodesia—Zambia

In another case—that of Northern Rhodesia, subsequently Zambia—all parties concerned took prophylactic action over the claim of the British South Africa Company. Originally, the Company had considered itself entitled to ownership in perpetuity of all mineral rights in Northern Rhodesia which, in its turn, the Company farmed out to operating concessionaries.

In 1950, the Company concluded an agreement with the United Kingdom Government, relinquishing its rights by 1986.[10] Under the Agreement, the Government of the United Kingdom undertook that if, at any time, it were to abandon its responsibility for the government of Northern Rhodesia, it would attempt, before any such transfer of authority, to ensure "so far as it is possible to do so" that the government which would assume such responsibility would be "bound to observe the provisions of this Agreement."[11]

Actually, shortly before the grant of independence to Northern Rhodesia,

[6] See, for instance, Article 3 of the Agreement of March 30, 1950, between Israel and the United Kingdom, Cmd. 7941 (1950), p. 3, and Article 3 of the Agreement of May 1, 1951, between Jordan and the United Kingdom for the Settlement of Financial Matters outstanding as a result of the Termination of the Mandate for Palestine, Cmd. 8255 (1951), pp. 2–3; the Public Officers' Agreement of February 22, 1965, between The Gambia and the United Kingdom, Cmnd. 2772 (1965); the Exchange of Notes of April 15, 1965, between the Governments of Israel and the United Kingdom on the Settlement of Outstanding Financial Matters, Cmnd. 2689 (1965), p. 3 *et seq.*; the Public Officers' Agreements of February 17, 1967, between Lesotho and the United Kingdom, Cmnd. 3393 (1967) and of March 12, 1968, between Mauritius and the United Kingdom, Cmnd. 3668 (1968), and O'Connell, *loc. cit.* in note 2 above, Vol. I, p. 465 *et seq.*

[7] Not yet concluded.

[8] Cmd. 7360 (1948), p. 6.

[9] *Ibid.*, p. 7.

See also below, p. 92.

[10] Northern Rhodesia. White Paper on *The British South Africa Company's Claims to Mineral Royalties in Northern Rhodesia* (Lusaka—1964), Section 73 (p. 31).

[11] *Ibid.*, p. 31.

a compromise was reached between the Government of the United Kingdom and the Company in which the government of the new State-to-be concurred. From the date of Zambia's independence, the mineral rights in Zambia granted to the British South Africa Company were to be vested in the President of Zambia and, on an *ex gratia* basis, the Company was to receive £2 million from the British Government and a further £2 million from the Zambian Government, free of Zambian taxation.[12]

This arrangement is open to a number of interpretations.[13] It appears advisable to err on the side of caution. On the basis of the White Paper published at Lusaka in the last weeks of British rule, the Northern Rhodesian Government which, shortly after, became the Government of independent Zambia, made it clear that it considered the agreements made in the past between the British authorities and the British South Africa Company as incompatible with the public interest of the Colony. Irrespective, therefore, of what, otherwise, might have been the duties of the new State in relation to such a concession agreement under international law,[14] the Government of Northern Rhodesia announced that, after independence, it would not consider itself bound to honour the 1950 Agreement between the United Kingdom Government and the British South Africa Company.

In the circumstances, all concerned thought it wiser to settle the issue prior to Zambia's independence.

Assuming that the facts disclosed in the White Paper are correct,[15] the United Kingdom owed it to itself not to press the Company's claims any harder.

2—Rescue Agreements

In a variety of ways, the Government of the United Kingdom—like those of a number of other capital-exporting countries—has indirectly given a helping hand to exporters and investors abroad by monetary assistance and loans to debtor countries which, otherwise, would or could not meet their international obligations. In a *double entendre* which may apply to the bondholders, creditors or investors concerned as much as to the governments of the debtor States, these agreements may be described as rescue agreements.

(a) Bilateral Operations

In some cases, the United Kingdom has assisted in settlements being made on behalf of British investors with foreign governments by the Council of the Corporation of Foreign Bondholders in London. In others, it has consented to these arrangements being incorporated in exchanges of notes

[12] See B.P.I.L. 1964 (II), p. 142.
[13] See *ibid.*, p. 143 *et seq.*, and O'Connell, *loc cit.* in note 2 above, Vol. I, pp. 344–345.
[14] See above, p. 5 *et seq.*
[15] See *loc. cit.* in note 10 above, for instance, *Introduction*: Sections 5 (p. 2), 11 (p. 3), 14 (p. 3); Part II: Sections 2 (pp. 4–5), 5 (p. 5), 26 (p. 13) and 64–65 (pp. 26–27).

with the governments concerned and, thus, given them the additional protection of inter-governmental agreements. The Exchanges of Notes of November 21, 1952, between the Governments of Japan and the United Kingdom on the Settlement of the Japanese Pre-war External Debts (Sterling Bonds)[16] and of May 31, 1954, and October 14, 1954, between the Governments of Austria and the United Kingdom on the Validation in Austria of Foreign Currency Bonds illustrate this type of agreement.[17]

Another type of agreement is concerned with the liquidation of commercial debts which residents in certain countries had incurred irrespective of the international payment position of these countries, but in reliance on the approval of applications for Pounds Sterling made, for instance, to the Bank of Brazil by Brazilian importers. In this particular case, the agreed solutions were delayed payments and moratory interests of 3½ per cent. from the date of the Agreement until the date of the remittance of funds for the discharge of each debt.[18]

(b) Bilateral-Multilateral Operations

In more complex cases, the Government of the United Kingdom, together with other capital-exporting countries and international institutions, stepped into the breach with governmental loans and bilateral transfer schemes to safeguard United Kingdom creditors as well as it could.

(1) *Turkey.* On the basis of the multilateral Paris Agreement of May 11, 1959,[19] Turkish commercial debts were to be transferred under an instalment scheme, with moratory interests of 3 per cent. regarding payments in the process of transfer.

In 1965, the United Kingdom, as a member of the Turkish Consortium, further agreed to give a loan of over £5 million to Turkey, payable over

16 Cmd. 9370 (1955).

See also Council of the Corporation of Foreign Bondholders, London, 94th *Annual Report* (1967), p. 195 *et seq.*

17 Cmd. 8763 (1953).

See also Council of the Corporation of Foreign Bondholders, London, 94th *Annual Report* (1967), p. 58 *et seq.*

18 See, for instance, the Exchanges of Notes of October 1, 1953, and December 21, 1953, between the Governments of Brazil and the United Kingdom for the Settlement of Brazilian Commercial Arrears, Cmd. 8978 (1953) and 9034 (1954), and the Loan Agreement of October 16, 1964, between Brazil and the United Kingdom, Cmnd. 2569 (1964).

19 Cmnd. 2769 (1965).

See also the Agreement of January 17, 1955, on certain Financial Matters between Turkey and the United Kingdom, Cmd. 9373 (1955) and, on the collective efforts made to deal with Turkey's international insolvency, J. J. Kaplan, *The Challenge of Foreign Aid* (1967), p. 325 *et seq.*

For an interest-free loan by the United Kingdom to Turkey "towards the cost of the purchase of 300 buses, and spare parts, by the Istanbul Municipal Transport Authority," see the Agreement of March 4, 1968 (Cmnd. 3637 (1968)), as amended by the Agreement of May 2, 1968 (Cmnd. 3719 (1968)) and, for a further interest-free loan of £1½ million towards the cost of establishing a seamless steel pipe plant in Ankara, the Agreement of May 22, 1968, Cmnd. 3734 (1968).

three years and to be repaid from 1971 to 1975 without interest.[20] This loan corresponds to 60 per cent. of the amounts due, under the Paris Agreement of 1959, from the Turkish Government to British creditors from 1965 to 1967.[21]

(2) *Argentina.* The United Kingdom, together with the other capital-exporting OECD countries, provided assistance in 1966 to Argentina in refinancing her medium-term commercial debts. The object was to enable her to meet in the required foreign exchanges all obligations under contracts by persons or corporations resident in Argentina for the supply of goods or services which had been officially guaranteed, and the payments under which had fallen due in 1965.

The British share of the loan was 60 per cent. of the instalments due in 1965 and paid in Argentinian currency during that year or before March 31, 1966, up to a maximum of £3,500,000. Repayment of this loan is to take place in five gradually increasing instalments, spread over the period from 1968 to 1972.[22]

Participation of the United Kingdom in this loan was not made dependent on what, in an accompanying exchange of notes, is described as a "satisfactory settlement of outstanding claims by United Kingdom interests on the Argentine Government." All the Argentine Government undertook was to use its best endeavours to pursue direct negotiations then in progress in order to facilitate such a settlement.[23] The Agreement came into force on signature.[24] The Government of the United Kingdom did not consider it necessary to insist on a ratification clause to assist the Argentine Government in implementing speedily its good resolutions.

(3) *Ghana.* Under the transfer scheme agreed between the United Kingdom and Ghana (Agreement of February 27, 1967)[25] regarding the medium-term commercial debts (as defined in the Agreement) which were owed by the Government and residents of Ghana and due by June 30, 1967, 20 per cent. were to be transferred between July 1, 1967, and December 1, 1968. Of debts due between July 1, 1967, and December 31, 1968, 20 per cent. are to be transferred on maturity, and the remainder of 80 per cent. of all these debts in eight instalments between June 30, 1972, and 1979.

[20] *The Times* (London), October 22, 1965.
In 1965, payments for interests, dividends and debt amortisation absorbed more than 40 per cent. of Turkey's earnings of foreign exchange (Kaplan, *loc. cit.*, above, p. 51, note 19, p. 360).

[21] *The Times* (London), October 22, 1965.

[22] Cmnd. 3215 (1967). See also the Loan Agreement of June 5, 1963, between Argentina and the United Kingdom, Cmnd. 2164 (1963).

[23] Cmnd. 3215 (1967), p. 9.
See also below, p. 91.

[24] Article VIII, Cmnd. 3215 (1967), p. 5.
For an earlier agreement of the United Kingdom with Chile to assist her in refinancing her medium-term commercial debts, as defined in the Agreement of November 23, 1965, see Cmnd. 2872 (1966).

[25] Cmnd. 3247 (1967).
Between April 1, 1966, and June 1967, the Exports Credits Guarantee Department paid out to claimants regarding payments outstanding long after the date when they were due £8½ million (H.C.Deb., Vol. 748, col. 75, June 14, 1967).

(4) *Indonesia.* Under the transfer scheme with Indonesia (Agreement of August 1, 1967),[26] debts overdue or due by December 31, 1967, are to be transferred in thirty-two instalments extending from 1971 until 1978.

(5) *Laos.* In co-operation with Australia, France and the United States, the United Kingdom undertook in 1963 to establish a Foreign Exchange Operations Fund for Laos of U.S.$ 8 million. The maximal liability of the United Kingdom in this rescue operation was fixed at U.S.$ 1,700,000. These commitments by the rescue Powers were entered over and above the other aid programmes announced prior to this Agreement.[27]

One of the objectives of the operation was to " establish a solid foundation for sound economic development favourable to capital investment." [28] At least, the Royal Lao Government had the courtesy to thank that of the United Kingdom for its assistance and to express its " sentiments of gratitude." [29]

In assessing the effectiveness of this scheme, it is necessary to bear in mind that stabilisation of the deficit of the Lao budget on an agreed level was considered to be an essential feature of making the country " viable " on the international level. The figures stated in this and subsequent agreements appear to prove conclusively that this object has not yet been attained.

In the 1963 Agreement, the Lao Government undertook to restrict its overall budget deficit for 1964–65 to 5,803·7 million Kip.[30] In the 1965 Agreement, an additional difference between revenues and expenditure during this period of 1,400 million Kip was disclosed. It was agreed that this was to be covered by the sale of foreign exchange at the disposal of the Lao Government to the Foreign Exchange Operations Fund.[31] In the 1966 Agreement, it was agreed that the budgetary deficit for 1965–1966 should be increased to 10,400 million Kip. It was understood that the Lao Government would hold the deficit on this level,[32] which was nearly twice

26 Cmnd. 3528 (1968).

27 December 24, 1963, Cmnd. 2331 (1964).
See also the Loan Agreement of May 17, 1963, between Laos and the United Kingdom, Cmnd. 2072 (1963).

28 Cmnd. 2331 (1964), p. 5.

29 *Ibid.*, p. 7.

30 *Ibid.*, p. 5.
According to information received from the Bank of England, there are two rates for the Lao Kip. The official rate of Kip 240 = U.S.$ 1 (Kip 576 = £1) was established on January 1, 1964, replacing the former official rate of Kip 80 = U.S.$ 1 (in operation since 1958). This rate applies to imports of aid goods, government requirements and other specified transactions. The unofficial rate has stabilised at Kip 500 = U.S.$ 1 (Kip 1,200 = £1) and is used for all other foreign exchange transactions.

31 April 7, 1965, Cmnd. 2699 (1965), pp. 4–5.
Since 1965, also Japan is associated with this programme.

32 January 29, 1966, Cmnd. 2999 (1966), pp. 3–4.
For promised reductions in this Lao budget, see the further Agreement of January 11, 1967, between Laos and the United Kingdom, Cmnd. 3236 (1967), p. 37.
In the Agreement of June 7, 1968 (Cmnd. 3738—1968), it was provided that the Government of Laos should limit the budgetary deficit during the fiscal year 1967–68 to a maximum of 8,500 million Kip (p. 3).

that contemplated in 1963. In purely financial terms, it would be hard to consider the operation an unqualified success. It is arguable that overriding political and military reasons account for this failure and explain the further inflation of Lao budgets since 1963.

In any case, it may be doubted whether any of the rescue agreements discussed in this Section have succeeded in laying solid foundations—as, in one of these agreements, it was hopefully termed—for " sound economic development, favourable to capital investment." [33]

3—Agreements Terminating a Status Mixtus

Under the international quasi-order of the United Nations, a number of unverifiable situations of resort to force may arise. They belong to an ill-defined sphere of *status mixtus* between the states of peace and war.[34]

In the context of the protection of British property rights abroad, two post-1945 treaties by which such a *status mixtus* was terminated call for consideration: the Agreement of February 28, 1959, between the United Arab Republic and the United Kingdom on Financial and Commercial Relations and British Property in Egypt [35]—and subsequent supplementary agreements [36]—and the Exchange of Notes of December 1, 1966, between Indonesia and the United Kingdom concerning the losses incurred by the Government of the United Kingdom and British nationals as a result of the disturbances in Indonesia in September 1963.[37]

(a) The Treaty with the United Arab Republic

It is necessary to distinguish between three interrelated but, in law, separate sets of facts: the nationalisation by Egypt of the Suez Canal Company [38]; the interference by Egypt with the freedom of navigation in the Suez Canal,[39] and the measures of confiscation and sequestration taken by the Egyptian Government at various times since 1956 against British and other foreign-owned property.

[33] *Loc. cit.* above, p. 53, note 27, p. 5.

In May 1968, India and the Aid Consortium, established under the auspices of the International Bank for Reconstruction and Development and consisting of 11 members, agreed to a postponement of the repayment of part of India's foreign debt, which required debt servicing by repayment of capital and interest of $500 million a year (*The Economist*, June 1, 1968).

By the end of 1967, what are by the Ministry of Overseas Development described as developing countries had outstanding debts to the United Kingdom of £988 million in principal and interest (*The Times* (London), September 10, 1968).

[34] See, further, Vol. II, p. 50 *et seq.*

[35] Cmnd. 723 (1959).

[36] The Agreements of August 7, 1962 (Cmnd. 1820—1962), and April 24, 1967 (Cmnd. 3476—1967).

[37] Cmnd. 3277 (1967).

[38] See below, p. 84 *et seq.*

[39] See, for instance, B. Broms, *The Legal Status of the Suez Canal* (1961) and Y. van der Mensbrugghe, *Les Guaranties de la liberté de navigation dans le Canal de Suez* (1964); R. O. Matthews, 21 *International Organization* (1967), p. 79 *et seq.*; D. H. N. Johnson, 31 M.L.R. (1968), pp. 163–164, and the further literature cited in the *Manual*, p. 489. See also below, p. 85.

In this Section, we are concerned only with these measures of confiscation and sequestration. Those taken between 1956 and 1959 were alleged to have been retaliatory acts against the armed interventions in 1956 by the United Kingdom, France and Israel and the British acts of freezing Egypt's Sterling balances in London and other related British measures.[40]

In principle, the measures of appropriation of British property by the Egyptian Government without full or adequate, prompt and effective compensation were acts of illegal confiscation.[41] Even if, at the time, a state of war had existed between Egypt and the interventionist Powers, the Egyptian acts of appropriation of British property would have been contrary to international customary law. All that a belligerent may do is to sequestrate the property of enemy nationals.[42]

At best, the Egyptian measures of expropriation could be justified on the ground of retaliation against alleged breaches of the Charter of the United Nations by the interventionist Powers. It is, however, arguable that the acts of these Powers were justifiable as acts of self-defence on the part of Israel, and collective defence by France and the United Kingdom, against the persistent infiltration into Israel of Egyptian-trained irregular forces from Egyptian and Egyptian-held territories.[43] On this assumption, Egypt was unable to plead reprisals—that is, acts illegal in themselves, but legalised by a prior illegal act of the other party [44]—in justification of its acts of confiscation of British-owned property.

The position is different regarding the sequestration of property owned by nationals of the intervening Powers. In the relations between Egypt and Israel the armistice agreements had not terminated the state of war existing between the Arab States and Israel since Israel's foundation. At least, this was the Egyptian contention.[45]

In the relations between France and the United Kingdom, on the one hand, and Egypt on the other, the interventions of 1956 did not lead to a formal state of war. They created an armed conflict by which a *status mixtus* between the states of peace and war was created. In these circumstances, the Egyptian authorities were entitled to assimilate the treatment of private British and French property to that of enemy aliens. Thus, while the armed conflict lasted, they were free to subject such property to measures analogous to the treatment of enemy property, that is, a fiduciary administration similar to the sequestration of enemy property.[46]

It was the threefold object of the 1959 Agreement between the United Arab Republic and the United Kingdom to terminate the armed conflict

40 See, for instance, the Exchange Control (Payments—Egyptian Monetary Area) Order 1956 (S.I. 1956 No. 1163).

41 See above, p. 4 *et seq.*

42 See, further, Vol. II, p. 75 *et seq.*

43 See, further, the present writer's Letter to the Editor of *The Times* (London), November 8, 1956.

44 See, further, Vol. II, p. 37 *et seq.*

45 See, further, 21 C.L.P. (1968), p. 245, n. 5.

46 See, further, Vol. II, pp. 50 and 75 *et seq.*

between Egypt and the United Kingdom, " re-establish normal relations "[47] and settle the issues which had arisen from the Egyptian acts of appropriation and sequestration of British property.

This last object was attained on a rough and ready basis. The United Arab Republic undertook to make a lump-sum payment of £27,500,000 as compensation for the confiscation of the properties of United Kingdom nationals in the United Arab Republic and of the shares of such nationals in Egyptian enterprises and for any claims regarding injury or damage to such property before the signature of the Agreement.[48] For the rest, both sides agreed to terminate all restrictive measures taken in connection with the armed conflict of 1956[49] and waive all other claims against each other arising from this confrontation.[50]

Five aspects of the settlement of 1959, the subsequent subsidiary Agreements of 1962 and 1967, and the treatment of British claimants by the United Kingdom Government are noteworthy:

(1) The claims for compensation by United Kingdom nationals were estimated to amount to about £80 million.[51] Thus, claimants under the 1959 Agreement fared better than those under some of the post-1945 nationalisation agreements concluded by the United Kingdom.[52]

(2) The position of these claimants was further improved by additional compensation granted out of United Kingdom funds. This action was considered to be justified on the special grounds which had put these properties in jeopardy.[53]

(3) The special responsibilities accepted by the United Kingdom in these cases also explain another exceptional feature in the treatment of the claimants. Claimants for small amounts—actually, as estimated by Lord Hume, 90 per cent. of the claimants—did not merely receive *pro rata* compensation of their claims but, on grounds of equity, full compensation.[54]

(4) It may be wondered why the United Kingdom did not use more effectively the Sterling balances of about £140 million, held by Egypt in London, to obtain a more satisfactory settlement. It has been suggested that to have taken this course would have ruined the United Kingdom's reputation as an international banker. Another and, perhaps, even more potent reason may have been that the value of British properties exposed

47 Preamble, Cmnd. 723 (1959), p. 3.
See also the reference in one of the exchanges of letters of February 28, 1959, to the action which the two Governments agreed to take " with a view to resuming normal commercial relations " (*ibid.*, p. 16).
48 Article IV (*ibid.*, p. 4).
49 Article II–III (*ibid.*, p. 3).
50 See the Exchange of Letters of February 28, 1959 (*ibid.*, p. 19).
51 Lord Killearn (H.L.Deb., Vol. 243, col. 414 (August 2, 1962). See, however, the Chancellor of the Exchequer, H.C.Deb., Vol. 601, cols. 37–38 (March 2, 1959).
On the Foreign Compensation Act 1962 (11 Eliz. 2, c. 4), under which these claimants received compensation, see *Contemporary Practice* 1962 (II), p. 198 *et seq.*; B.P.I.L. 1963 (I), p. 28, and Lillich (1967), p. 149 *et seq.*
52 See above, p. 40 *et seq.*
53 H. Gaitskell, as quoted by Lillich (1967), p. 136.
54 As quoted by Lillich (1967), p. 19, n. 113.

to Egyptian counter-measures, and to be returned to their owners under the 1959 Agreement was estimated to be of about the same order as the Egyptian Sterling balances in London.[55]

(5) The Supplementary Exchange of Notes of April 24, 1967, makes salutary reading. Under the heading of " recent measures of sequestration," it lists further measures of sequestration imposed by the Egyptian Government on British-owned property between the date of signature of the 1959 Agreement and March 24, 1964.[56]

In 1965, the Egyptian Government broke off diplomatic relations with the United Kingdom over Rhodesia.[57] It would be ironical if resumption of these relations were to be followed by a post-1945 reversal of pre-1914 gunboat diplomacy: accommodation, however temporary, of difficult small States or small-Power law-breakers by the grant of additional economic aid.[58]

(b) The Agreement with Indonesia

By the Agreement of December 1, 1966, between Indonesia and the United Kingdom the British property claims arising out of the Jakarta incidents of 1963 were settled. After a series of acts which amounted to a complete breakdown of law and order, it was, to crown it all, Indonesia—and not the United Kingdom—which had broken off diplomatic relations.

The subsequent change in the Indonesian régime enabled the United Kingdom to dispense with the need to decide on whether it should insist on formal apologies and satisfaction for the non-material injuries suffered. It was able to content itself with reparation for the costs of reconstruction and complete reinstatement of the British Embassy buildings in Jakarta and further payments in full settlement of any claims for loss or damage suffered by United Kingdom nationals, " directly or indirectly, during or as a consequence of the riots and public disorders in Indonesia between 10 and 30 September, 1963." [59]

To attempt to analyse the Agreement in isolation would mean missing an essential point. This settlement—like that made also in 1966 between Indonesia and the Netherlands—has to be evaluated in a wider setting: the phase then reached in the three-cornered global struggle for Indonesia.

In this perspective, the restraint shown by the victims of the Sukarno régime and the international rescue operation mounted by the major capital-exporting countries in O.E.C.D. make sense. They form integral parts of a sustained effort to remove Indonesia from the Chinese sphere of influence.[60]

[55] Estimates submitted by the Chancellor of the Exchequer to the House of Commons on March 16, 1959. See *Contemporary Practice*, 9 I.C.L.Q. (1960), p. 290.
[56] Appendix B (Cmnd. 3476 (1967), p. 4 *et seq.*).
[57] The Egyptian action was taken on December 15, 1965, in implementation of a Resolution of the Organisation for African Unity, passed December 5, 1965 (*Keesing's Archives*, p. 21182).
[58] See below, p. 90 *et seq.*
[59] Point (1) (c), Cmnd. 3277 (1967), p. 2. See, further, *Inductive Approach*, pp. 172–173.
[60] For footnote, see p. 58.

4—Regional and Sectional Agreements

In the post-1945 period, the United Kingdom increasingly put its faith in the attempts made to protect property abroad on a multilateral basis.

These efforts were made against the background of the two lapidary, if legally not-binding, propositions on the subject enunciated in the Universal Declaration of Human Rights, adopted by the General Assembly of the United Nations in 1948:

1. "Everyone has the right to own property alone as well as in association with others."

2. "No one shall be arbitrarily deprived of his property."[61]

In the drafting of the International Covenants, adopted by the General Assembly in 1966, the protection of property rights suffered from a process of shrinkage, characteristic of post-1945 international attempts at transforming moral duties into legally binding obligations. While, by itself, the adoption of the Covenants by the General Assembly could not produce this effect, these Covenants are intended to become legally binding through the regular processes of signature and ratification or accession.[62]

Five features of these Covenants are directly relevant:

(1) Property rights as such are not protected.[63]

(2) The word *property* is mentioned merely as one of several grounds of illegal discrimination, detracting from equal enjoyment by all of the rights granted under the Covenants, in particular equality before the law and equal protection of the law.[64]

(3) The door for one form of discrimination is left open. Developing countries—although left undefined[65]—"with due regard to human rights and their national economy, may determine to what extent they would guarantee the economic rights recognised in the present Covenant to non-nationals."[66]

60 See above, p. 53, and below, p. 95

For the Agreement of September 7, 1966, between Indonesia and the Netherlands on outstanding financial problems, see 6 I.L.M. (1967), p. 45 *et seq.*

It is provided in the Agreement that, in the case of expropriation or nationalisation of property owned by nationals of the other party, the State taking such measures "shall make provision for the payment of an effective and adequate indemnity in conformity with the law of nations" (Article VIII—*ibid.*, p. 49).

61 Article 17, Gen.Ass.Res. 217 (III).

On slavery and servitude, see *ibid.*, Article 4.

62 Article 26 of Covenant I; Article 48 of Covenant II (Cmnd. 3220 (1967), pp. 9–10 and 27).

63 Proposals to this effect were made by France, the United States of America and Uruguay. See, further, M. S. McDougal and G. Bebr, 58 A.J.I.L. (1964), p. 626.

On slavery and servitude, see Article 8 of Covenant II (Cmnd. 3220 (1967), p. 15).

On the reasons for the exclusion of respect for private property from his draft of a bill of human rights, see H. Lauterpacht, *An International Bill of the Rights of Man* (1945), p. 163, and *International Law and Human Rights* (1950), p. 342, n. 39.

64 Article 2 (2) of Covenant I and Article 2 (1) of Covenant II (Cmnd. 3220 (1967), pp. 3 and 13).

65 See above, pp. 15–16.

66 Article 2 (3) of Covenant I, Cmnd. 3220 (1967), p. 3.

(4) On the basis of the discussions in the General Assembly on permanent sovereignty over natural resources and the spate of resolutions adopted by that body on a subject of increasingly ritual significance,[67] the relevant proposition is couched in the form of a collective economic right in the Covenant on Economic, Social and Cultural Rights: "All peoples may, for their own ends, freely dispose of their natural wealth and resources, without any prejudice to any obligations arising out of international economic co-operation, based upon the principle of mutual benefit, and international law. In no case may a people be deprived of its own means of subsistence." [68]

As in the corresponding Resolutions of the General Assembly, the right of the disposal of natural wealth and resources includes the freedom under international customary law to limit this state of affairs. Similarly, mutual benefit is open to different interpretations according to the society or community context of such engagements. Moreover, even in highly developed legal systems, requirements such as consideration or *causa* tend to become rather formal types of reciprocity.[69] Finally, experience appears to prove that, from the angle of the recipient, the adequacy of any consideration looks different before and after the conclusion of an agreement which is intended to provide substantive benefits to both sides.[70]

(5) Both Covenants contain identical clauses for their interpretation in relation to the right of permanent sovereignty. None of their provisions is to be interpreted as "impairing the inherent right of all peoples to enjoy and utilise fully and freely their natural wealth and resources." [71]

The term "inherent" right is as meaningless in this context as in Article 51 of the Charter of the United Nations.[72] In both cases, the exercise of the inherent right may be limited by consent like that of any other right under international law. All these Articles mean is that any other right affirmed in the Covenants must be interpreted restrictively so as not to interfere with the right of enjoyment and full and free use of natural wealth and resources.

It will remain to be seen whether the United Kingdom will become a party to these Covenants. The real difficulty is that, on a global level, the precondition of the effective application of such Covenants is lacking in contemporary world society: the requisite ethical common denominator.[73]

[67] See above, p. 9, and below, p. 189.

See also Resolution No. 1932 (XVIII) on Means of Promoting Agrarian Reform, adopted by the General Assembly on December 11, 1963.

In explaining his affirmative vote in the Second Committee, the United Kingdom representative endorsed the view expressed by the delegate of the United States of America that nothing in the draft Resolution affected the obligations of States under international law, B.P.I.L. 1963 (II), p. 124.

[68] Article 1 (2) of Covenant I. Similarly, Article 47 of Covenant II (Cmnd. 3220 (1967), pp. 3 and 27).

[69] See, further, *The Frontiers*, p. 15 *et seq.*

[70] See, further, below, p. 65 *et seq.*

[71] Article 25 of Covenant I and Article 47 of Covenant II (Cmnd. 3220 (1967), pp. 9 and 27).

[72] See *Fundamental Principles*, p. 327 *et seq.*

[73] See, further, *The Frontiers*, p. 294 *et seq.*

The mere incantation in the Covenants of the postulate of a " democratic society " is no commensurate substitute.[74]

On levels falling short of universal aspirations, it assists in clarifying thought to distinguish between attempts on a genuinely regional basis, intended to include every sovereign State in a functionally determined area, and others on a sectional footing.[75] In so far as the protection of property rights is concerned, it is especially advisable to bear in mind the elements of ideology and vested interests which may enter the picture and make it more appropriate to be strict in classifying an apparently regional institution as a sectional organisation.

From this angle, two of the three relevant institutions—the Council of Europe and the Organisation for Economic Co-operation and Development—are ambivalent. The Council of Europe has its regional and ideological aspects.[76] Similarly, the predecessor of O.E.C.D., the Organisation for European Economic Co-operation, started its career as a regional organisation. Yet, subsequently, it became an unmistakably sectional organisation, dominated by its major capital-exporting members.[77]

In analysing the conventions to be considered under this head, the dual character of the institutions sponsoring these agreements should be recalled.

(a) The 1952 Protocol

The founder-members of the Council of Europe thought of themselves as being sufficiently " like-minded " and sharing an adequate " common heritage of political traditions, ideals, freedom and the rule of law " to implement further certain of the rights stated in the Universal Declaration of 1948.[78] The reassertion of the prohibition of slavery and servitude apart,[79] property rights are covered with oblivion in the Rome Convention of November 4, 1950, for the Protection of Human Rights and Fundamental Freedoms.[80] As in the International Covenants of 1966, the word " property " appeared merely as a criterion of illegal discrimination.[81]

It took a separate Protocol of March 20, 1952, to the Convention to

74 See Articles 4 and 8 of Covenant I (Cmnd. 3220 (1967), pp. 3–4).

75 See, further, *The Frontiers*, p. 285, and the *Manual*, p. 337 *et seq.*

76 See below under (a), and, further, the *Manual*, p. 344 *et seq.*

77 See, further, the *Manual*, p. 350 *et seq.*

78 Preamble of the Convention of November 4, 1950, for the Protection of Human Rights and Fundamental Freedoms (Cmd. 8969 (1953), p. 2).

79 Article 4 (*ibid.*, p. 2).

80 Until the publication of the preparatory material on the 1950 Convention and the 1952 Protocol, merely indirect evidence for this omission is available. It points to a veto by the United Kingdom in the Committee of Ministers of a draft clause, recommended by the Consultative Assembly and drafted on lines similar to those incorporated in Article 1 of the 1952 Protocol. See, further, K.-H. Böckstiegel, *Die allgemeinen Grundsätze des Völkerrechts über Eigentumsentziehung* (1963), p. 11 *et seq.*, and E. Schwelb, 13 A.J.C.L. (1964), p. 533 *et seq.*

81 See Article 14 (Cmd. 8969 (1953), p. 8) and above, p. 58.

repair this omission. The form in which this was done was less than perfect.

According to the English text,

> " Every natural or legal person is entitled to the peaceful enjoyment of his possessions. No one shall be deprived of his possessions except in the public interest and subject to the conditions provided for by law and by the general principles of international law.
>
> The preceding provisions shall not, however, in any way impair the right of a State to enforce such laws as it deems necessary to control the use of property in accordance with the general interest or to secure the payment of taxes or other contributions or penalties." [82]

In the equally authoritative French text of Paragraph 1 of Article 1 of Protocol 1, no exact equivalent to the " peaceful enjoyment " of one's possessions is to be found. Instead, everybody " *a droit au respect de ses biens*." In the second sentence of the French text of the first Paragraph, the equivalent for " possessions " is " *propriété*." Thus, it appears that the term " possessions " in the English text has no technical meaning in contrast to property, but must be read as being synonymous with it.

Similarly, the general principles of international law referred to are neither the general principles of law recognised by civilised nations nor any general principles of international law as distinct from operative rules of international law.[83] What the draftsmen meant were the rules of general international law on the expropriation of foreign property. In this way, but without saying so expressly, they intended to incorporate into Article 1 the requirement of compensation for expropriation, as postulated by international customary law.[84]

It is doubtful whether, under the Protocol, this protection of property rights extends to nationals of the Contracting Parties. In the European Commission on Human Rights, a tendency appears to exist to reject such an interpretation.[85] Yet, in the context of a convention which is intended to implement universal human rights, it is difficult to accept so restrictive a construction of the Article.[86]

The United Kingdom has accepted the jurisdiction of the European Commission of Human Rights to receive petitions, *inter alia*, on Article 1 of the 1952 Protocol, and also the jurisdiction of the European Court of Human Rights regarding the interpretation and application of this provision.[87]

[82] Cmd. 9221 (1954), p. 2.

[83] See, further, *Inductive Approach*, p. 72 *et seq.*

[84] See above, p. 4 *et seq.*

[85] *Gudmundsson* v. *Iceland* (1960), 3 *Yearbook of the European Convention on Human Rights* (1960), p. 394, at pp. 424 *et seq.*

[86] For a brilliant refutation, see Schwelb, *loc. cit.* in note 80 above, p. 518 *et seq.*

[87] Declaration of September 12, 1967, Cmnd. 3475 (1967).

On the need for prior exhaustion of all local remedies, " according to the generally recognised rules of international law," as a precondition of the Commission's jurisdiction, see Article 26 of the 1950 Convention (Cmd. 8969 (1953), p. 12) and, further,

(*ctd. overleaf*)

(b) The European Establishment Convention

The European Convention on Establishment of December 13, 1955, has been in force since February 23, 1965. In 1956, the United Kingdom signed but, so far, has not ratified the Convention.[88]

The Convention is primarily based on the standard of national treatment, that is, the treatment of nationals of other Contracting Parties on a footing of equality with those of the Contracting Party where they sojourn or are resident. In principle, this applies to the possession and exercise of all private rights, including those relating to property.[89] The term "possession" in this context becomes clearer from comparison with its equivalent in the French text: "*jouissance*" (enjoyment).

Provision is made for the maintenance of existing restrictions on the acquisition, possession or use of certain categories of property by nationals of other Contracting Parties [90] and the imposition of further restrictions on grounds of national necessity or defence.[91]

The judicial and administrative guarantees of the protection of property offered in the Convention are also secured on a basis of equality of all nationals of Contracting Parties.[92] It is made clear in the Convention that the standard of national treatment is not intended to derogate from the minimum standard applicable to foreign nationals under international customary law or from the obligations entered into by Contracting Parties under the 1952 Protocol on Human Rights [93]: in the event of expropriation or nationalisation of their property by any other Party, they are to be treated "*at least* as favourably as nationals of the latter Party." [94]

Equality on a national footing applies also to duties, charges, taxes or contributions but subject to provisions on double taxation in agreements previously concluded or to be concluded.[95]

In the last resort, the International Court of Justice is authorised under the Convention to deal with any dispute between the Parties on the interpretation and application of the Convention.[96]

(*Note 87 ctd.*)
F. Monconduit, *La Commission Européenne des Droits de l'Homme* (1965), p. 302 *et seq.*; N. Antonopoulos, *La Jurisprudence des organs de la Convention Européenne des Droits de l'Homme* (1967), p. 47 *et seq.*, and C. C. Morrisson, *The Developing European Law of Human Rights* (1967), p. 78 *et seq.*

88 *European Treaty Series* No. 19.
The signature of the United Kingdom is subject to reservations regarding Articles 9, 15 and 21.
For a statement in the House of Commons by the Joint Under-Secretary of State for Home Affairs made on July 7, 1964, which could be taken to imply that the United Kingdom was bound by the Convention, see B.P.I.L. 1964 (II), p. 193.
Neither, so far, is the United Kingdom a party to the European Convention on the Establishment of Companies, opened for signature on January 20, 1966 (*European Treaty Series* No. 57).

89 Article 4 (*European Treaty Series* No. 19, p. 3).

90 Article 6 (a) (*ibid.*, pp. 3–4).

91 Article 5 (*ibid.*, p. 3).

92 Articles 7–9 (*ibid.*, pp. 4–5).

93 See above, p. 60 *et seq.*

94 Article 23 (*European Treaty Series* No. 19, p. 10).

95 Article 21 (1) (*ibid.*, p. 9).

96 Article 31 (1) (*ibid.*, p. 13).

(c) The European Convention for the Peaceful Settlement of Disputes

In addition to the commitments entered into under the Optional Clause of the Statute of the World Court [97] and those discussed in a previous Section,[98] the United Kingdom is a party to the European Convention for the Peaceful Settlement of Disputes of April 29, 1957. The Convention has been in force since April 30, 1958. Subject to far-reaching reservations authorised,[99] the Convention provides for a comprehensive system for the pacific settlement of disputes by international adjudication, conciliation and arbitration.[100]

(d) The O.E.C.D. Code of Liberalisation of Capital Movements of 1965, as amended in 1968

This Code, in force since 1965 and amended in 1968, rests on a decision of the Council of the Organisation for European Economic Co-operation of December 4, 1959, and subsequent decisions of the Council of the Organisation for Economic Co-operation and Development.

Under the Code, members of the Organisation have undertaken general and specific obligations to eliminate restrictions on the movement of capital. Measures to this effect are termed measures of liberalisation. Members are generally committed to the progressive abolition of restrictions on movements of capital from one member State to another. The criterion is the extent necessary for effective economic co-operation.

Moreover, the members have agreed to endeavour to treat all assets owned by non-residents on a footing of equality, irrespective of the date of their creation, and to permit the liquidation of such assets and the transfer of such assets or of the proceeds of their liquidation.[101]

97 Declaration of November 27, 1963 (International Court of Justice, *Yearbook 1966–1967*, p. 70).

98 See above, p. 61.

99 Articles 34 and 35 (5 *European Yearbook*, p. 359).

These reservations are not stated in Cmnd. 1298 (1961), but are available in a *corrigendum* slip. They are also not contained in the *European Treaty Series* or the *European Yearbook*.

In accordance with these reservations, contained in the *procès-verbal* of the deposit of the instrument of ratification (December 7, 1960), the United Kingdom is not bound by Chapter III of the Convention on Arbitration but, so far as relevant, the reservations made by the United Kingdom in its Declaration under the Optional Clause of the Statute of the I.C.J. apply also to this Convention. Moreover, Chapter II of the Convention on Conciliation does not apply to non-metropolitan territories of the United Kingdom other than the Channel Islands and the Isle of Man.

100 In the case of disputes other than those to be submitted under Article 1 to the International Court of Justice or settled by way of conciliation, *ex aequo et bono* arbitration is provided for all remaining disputes, "having regard to the general principles of international law, while respecting the contractual obligations and the final decisions of international tribunals which are binding on the parties." (Article 26—*ibid.*, p. 355.)

Under Article 28 (2) (*ibid.*, p. 357), the Convention does not affect the application of the provisions discussed above for the settlement of disputes under the Rome Convention of 1950 on the 1952 Protocol (see above, p. 60).

On the 1966 Convention on the Settlement of Investment Disputes, to which the United Kingdom is also a party, see below, p. 135 *et seq.*

101 Article 1 (No. 18085/June 1965, p. 9).

See, further, H. J. Hahn, 13 *A.V.R.* (1967), p. 197 *et seq.*

Beyond this, the members are to grant any authorisation that may be required for the conclusion or execution of transactions and for transfers specified in the Code.[102]

In 1964, the O.E.C.D. Council decided to treat three of its members—Greece, Turkey and Iceland—as being justified in invoking one of the derogation clauses of the Code because of their precarious economic and financial situation. Under this clause, a member State need not take the whole of the liberalisation measures set out in Article 2 of the Code.[103]

(e) The EFTA Agreement

Article 16 of the Stockholm Convention of January 4, 1960, establishing the European Free Trade Association, contains a directly relevant provision.[104] As in the European Convention on Establishment,[105] provision is made in the EFTA Agreement for national treatment. The test is whether such treatment is necessary to avoid frustration of the benefits to be expected from the removal or absence of duties and quantitative restrictions on trade between member States.

[102] Article 2 (a) (No. 18085/June 1965, p. 10).

[103] *Ibid.*, p. 3.
See also the complementary Code of Liberalisation of Current Invisible Operations of 1967 (No. 22987), the obligations of which also do not, at present, apply to Greece and Turkey.

[104] Cmnd. 1026 (1960), p. 22.
For a decision taken under Article 16 at the meeting of May 12–13, 1966, of the EFTA Council and the Joint Council of EFTA and Finland, see 5 I.L.M. (1966), p. 784.

[105] See above, p. 62.

CHAPTER 6

EVALUATION:

I—TWO TEST CASES

IT remains to evaluate more fully the British treaty programme of the post-1945 era. What is needed is not any impressionist overall evaluation, be it positive or negative, but an assessment which is rationally verifiable and as concrete as possible.

A criterion that appears to meet these requirements is the prophylactic value of these treaties: If the treaty had not been concluded, what difference, if any, would this have made for the actual protection of the investments concerned?

From this point of view, primarily retrospective treaties—peace settlements [1] and nationalisation agreements [2]—are, at the most, of indirect relevance. Unequivocal reaffirmation, even if retrospective, of governing legal rules and principles has some protective value beyond the parties directly involved. Yet, this test is more fully applicable to the other types of treaty—general economic agreements,[3] devolution agreements,[4] rescue agreements [5] and germane regional and sectional agreements.[6]

If all available cases of relevant conflict situations were examined, this would provide a reliable picture of the value of these British treaties for the direct and indirect protection of foreign investments. To perform adequately the task of such an evaluation, it would be necessary to provide detailed studies of each of the pertinent conflict situations. If corresponding investigations were carried out into the prophylactic functions fulfilled by the treaty programmes of the other major capital-exporting States, this would be even more valuable. Allowing for differences in metalegal forms of pressure available in individual cases, such a procedure would make it possible to reach well-founded conclusions on the comparative value of certain patterns of treaty and individual clauses in such treaties.

Nothing so ambitious can be attempted within the compass of this book. All that it is possible to do is to select the two most significant disputes in the field of the protection of foreign investments in which, since 1945, the United Kingdom was involved and apply to them the test of the relevance of the governing treaties, especially those designed to anticipate

[1] See above, p. 30 *et seq.*
[2] See above, p. 40 *et seq.*
[3] See above, p. 32 *et seq.*
[4] See above, p. 48 *et seq.*
[5] See above, p. 50 *et seq.*
[6] See above, p. 58 *et seq.*

and avoid any dispute. They are the Anglo-Iranian Oil Dispute and the Nationalisation of the Suez Canal Company.

1—The Anglo-Iranian Oil Dispute

For at least eight reasons, the Anglo-Iranian Oil Dispute of 1949–54 provides a test case *par excellence*:

(1) The oil wells and refineries of the Anglo-Iranian Oil Company constituted one of the most highly prized British investments abroad. Actually, the Government of the United Kingdom itself was the majority shareholder in A.I.O.C.[7]

(2) The investment was situated in a capital-importing country which was hardly more unstable than most.[8] Moreover, at the time, the United Kingdom could bring into operation in this area a credible display of military, naval and air forces.

(3) Iran had become a sensitive spot on the world frontier between the two hegemonial world Powers. This made any Anglo-Iranian dispute a matter of concern to both the Soviet Union and the United States of America.[9]

(4) On the legal plane, the British oil investments in Iran were considered to be protected not only by international customary law, but also by bilateral treaties of commerce, an Iranian Declaration under the Optional Clause of the Statute of the World Court and a concession agreement, bristling with safeguards in favour of A.I.O.C.

(5) The dispute gave opportunities to a number of international institutions—the International Court of Justice, the Security Council of the United Nations and the International Bank for Reconstruction and Development—to prove themselves.

(6) The United States of America and the American oil companies actively participated in the attempts made to settle the dispute. In its turn, the Soviet Union discreetly assisted Iran from the side-lines.

(7) In the penultimate phase of the dispute, the United Kingdom applied against Iran increasingly stringent economic and financial means of pressure, and A.I.O.C. engaged in a worldwide campaign of threatening potential purchasers of Iranian oil with legal action in national courts.

(8) Finally, the actual settlement of the dispute itself is significant.

(a) Factual Aspects

It is a matter of argument how to date the dispute with reasonable accuracy. It probably has its deepest roots in the reaction of Iranian

[7] Cmd. 7419 (1914) and, further, Bin Cheng, 5 *World Affairs* (1951), p. 387 *et seq.*, and B. Shwadran, *The Middle East, Oil and the Great Powers* (1959), p. 22 *et seq.*
See also below, note 9.

[8] See, further, *Power Politics*, p. 495 *et seq.*

[9] See, further, J. Frankel, 6 Y.B.W.A. (1952), p. 56 *et seq.*, and R. Engler, *La politica petrolera* (1966).
See also above, note 7.

nationalism to the great-Power struggle in the Middle East since the second half of the nineteenth century and the treatment of Iran as a pawn in this game.

A more immediate cause of the confrontation was the desire of the Iranian Government to change in its favour the 1933 Concession Agreement of A.I.O.C.[10] This Agreement itself was the outcome of an earlier dispute between Iran and the United Kingdom which, in 1932, was settled under the auspices of the League of Nations, with Edward Benes as Rapporteur of the League Council and successful mediator.[11]

In 1949, a Supplemental Agreement to the 1933 Agreement was signed by A.I.O.C. and the Iranian Government. Under this Agreement, A.I.O.C. made substantial concessions regarding royalty payments to the Iranian Government but, in exchange, obtained a confirmation of its other rights under the 1933 Concession. Yet, the Supplemental Agreement failed to obtain the consent of the Lower House of the Iranian Parliament and, from 1950 onwards, pressure mounted in Iran for the nationalisation of the Iranian oil industry, which, in fact, was A.I.O.C.[12]

When this battle of words was drawing to a close, the Government of the United Kingdom formally notified the Iranian Government on March 14, 1951, that it considered the proposed nationalisation to be illegal. In particular, it pointed out the difference between a policy of nationalisation, unincumbered by international obligations,[13] and the expropriation of an industry which had been operating in Iran on the security of a regularly negotiated agreement valid until 1993, and "relying on that security, has in all good faith spent enormous sums of money in development."[14]

On March 15, 1951, the Lower House of the Iranian Parliament passed a Single-Article Bill, in accordance with which all operations of exploration, extraction and exploitation of oil in Iran were to be carried out by the Government. The Senate passed the Bill on March 20, 1951. This Bill,[15] and the Oil Nationalisation Law implementing the Single-Article Law, came into force on May 1, 1951, on signature and promulgation by the Shah.[16]

The day after, A.I.O.C. informed the Iranian Government that it requested arbitration under the Concession Agreement of 1933.[17] It also

[10] The Agreement was embodied in a Convention of April 29, 1933, between what then were termed the Imperial Government of Persia and the Anglo-Persian Oil Company, *I.C.J. Pleadings, Anglo-Iranian Oil Co. Case* (*United Kingdom* v. *Iran*), p. 247 *et seq.* The French text of the Convention is the authoritative text.

[11] See *ibid.*, p. 235 *et seq.*

[12] *Ibid.*, p. 274 *et seq.*, and Cmd. 8425 (1951), pp. 3–4. See, further, A. W. Ford, *The Anglo-Iranian Oil Dispute 1951–1952* (1954), p. 48 *et seq.* (useful bibliography, p. 329 *et seq.*).

[13] See above, p. 5 *et seq.* and below, pp. 121 and 161.

[14] Cmd. 8425 (1951), p. 26.

[15] *Ibid.*, p. 27.

[16] *Ibid.*, p. 29.

[17] Article 22 (*loc. cit.* in note 10 above, p. 256).

announced the appointment of Lord Radcliffe as its arbitrator. At the same time, further inconclusive negotiations were proceeding between the Governments of Iran and the United Kingdom.

On May 15, 1951, it was announced in London that a brigade of paratroops was held in readiness in the United Kingdom to protect, if necessary, British lives and property in Iran. In Tehran, the British Ambassador made it clear that the Government of the United Kingdom reserved its right to take the dispute to the International Court of Justice if Iran refused the Company's request for arbitration.

On May 20, the Iranian Government refused the Company's request for arbitration. On May 25, the British brigade of parachutists was moved from the United Kingdom to Cyprus. The day after, A.I.O.C. informed the Iranian Government of its request to the President of the International Court of Justice, in accordance with the Concession Agreement of 1933, to appoint a Sole Arbitrator.[18]

On May 27, the United Kingdom filed its own Application against Iran with the International Court of Justice.[19] The following day, the President of the Court informed the Chairman of A.I.O.C. that some of the questions raised in the Application made by the United Kingdom were in certain respects the same as those arising from the Company's request. Thus, for the time being, he could not take any action regarding the appointment of a Sole Arbitrator under the Concession Agreement.[20]

In June, 1951, an A.I.O.C. delegation from London entered into negotiations with the Iranian Government in Tehran. It stood by its earlier offers—made in February, 1951—of a fifty-fifty division of profits between the Company and the Iranian Government. According to an A.I.O.C. press statement,[21] the delegates also pointed out to the Iranian Government some of what they considered to be realities of the situation: that nobody but A.I.O.C. could provide the capital of £100 million for the needed pipe line from Khorramshahr to the Mediterranean; that, in one year, crude-oil production at Kuwait alone could be raised above the level of Iranian production; that, within three years, the loss of Abadan's refining capacity could be replaced, and that the Company could usefully employ its tanker fleet elsewhere.

On June 20, 1951, the Foreign Secretary of the United Kingdom reassured British subjects that, if required, they would receive protection from the Government of the United Kingdom. The A.I.O.C. delegation left Tehran, without having achieved any visible results and, on June 22, the Government of the United Kingdom filed a request with the International Court of Justice, for provisional measures of protection to be ordered by the Court, pending the final settlement of the dispute.

18 Article 22 (D), *ibid.*, p. 268.
19 *Loc. cit.* in note 10 above, p. 45 *et seq.*
20 I.C.J.Y.B. 1950–1951, p. 48.
21 Ford, *loc. cit.* in note 12 above, pp. 64–65.

On June 26, A.I.O.C. ordered its tankers at Abadan to pump their oil ashore and leave the port. Simultaneously, the Foreign Secretary of the United Kingdom announced that the cruiser *Mauritius* had been ordered to move into the neighbourhood of Abadan.

The Iranian Government denied the jurisdiction of the International Court of Justice to order provisional measures and was not represented at the Court's hearing of the United Kingdom's request for such interim measures. On July 5, 1951, the Court issued an Order, indicating the measures it considered appropriate to preserve the rights of both parties, pending final judgment.[22]

On July 9, 1951, the Iranian Government denounced its Declaration on the jurisdiction of the International Court of Justice under Article 36 of the Court's Statute.[23]

Almost simultaneously, President Truman offered to the Iranian Prime Minister to send to Tehran Mr. Averell Harriman, his adviser on foreign policy, to discuss the whole situation. Dr. Musaddiq accepted the offer and, in fact, Mr. Harriman acted as mediator between the Governments of Iran and the United Kingdom. He also assured the Iranian Government that, in any case, the United States was willing to help Iran under the Point Four Programme of technical assistance.[24]

On July 31, 1951, more British warships arrived in Iraqi waters and, on September 6, A.I.O.C. announced that it would take legal action against any purchasers of oil from the Iranian Government.[25] Four days later, the United Kingdom Treasury cancelled the special convertibility privileges regarding Iranian Sterling balances in London. This measure deprived Iran of most of her Dollar exchange. Beyond this, all United Kingdom licences for the export to Iran of scarce materials, such as railway track equipment and sugar, were withdrawn.

On September 15, 1951, the Iranian Government announced the conclusion of a new barter agreement with the Soviet Union. Among other things, this enabled Iran to obtain the sugar she was no longer able to obtain from the United Kingdom. As the irony of fate would have it, the United Kingdom also turned to the Soviet Union. It bought 200,000 tons of fuel oil from Sovrom Petrol, a Russian-Rumanian joint company. A piquant point was that Sovrom operated expropriated Belgian, British, French and United States oil fields and production facilities in Rumania, for which Rumania had failed to pay compensation.[26]

22 *I.C.J. Reports 1951*, p. 89 *et seq.*

23 I.C.J.Y.B. 1950–1951, p. 199.

24 Ford, *loc. cit.* in note 12 above, pp. 100–123.
On the interest of some of the United States oil companies in these areas since the First World War, see *ibid.*, pp. 20–22.

25 On the contract for the sale of $3·5 million worth of oil to the Afghan Government, to be delivered at the border, which A.I.O.C. chose to distinguish from other contracts, see *ibid.*, pp. 121–122.

26 *Ibid.*, pp. 122–123.
See also above, p. 41 *et seq.*

By September 27, further British army, navy and air force units assembled in the eastern Mediterranean and near the Persian Gulf. In its turn, the Iranian Government gave orders to the Iranian army to blow up the oil installations at Abadan if any foreign troops attempted to land.

On September 28, the United Kingdom Government requested the Security Council of the United Nations to call on the Government of Iran to comply with the provisional measures indicated in the July Order of the International Court of Justice. The Iranian Government contested the Council's jurisdiction on the ground that the dispute was a matter essentially within its domestic jurisdiction. On October 19, the Security Council adjourned its discussion on the substance of the issue until the International Court of Justice had ruled on the Iranian objection to its jurisdiction regarding the British Application.

On December 23, 1951, a survey mission of the International Bank for Reconstruction and Development arrived in Iran. Among other proposals, it suggested resumption of Iranian oil production under a neutral top executive, chosen by and responsible to I.B.R.D.

On January 12, 1952, the Iranian Government ordered all British consulates in Iran to be closed. On January 20, Iran and the United States of America reached agreement on economic and technical aid to Iran of $23 million under the Point Four Programme.

Further I.B.R.D. missions sent to Iran in February and March, 1952, also proved unsuccessful. After the failure of these I.B.R.D. attempts at mediation, President Truman informed the Iranian Government that it could not expect a major United States loan. This had first been mooted in the autumn of 1951 during Premier Musaddiq's visit to Washington and was expected to be in the neighbourhood of $120 million.

During this visit to Washington, the Iranian Prime Minister had refused to sign an agreement for economic and military aid under the United States Mutual Security Act as being incompatible with Iran's neutralist policy. Yet, by April, 1952, he thought it advisable to agree to the resumption of the shipment of military aid, suspended since January, 1952.[27]

On July 22, 1952, the International Court of Justice declined its jurisdiction regarding the British Application.[28] In October, Iran broke off diplomatic relations with the United Kingdom, but resumed them again in December, 1953.

On August 5, 1954, the outlines of a settlement of the dispute, which had the support of the Governments of the United States, the United Kingdom and Iran, were announced. It provided for the payment of compensation by Iran to A.I.O.C.; arrangements between an international consortium of oil companies (the Iranian Oil Consortium 1954) and the Iranian Government for the restoration of the Iranian oil industry in

[27] Ford, *loc. cit.* in note 12 above, p. 153 *et seq.*
[28] *I.C.J. Reports 1952*, p. 93 *et seq.*

southern Iran, outlets for Iranian oil to the world markets, and payments arrangements between the Iranian and United Kingdom Governments, which were to come into operation on ratification by the Iranian Government of the Consortium and Compensation Agreements comprised in the Government Agreement.

The Government Agreement regarding the Iranian Oil Consortium 1954 came into force with the issue of an Iranian Royal Decree on October 29, 1954. It was published on November 15, 1954 in the *Iranian Official Gazette*. In 1965 and 1967, two Supplemental Agreements were concluded.[29]

In the Iranian Oil Consortium—incorporated in the United Kingdom as Iranian Oil Participants, Ltd.—A.I.O.C., subsequently renamed British Petroleum Company, obtained a holding of 40 per cent., and Royal Dutch Shell (Netherlands Iranian Oil Trading Company) a share of 14 per cent. The remainder was allocated to United States (40 per cent.) and French (6 per cent.) oil companies. Under the Agreement, the Consortium was to form two Operating Companies. Actually, these had been incorporated in the Netherlands before the Agreement came into force. They were to be registered in Iran and also to become parties to the Agreement. They came to be known as the Iranian Oil Exploration and Producing Company and the Iranian Oil Refining Company. These two companies, wholly owned by the Iranian Oil Participants, Ltd., were to be responsible for producing and refining operations in Iran. The Boards of Directors of each Company were to consist of seven directors, two of whom were to be nominated by the National Iranian Oil Company.

The members of the Consortium were to nominate subsidiaries of theirs as Trading Companies under the Agreement and were permitted to assign to them a part or all of their rights and obligations regarding purchases and resales under the Agreement. Any Trading Company to which such an assignment was made was deemed to become a party to the Agreement.[30]

(b) Legal Aspects

A number of legal instruments call for consideration: relevant inter-State agreements; the Iranian Declaration under the Optional Clause, as interpreted in the 1952 Judgment of the International Court of Justice; the 1951 Provisional Measures Order of the same Court; the A.I.O.C. Concession Agreement in 1933, and the Iranian Government Agreement of 1954, as amended in 1965 and 1967.

(1) *Relevant inter-State Agreements.* Under the Treaty of Paris of March 4, 1857,[31] and the Commercial Convention of February 9, 1903,[32]

[29] Printed texts, Tehran 1965 and 1967.

The First Supplemental Agreement received the Royal Assent on January 21, 1965, and, in accordance with Article 9 of the Agreement, became effective as from January 1, 1964.

The Second Supplemental Agreement received the Royal Assent on July 15, 1967.

[30] Article 18 B of the Consortium Agreement.

[31] Article IX (47 B.F.S.P., p. 43).

[32] Article II (96 *ibid.*, p. 51).

the treatment of British and Iranian subjects and their trade was based on the most-favoured-nation standard. By these clauses, British subjects became entitled to the benefits of a number of other treaties, concluded subsequently between Iran and third States in which the international customary law on the minimum standard of treating foreign nationals and their property were codified.[33]

In the British-Iranian Exchange of Notes of May 10, 1928, on the abolition of capitulations in Iran, the Iranian Government undertook that on the basis of perfect reciprocity, British nationals were to be admitted and treated on Iranian territory in conformity with the rules and practice of international law, were to enjoy the fullest protection of the Iranian laws and authorities, and were to receive the same treatment as Iranian nationals.[34]

Whether these consensual engagements remained on the same plane of auto-interpretation as Iran's obligations on these issues under international customary law would depend on the scope of the Declaration made by Iran under the Optional Clause of the Statute of the World Court.

(2) *The Iranian Declaration under the Optional Clause.* As was proved by the Judgment of the International Court of Justice in the *Anglo-Iranian Oil Co.* (Jurisdiction) case (1952), the Declaration was ambiguous.

It was possible to interpret the Declaration so that it was not only limited to relevant situations or facts arising after the Declaration became operative on September 19, 1932, but also to treaties or conventions accepted by Iran after the ratification of her Declaration.[35]

On this assumption, for the purpose of establishing the Court's jurisdiction, the United Kingdom could rely merely on consensual engagements entered into by Iran after this crucial date. All the treaties which the United Kingdom itself had concluded with Iran antedated this event. Thus, for *this* purpose, the treaties subsequently concluded between Iran and third parties were irrelevant.

Most-favoured-nation clauses operate so as to incorporate such later treaties into the relevant master agreements, but not the other way round.[36] If anything, the overstressed reliance on a supposed tacit agreement between Iran and the United Kingdom, which, in the latter's submission, was to have been contemporaneous with the conclusion in 1933 of the Concession Agreement between Iran and A.I.O.C., indicated some uneasiness on this flaw in the United Kingdom's legal argument.[37]

(3) *The Court's Provisional Measures Order of 1951.* When the International Court of Justice declined its jurisdiction in the *Anglo-*

[33] For a list of 10 relevant treaties, see *loc. cit.* in note 10 above, pp. 150–151.
[34] *Ibid.*, p. 176.
[35] *I.C.J. Reports 1952*, p. 93, at p. 103 *et seq.*
[36] See *Most-Favoured-Nation Standard*, p. 104.
[37] See President McNair's Ind. Op. in the *Anglo-Iranian Oil Co.* (*Jurisdiction*) case. *I.C.J. Reports 1952*, p. 93, at p. 121, and Vol. I, pp. 147–148.

Iranian Oil Company case, the provisional measures indicated in its Order of July 5, 1951,[38] automatically lapsed.

Even while the dispute was pending, it was doubtful whether the Court's Order had the obligatory character attached to it by the United Kingdom. Under the Statute and Rules of Court, the general dividing line between orders and judgments of the Court is that the former lack the binding force and final effects of a judgment.[39] On the specific issue of the binding or non-binding character of interim measures of the Permanent Court of Justice Doctrine had been divided.[40]

It is arguable that if, by themselves, orders of the International Court of Justice are not binding, this quality is given to them by Article 94 (1) of the Charter of the United Nations: "Each Member of the United Nations undertakes to comply with the decision of the International Court of Justice in any case to which it is a party." Orders, like judgments, of the Court are decisions. Yet, Article 94 (1) does not refer to decisions of the Court in the plural, but to "the decision." This rather suggests the final decision, that is, the judgment in the case to which a member State is a party.[41]

What is reasonably certain is that an order is not a judgment in the technical sense which would entitle the Security Council to make recommendations or decide upon measures to give effect to it under Article 94 (2) of the United Nations Charter.[42] Yet, even if an order of the Court could be assimilated to a judgment, the veto would apply to any recommendation or decision under this provision.[43]

(4) *The 1933 Concession Agreement.* In the Concession Agreement of April 29, 1933, between the Iranian Government and A.I.O.C., the

[38] *Loc. cit.* in note 22 above.

[39] P.C.I.J. in *Free Zones of Upper Savoy and the District of Gex* (1929) between France and Switzerland, Series A 22, p. 13.

See, further, S. Rosenne, *The Law and Practice of the International Court* (1965), pp. 630–631.

[40] Against the binding character of interim measures, A. P. Fachiri, *The Permanent Court of International Justice* (1932), p. 111; M. O. Hudson, *The Permanent Court of International Justice* (1934), p. 415, and A. Hammarskjöld, *Juridiction internationale* (1938), p. 313.

For the binding character of such interim measures, M. O. Hudson, *The Permanent Court of International Justice*, 1920–1942 (1943), p. 426, and 46 A.J.I.L. (1952), pp. 22–23.

On a difference of opinions on this matter which arose during the 1931 revision of the P.C.I.J. Rules of Court, see Rosenne, *loc. cit.* above, note 39, p. 141, n. 3.

See also Hersch Lauterpacht, *The Development of International Law by the International Court* (1958), pp. 112–113 and 347, n. 29.

[41] See, further, H. Kelsen, *The Law of the United Nations* (1950), pp. 720–721 and E. Tunçel, *L'Exécution des Décisions de la Cour Internationale de Justice selon la Charte des Nations Unies* (1960), p. 51.

[42] See, further, Ford, *loc. cit.* above, p. 67, note 12, p. 93, and Rosenne, *loc. cit.* above, note 39, pp. 141 and 158–159 and below, p. 133.

[43] Such recommendations and decisions are matters of a substantive character and fall under Paragraph 3 of Article 27 of the U.N. Charter.

On the usefulness of the Order of the I.C.J. in subsequent proceedings instituted by A.I.O.C. in national courts, see below, p. 83, and Rosenne, *loc. cit.* above, note 39, p. 132, n. 1.

Company was strongly safeguarded against unilateral interference by the Iranian Government with the concession.

The Company's rights were protected in five different ways:

First, good faith as the basis: Both parties declared that they based the performance of the Agreement on " principles of mutual good will and good faith as well as on a reasonable interpretation " of the Agreement.[44] In other words, they intended the convention to be interpreted as *jus aequum*.[45]

Secondly, prohibition of annulment: The parties agreed that the Concession was " not to be annulled " by the Iranian Government, nor were its terms to be " altered either by general or special legislation in the future, or by administrative measures or any other acts whatever of the executive authorities." [46]

Thirdly, a comprehensive system for the settlement of disputes: " Any differences between the parties of any nature whatever and in particular any differences arising out of the interpretation of this Agreement and of the rights and obligations therein contained as well as any differences of opinion which may arise relative to questions for the settlement of which, by the terms of this Agreement, the agreement of both parties is necessary, shall be settled by arbitration." [47]

The party requesting arbitration was to notify the other party in writing to this effect. Each party was to appoint an arbitrator and, before proceeding to arbitration, the two arbitrators were to choose an umpire. If, within two months, the arbitrators could not agree on the person of the umpire, he was to be nominated, at the request of either of the parties, by the President of the World Court or if, on grounds of nationality, the President was disqualified, by the Court's Vice-President.[48]

If one of the parties failed to appoint its arbitrator or advise the other of the appointment, the other party had the right to ask the President or the Vice-President of the World Court to nominate a Sole Arbitrator. In this case, the Sole Arbitrator was to settle the dispute.[49]

The award was to be based on " the juridical principles contained in Article 38 " of the Statute of the World Court, that is, the rules of international customary law, relevant treaties and the general principles of law recognised by civilised nations and, regarding evidence of international law, on the law-determining agencies and elements of such law-determining agencies enumerated or implied in this Article.[50]

Fourthly, termination of the Concession: The grounds on which, before December 31, 1993, the Concession could be lawfully terminated were exhaustively enumerated in the Agreement.

[44] Paragraph 1 of Article 21 (*loc. cit.* in note 10 above, p. 256).
[45] See, further, Vol. I, p. 53, and Index *sub nomine*.
[46] Paragraph 3 of Article 21 (*loc. cit.* in note 10 above, p. 256).
[47] Article 22 (A) (*ibid.*, p. 256).
[48] Article 22 (B) (*ibid.*, p. 256).
[49] Article 22 (D) (*ibid.*, p. 256).
[50] See, further, *Inductive Approach*, p. 19 *et seq.*

On two years' notice to the Iranian Government, the Company had the right to terminate the Concession at the end of any Christian calendar year.[51] Otherwise, the Concession could be annulled only by the arbitration tribunal provided in the Convention, but not unless the Company failed to perform the agreement. Default under the Agreement was limited to the failure of payment within one month of the award of any sum awarded to Iran by the tribunal or a decision on the voluntary or compulsory liquidation of the Company.[52]

In any other case of breach of the Agreement by one of the parties, the arbitration tribunal was to establish the responsibilities and determine their consequences.[53]

Fifthly, specialised forms of protection: (i) The Company had the right to determine the position of its pipelines and was protected against having to pay inflated prices for land it required for the construction of its pipe-lines.[54]

(ii) The Company was authorised to import materials for its operations without any licence and exempt from any taxes or payments to the State or local authorities.[55]

(iii) The export of petroleum by the Company enjoyed Customs immunity and was similarly exempted from any taxes or payments.[56]

(iv) The Company was protected against harmful interference by holders of other concessions.[57]

(v) The Company was under no obligation to convert into Iranian currency any part of its funds, including proceeds of the sale of its exports from Iran.[58]

(vi) For the first thirty years of the Concession, the Company was completely exempted from any taxation "present or future" of the Iranian State or local authorities. In exchange, the Company had to pay stipulated petroleum royalties. Before 1963, the parties were to reach agreement on the annual payments to be made by the Company in consideration of an extension of these tax privileges during the following thirty years.[59]

(5) *The Government Agreement of 1954, as amended in 1965 and 1967.* The Agreement is divided into two Parts. The one contains an Oil Consortium Agreement between the Iranian Government and the National Iranian Oil Company as First Parties, and the United States, United Kingdom, Netherlands and French Oil companies as the Second Parties

51 Article 25 (*loc. cit.* in note 10 above, p. 257).
52 Paragraphs 2 and 3 of Article 26 (*ibid.*, p. 258).
53 Paragraph 4 of Article 26 (*ibid.*, p. 258).
54 Articles 3–4 (*ibid.*, pp. 248–249).
55 Article 6 (A)–(C) (*ibid.*, p. 250).
56 Article 6 (D) (*ibid.*, p. 250).
57 Article 7 (C) (*ibid.*, p. 250).
58 Article 8 (*ibid.*, p. 250).
59 Article 11 (*ibid.*, pp. 252–253).

(Oil Consortium Agreement). The other consists of the Compensation Agreement between the First Parties and A.I.O.C. as the Third Party,[60] which it is convenient to discuss first.

The Compensation Agreement. In calculating the amount of compensation due to A.I.O.C. the parties agreed to consider Iran as being entitled in equity to the increased royalties which, if Iran had ratified the Supplemental Agreement of 1949,[61] she would have received.[62] Taking into account this amount, Iran paid in full settlement of all claims of A.I.O.C. to the Company £25 million, free of interest, in ten equal and annual instalments, payable in London.[63]

A.I.O.C. retained a 40 per cent. share in the Oil Consortium. The companies which took up the other 60 per cent., paid A.I.O.C. £214 million for their shares in the Consortium. Moreover, A.I.O.C. retained £51 million from a special contingency account which, if Iran had ratified the Supplemental Agreement of 1949, would have been due to the Iranian Government.

At the time of nationalisation, A.I.O.C.'s compensation claims were estimated at about £350 million. Actually, the Company received from the sources mentioned above about £300 million and maintained a 40 per cent. interest in the Consortium. The rights granted to the Consortium were, however, considerably more limited in their geographical and functional scope than had been those under the 1933 Concession.

A relevant, if not necessarily accurate pointer to the Company's prospects under the 1954 Settlement was the rise of the Company's shares, after the signature of the Government Agreement in 1954, to more than three times their value, as compared with their value at the time of the nationalisation of the Company's Iranian assets in October, 1951. After Iran had ratified the Agreement, the Company also announced to its shareholders a free issue of four new shares for every registered share.[64]

The Agreement between Iran and the Oil Consortium: In addition to the points mentioned above,[65] attention should be drawn to the following:

(i) *General*: Compared with earlier concession agreements, the functions, rights, powers and obligations of all concerned—the Iranian Government, the National Iranian Oil Company, the Operating Companies and Trading Companies—are defined more precisely in the 1954 Agreement. In particular, this applies to the list of obligations owed by the Operating Companies to Iran and the National Iranian Oil Company.[66]

(ii) *Jus aequum*: As in the 1933 Agreement, the Parties express the intention that, for the purposes set out in the Preamble, the provisions of

60 Part One consists of 51 Articles, and Part Two of 5 Articles.
61 See above, p. 67.
62 Paragraph 5 of the Preamble to Part II.
63 Article 1.
64 Shwadran, *loc. cit.* above, p. 66, note 7, p. 189.
See also the assessment by Lord Shawcross, 102 Hague *Recueil* (1961), pp. 348–349.
65 See above, p. 70.
66 Article 4 F.

the Agreement " shall be carried out in a spirit of good faith and goodwill." In a subsequent Article, they repeat their firm intention of living up to these standards: " The parties undertake to carry out the terms and provisions of this Agreement in accordance with the principles of mutual goodwill and good faith and to respect the spirit as well as the letter of the said terms and provisions." [67]

(iii) *Guarantee of rights*: subject to one exception, the rights and powers granted to the Operating Companies under the Agreement may not be revoked or modified at any time during the term of the Agreement. The exception is a finding by the Arbitration Board or Sole Arbiter that the Agreement has been terminated by breach or dissolved by total impossibility of performance.[68]

(iv) *Duties of disclosure*: To enable Iran and the National Iranian Oil Company to satisfy themselves that the Operating Companies carry out their obligations under the Agreement, provision is made for special audits of the accounts of the Operating Companies and the supply of relevant scientific and technical information by the Operating Companies to the National Iranian Oil Company.[69]

(v) *Land prices*: If the Operating Companies require any further land in the areas allocated to them, such land is to be made available to them by the National Iranian Oil Company at a reasonable purchase price or rent. Prices must be based on the existing use of the land and not be in excess of the market price or rent for similar land in the same district.[70]

(vi) *Fees*: The fees to be paid by the Trading Companies to the Exploration and Producing Company and the Refining Company are fixed at one shilling per cubic metre of crude oil delivered or refined.[71]

(vii) *Nationality of Trading Companies*: Each Trading Company is to be registered in Iran. In principle, it is to have the same nationality as the Consortium member by which it is nominated. Yet an exception clause, characteristic of the style of the " transnational " companies of our time, follows: " unless such Consortium member considers that tax or foreign exchange requirements outside Iran make another nationality desirable." In this case, the Consortium member " may choose such other nationality for the Trading Company in question." [72]

(viii) *Level of exports*: The Consortium members agree to pursue a policy, " assuming favourable operating and economic conditions in Iran," of exporting Iranian oil in such a manner as " would reasonably reflect the trend of supply and demand for Middle East crude oil." [73]

67 Article 41 A. See also Paragraph 7 of the Preamble to Part I.
68 Articles 40 and 41C. See also Article 45, and below, p. 79 *et seq.*
69 Article 4 G.
70 Article 7 B (1).
71 Article 13.
72 Article 18 C.
73 Article 20 B.

(ix) *Royalties*: The Trading Companies are to pay the National Iranian Oil Company for this oil at the rate of 12½ per cent. of the applicable posted price of crude oil.[74]

(x) *Tax guarantees*: The Trading and Operating Companies are protected against any unilateral change to their disadvantage in the Iranian law relating to income tax and the rates of such taxation. Subject to exceptions stated, the members of the Consortium, the Trading Companies and Operating Companies are exempt from taxation to any central or local Iranian authority. The same applies to dividends paid by them out of income derived from their activities.[75]

It is expressly provided that any dispute between Iran and any Trading or Operating Company on such tax matters is arbitrable under the Convention.[76]

(xi) *Exemptions from import and export duties*: All machinery and equipment required for the National Iranian Oil Company or the Operating Companies may be imported into Iran without any licence and is exempt from import or other Customs charges.[77] Similarly, the Trading Companies may freely sell or otherwise dispose abroad of the crude oil and natural gas purchased from the National Iranian Oil Company and any products manufactured therefrom by the Operating Companies. Such exports are exempt from Customs duties and export taxes. The companies must, however, give precedence to Iranian requirements for purposes of internal consumption.[78]

(xii) *General prohibition of unilateral Iranian action*: In a formulation reminiscent of the Concession Agreement of 1933, it is stipulated that "no general or special legislative or administrative measures or any other act whatsoever of or emanating from Iran or any governmental authorities in Iran (whether central or local) shall annul this Agreement, amend or modify its provisions or prevent or hinder the due and effective performance of its terms. Such annulment, amendment or modification shall not take place except by agreement of the parties to this Agreement."[79]

As with the rights and powers granted to the Operating Companies,[80] so the Agreement as a whole can be terminated or dissolved against the will of one of the parties concerned in one way only: a decision by the

[74] Article 22 of the Consortium Agreement of 1954, as amended by the Supplemental Agreement of 1965.

Posted prices are the prices published by the oil companies for f.o.b. sales at a sea port terminal in single cargo lots. See, further, H. Cattan, *The Evolution of Oil Concessions in the Middle East and North Africa* (1967), pp. 51–52.

On the difference between *posted* and *realised* prices, see ibid., p. 79, and for the meaning of the terms *posted price* and *applicable posted price* in the Iranian Government Agreement of 1954, see Article 1 N and O of the Consortium Agreement and, on *stated payments*, see Article 22 (A) and (C).

[75] Article 28, as amended by Article 3 of the Supplemental Agreement of 1965.

[76] Article 29.

[77] Article 34 A.

[78] Article 35.

[79] Article 41 B.

[80] Article 4 D.

Arbitration Board or Sole Arbitrator under the Agreement that it has been terminated by breach or dissolved by total impossibility of performance.[81]

(xiii) *Conciliation and arbitration machinery*: Disputes on alleged defaults in the performance of obligations under the Agreement may be referred to a mixed Conciliation Committee. This consists of four members, two of whom are nominated by each party. For the ruling to be binding, it must be unanimous.[82]

Any complaint which either party does not wish to refer to a Conciliation Committee, or which is not determined by a binding ruling of such a Committee, may be submitted by the complainant to arbitration.

Special rules apply to disputes on the purchase of Iranian currency at the commercial bank rate of exchange and without discrimination. They are to be submitted to a Sole Arbitrator, appointed by the Managing Director of the International Monetary Fund.[83]

If the dispute relates to a technical or accounting question, it may, by agreement between the parties, be referred to a single expert or a body of three experts.[84]

In the last resort, any dispute under the Agreement can be brought before a Board of Arbitrators, consisting of three members. One is appointed by each of the parties, and these two arbitrators appoint an umpire who shall be the President of the Arbitration Board.

For the rest, the procedure for the constitution of the Arbitration Board is based in most of its essentials on the corresponding provisions of the Concession Agreement of 1933.[85] Failing appointment, in the contingencies envisaged in the Agreement, of one of the arbitrators being made by the President or Vice-President of the International Court of Justice, the President of the Swiss Federal Tribunal or the highest judge of Denmark, Sweden or Brazil (in the order stated) are to fulfil this function.[86] Neither party may question the exercise of this discretion.[87]

The award may be given by a majority decision, and the parties are to comply with it in good faith.[88] Provision is also made for proceedings in the absence or default of one of the parties.[89]

Pending the issue of a decision or award, the operations or activities which have given rise to the arbitration need not be discontinued. If the complaint is justified, the complainant may be entitled to receive "reparation."[90] It deserves to be noted that, at least in international

81 Article 41 C.
82 Articles 42–43.
83 Article 31 A (3).
84 Article 44 B (1).
85 Article 44 C–K. See also above, p. 74 *et seq.*
86 Article 44 C (3).
87 Article 44 C (4).
88 Article 44 C (5).
89 Article 44 E.
90 Article 44 F.

customary law, " reparation " means primarily restoration of the *status quo* existing before the wrongful act was committed.[91]

Either party may request the experts or arbitrators to interpret their decisions or awards.[92]

If the decision or award is for a defined sum of money payable to Iran or the National Iranian Oil Company, then, after the lapse of the time stipulated in the decision or award, and otherwise within three months of the decision or award, Iran may prohibit until the sum is paid all export of crude oil and petroleum products from Iran by the party in default.[93]

In other cases of non-compliance with a final award, and latest after six months, the party in whose favour the award has been given may seek the termination of the Agreement by a decision of an Arbitration Board or Sole Arbitrator. If possible, proceedings must take place before the Board or Arbitrator who had made the final award.[94]

(xiv) *Interpretation and application of the Convention*: Compared with the corresponding Article in the Concession Agreement of 1933,[95] the emphasis has shifted from international law to the general principles of law recognised by civilised nations: " In view of the diverse nationalities of the parties to this Agreement, it shall be governed by and interpreted and applied in accordance with principles of law common to Iran and the several nations, in which the other parties to this Agreement are incorporated, and in the absence of such common principles, then by and in accordance with principles of law recognised by civilised nations in general, including such of those principles as may have been applied by international tribunals." [96]

One particular type of situation which, under synonyms such as an act of God, *vis major*, *force majeure* or *höhere Gewalt*, constitute a generally recognised ground of exculpation for non-performance of an obligation under *jus aequum* is specifically dealt with in the Agreement.[97]

(xv) *Authoritative texts*: Both the Persian and English texts are authoritative. In case of any discrepancy the English text prevails.[98]

(xvi) *Duration*: The term of the Agreement is twenty-five years from the date when the Agreement came into force, or such additional periods

[91] See also above, p. 17.

It is a moot question of comparative law whether, in accordance with the " principles of law common to Iran and the several nations in which the other parties to this Agreement are incorporated " or, in the absence of such common principles, in accordance with the general principles of law recognised by civilised nations (see below under (xiv)), reparation in this clause means primarily restitution or compensation.

See also the United Kingdom Memorial in the *Anglo-Iranian Oil Co.* case (*loc. cit.* above, p. 67, note 10, p. 114 *et seq.*).

[92] Article 44 K.

[93] Article 45 A.

[94] Article 45 B and C.

[95] See above, p. 74.

[96] Article 46.

[97] Article 47.

[98] Article 48.

during which, in accordance with its provisions, the Agreement is continued.[99]

Evaluation: The 1954 Agreement is of major significance for, at least, nine reasons:

(1) It represents a significant type of co-operation between a capital-importing State and some of the West's most powerful transnational companies.[100]

(2) It offers a model illustration of three decisive conditions on which it depends whether States other than the super-Powers can effectively support investments as immobile and vulnerable as oil or mineral concessions:

(i) An interest—political, economic or military—of the hegemonial Power involved in the maintenance of an elastic *status quo* in the area concerned.

In relation to Iran, the United States firmly declared this interest.[101] Moreover, since the end of the First World War the United States Administration—if anything, more than the United States oil companies [102] —had resented the British oil monopoly in Iran and was ready to break it when a suitable opportunity offered itself. Yet, in advising the Government of the United Kingdom and A.I.O.C. well in time on the need to make timely concessions and in making themselves available as a *de facto* mediator, the United States acted throughout as fairly as could be expected.[103]

(ii) Limitation of threatening military postures to demonstrations acceptable to the hegemonial Power which, ultimately, is likely to become involved in any escalation of the conflict.

(iii) Realisation of the inherent advantages of applying the principle of reciprocity.

In a situation such as that in which A.I.O.C. found itself, this means more than awareness of the fact that a host country needs the capital, know-how and market facilities of the international oil industry. It calls for appreciation that it is in the best interest of even combines as powerful

[99] Article 49.

[100] See, further, E. Penrose, 18 Y.B.W.A. (1964), p. 150 *et seq.*, and M. El-Sayed, *L'Organisation des Pays Exportateurs de Pétrole* (1967), p. 9 *et seq.* (useful bibliography, p. 205 *et seq.*).

On the partnership between the National Iranian Oil Company and Assienda Generale Italiana Petroli (AGIP) in Société Irano-Italienne des Petroles (SIRIP), amounting to a profit-sharing arrangement of 75–25 per cent., see E. H. Wall, 7 I.C.L.Q. (1958), p. 736 *et seq.*; W. G. Friedmann and G. Kalmanoff (eds.), *Joint International Business Ventures* (1961), p. 184 *et seq.*, and H. Cattan, *The Evolution of Oil Concessions in the Middle East and North Africa* (1967), p. 129 *et seq.*

[101] See, further, *loc. cit.* above, p. 66, note 9.

[102] See, further, *loc. cit.* in note 24 above.

[103] See, further, Shwadran, *loc. cit.* in note 7 above, pp. 62 and 179 *et seq.*, and, on United States warnings given in 1950 to the United Kingdom to intercede between A.I.O.C. and the Iranian Government, Ford, *loc. cit.* in note 24 above, p. 50.

See also President Eisenhower's letter of June 29, 1953, to the Iranian Prime Minister (*Whiteman Digest*, Vol. 8 (1967), p. 1080 *et seq.*).

as the oil giants to avoid the impression of pursuing policies which are open to misinterpretation of being grossly unfair. Such impressions may be created, for instance, by—in relation to profits—disproportionately small royalties; policies of secretiveness regarding facts and figures affecting the host country, and any unfair exclusion of qualified nationals of the host State from the higher echelons of companies operating in the territory of the host State.

(3) While the 1954 Convention embodies considerable concessions to Iran, the needs compelling Iran to conclude the 1954 Convention were hardly less compelling than those inducing her to accept the Concession Agreement of 1933.[104] Once the major Western Powers involved and the major oil companies had reached agreement among themselves, no other constructive alternative existed for a country and regime which preferred United States military and economic assistance to subversion, civil war, Russian intervention under the Soviet-Iranian Treaty of 1921 and, in this eventuality, the risk of becoming a battlefield in an armed collision between the two world Powers.

(4) The Security Council of the United Nations provided the necessary safety valve which enabled Labour and Conservative Governments of the United Kingdom, under pressure from public opinion at home to show armed strength, to de-escalate and gradually withdraw their concentrations of military, naval and air power. In a bipolarised world and in circumstances in which the Western hegemonial Power had politely but firmly detached itself from any responsibility for any such move, these postures lacked the requisite credibility.

In international organs which are as much in the centre of power politics in disguise as is the Security Council, the legal arguments of the parties involved tend to err on the side of mediocrity. As, in addition, the applicable law involved was rather vague, argument and interest coincided to an extent which reduced most of these exercises to stereotyped forms of special pleading.[105]

(5) Similarly, the International Court of Justice was merely of limited usefulness. Yet, its existence allowed for additional exercises in shadow-fighting which helped in reducing an overheated atmosphere.

(6) The survey missions of the International Bank for Reconstruction and Development also had their uses. They maintained contacts at a time when the chief parties involved were no longer on speaking terms with each other. Moreover, they obtained and checked information in a manner which proved invaluable to all concerned in the subsequent phase of the dispute, leading to the consortium deal.

(7) If no more, the relevant Anglo-Iranian treaties of the pre-1914 era provided a plausible basis for the case presented by the United Kingdom

[104] See above, p. 67.

[105] See, further, Ford, *loc. cit.* above, p. 67, note 12 and p. 124 *et seq.*, and M. S. Rajan, *United Nations and Domestic Jurisdiction* (1961), p. 297 *et seq.*

before the International Court of Justice. Otherwise, they helped little more on the legal plane than would have reliance on the protection of the British properties concerned under the governing rules of international customary law. Yet the existence of these treaties assisted in aligning the United States with the United Kingdom in its demand for substantial compensation and, in the eyes of world public opinion, they lifted the British stand from a post-imperial quarrel to the level of legal and moral principle.

Similarly, it is possible to differ on the validity of the legal arguments employed in the proceedings instituted by A.I.O.C. in national courts.[106] Yet, in practice these actions, and others threatened, had some deterrent effect on potential purchasers of the oil in dispute.

(8) As is proved by the two Supplemental Agreements of 1965 and 1967, the parties to the 1954 Government Agreement succeeded in adjusting amicably issues as sensitive as the financial benefits derived by Iran from the Agreement and the reduction by one-quarter of the exploration area allocated to the foreign oil companies.[107] The overall effect of these changes was to meet further pressure to modify the 1954 Agreement in Iran's favour.

(9) In an overall situation which was conditioned by political factors beyond the control of the players most directly involved, Iran considered it advisable to come to terms with forces more diversified than those Musaddiq had chosen to challenge.

In their turn, A.I.O.C. and the other Western oil companies which had muscled into its formerly exclusive preserve had to make a basic decision of their own: Did they prefer a profitable deal to a confrontation of indefinite duration in which their chief arguments—capital resources, technological know-how and large-scale control of foreign market facilities for Iranian oil—might carry less weight than they imagined?

The Government Agreement of 1954 reflects these realities rather than any greater or lesser approximation to abstract legal standards or ideologies such as the doctrine of permanent sovereignty over natural resources.[108]

Similarly, the subsequent changes made on a consensual basis in the 1954 Agreement were the product of three governing metalegal factors: the Farouk-like appetite of the Iranian Exchequer; Iran's desire to prove to the other oil-exporting States her capacity to be second to none in wringing substantial concessions from the fixed foreign assets in her territory, and awareness of all concerned of the still profitable character of the enterprises of the Iranian Oil Consortium 1954.

106 See also above, p. 73, note 43, and below, p. 126 *et seq.*

107 *Loc. cit.* above, p. 71, note 29.

On the attempts made by the Iranian Government to induce the Iranian Oil Consortium to increase its production of Iranian oil—and, correspondingly, the Iranian royalties—see *The Economist*, March 2, 1968, pp. 47–48, and April 27, 1968, p. 70.

Iran's oil revenues from foreign oil companies are estimated at £333 million (*The Times* (London), April 13, 1968).

108 See above, p. 82, and further, below, pp. 189–190.

2—The Nationalisation of the Suez Canal Company

The nationalisation of the Universal Suez Company by Egypt in 1956 offers lessons confirmatory of, and complementary to, the nationalisation of the assets of the Anglo-Iranian Oil Company in Iran.

Seven aspects of this event deserve to be singled out:

(1) *The Prestige Aspect.* At the time of the nationalisation of the Suez Canal Company, more than half of its share capital was estimated to have been held by private, especially French, investors. Yet, since, in 1875, Disraeli acquired from the Khedive of Egypt 44 per cent. of the Company's share capital for the British Government, and Great Britain assumed a presence in strength in Egypt, the Sudan and Palestine, the Suez Canal and the Suez Canal Company became symbols of British power at home and abroad.[109]

(2) *The Political Context of the Nationalisation.* President Nasser's action was essentially an act of defiance against the Western Powers. It was a reaction to the United States and British withdrawal of their offers, made in 1955, of financial aid for the Aswan Dam scheme—themselves tactical moves in the East-West Cold War—an assertion of Egyptian independence and an affirmation of his policy of neutralism in the East-West Conflict.[110]

(3) *The Anti-Egyptian Front.* On the surface, the forces arraigned against Egypt by the Western Powers were impressive.[111] Actually, the countries invited, in addition to Egypt, to the first London Conference (August, 1956) were divided among themselves.

A majority of eighteen favoured a modified Dulles plan. This would have involved international control of all canal operations. A minority of African and Asian nations, supported by the Soviet Union, suggested a scheme of international guarantees and co-operation, falling short of international supervision.[112] With slight differences in emphasis in the two plans, the nationalisation of the Suez Canal Company was taken for

[109] On the historical background of the Dispute, see, for instance, 2b B.D.I.L. (First Phase), p. 193 *et seq.*, and R. O. Matthews, 21 *International Organisation* (1967), p. 80 *et seq.*
See also below, p. 87, note 128.

[110] See, further, Lok Sabha Secretariat, New Delhi, *Suez Canal* (1956), p. 15 *et seq.* and 10 *Chronique de Politique Étrangère* (1957), p. 24 *et seq.*

[111] Twenty-four countries were invited to this Conference either as Parties to the Suez Canal Convention of October 29, 1888, or as chief users of the Canal. The two countries which did not accept were Egypt and Greece, the latter because of the then still pending Cyprus Dispute with the United Kingdom. See, further, *The Suez Canal Conference. Selected Documents* (Cmd. 9853–1956) and 10 *Chronique de Politique Étrangère* (1957), p. 39.

[112] See, further, *The Suez Canal Conference. Selected Documents*, Cmd. 9853 (1956); Lok Sabha Secretariat, New Delhi, *Suez Canal. Nationalisation and After* (1956), p. 23 *et seq.*, and D. Rauschning, *Der Streit um den Suez Kanal* (1956), p. 157 *et seq.*
See also above, p. 54, note 39.

granted but provision was made for just and equitable compensation of the Company's shareholders.[113]

Three factors decisively shaped the further course of events. At short notice, Egypt proved that, with the help of foreign volunteers, she could handle competently the pilotage of ships through the Canal. Moreover, the United Kingdom, France and Israel alienated the United States of America by their armed interventions in Egypt. Finally, the Soviet Union came out increasingly firmly in Egypt's support.

Thus, the " consumer " front quickly disintegrated, and the nationalisation of the Suez Canal Company merged into the wider issue of settling the armed conflict between the three interventionist Powers and Egypt in a manner acceptable to the two world Powers and world public opinion.[114]

(4) *The Legal Status of the Suez Canal Company.* In accordance with the Statutes of the Suez Canal Company of 1856, approved by the Viceroy of Egypt, the Company had its seat (*siège social*)[115] at Alexandria and its administrative domicile in Paris.[116]

With Egyptian consent, the Company was organised as a joint stock company in analogy to French joint stock companies and governed by the " principles " of these companies.[117]

The appellative " universal " in the Company's name was intended to indicate that the Company sought support from investors everywhere. Yet, in the Concession Agreement of February 22, 1866, the Egyptian nationality of the Company was affirmed.[118] In principle, the Company was to be governed by the laws and customs of Egypt. Regarding its status as a company and relations between the shareholders, " by special agreement " the French law on joint stock companies was to apply. All

[113] See Cmd. 9853 (1956), pp. 8 and 11, and, for a statement in which, during the First London Conference of August, 1956, Mr. Chepilov (U.S.S.R.) expressed himself in favour of equitable compensation to be granted to the shareholders of the Suez Canal Company, R. Pinto, 2 *Annuaire français* (1956), p. 27.

[114] See, further, *The Annual Register of World Events 1956*, p. 276 *et seq.*

[115] See, further, Vol. I, p. 395.

[116] Article 3 (Society of Comparative Legislation and International Law, *The Suez Canal* (1956), p. 11).

See, however, P. de Visscher, 62 R.G.D.I.P. (1958), p. 429.

[117] Article 73 (*loc. cit.* above, note 116, *The Suez Canal*, p. 26).

[118] Article 16 (*ibid.*, p. 38).

See, further, J. A. Obieta, *The International Status of the Suez Canal* (1960), p. 91 *et seq.*; D. H. N. Johnson, 31 *Acta Scandinavica Juris Gentium* (1961), p. 190, and Y. van der Mensbrugghe, *Les Guaranties de la Liberté de Navigation dans le Canal de Suez* (1964), p. 187 *et seq.*, especially on the practice of the Mixed Courts in Egypt and former British assertions for purposes of private law, especially the conflict of laws, of the Egyptian nationality of the Suez Canal Company (*ibid.*, pp. 203–204).

On the Company's nationality, see, further, the opinions of U.K. Law Officers, reproduced in 2b B.D.I.L. (First Phase), pp. 220 and 254 *et seq.*, and T. J. Lawrence, *Essays on Some Disputed Questions in Modern International Law* (1884), p. 50.

In this context, the Shell Chemicals Distributing Company of Egypt Act, 1963 (c. iv–May 15, 1963)—a private Act of Parliament, passed at the Company's request, with the object of depriving the Company of its British nationality—deserves to be mentioned as a sign of the times. In this way, it was hoped to enable this English Company which was operating wholly in the territory of the United Arab Republic to continue its activities there in compliance with the local law without any break in its legal personality. See, further, B.P.I.L. 1963 (II), p. 128 *et seq.*

disputes of this type were to be settled in France by arbitrators, with a right of appeal to the Imperial Court in Paris. Disputes between the Egyptian Government and the Company were to be brought before Egyptian courts and decided by Egyptian law.[119]

In the Suez Canal Convention of October 29, 1888, the Contracting Parties took note of the engagements, undertaken by the Khedive of Egypt, and confirmed by the Turkish Sultan, towards the Suez Canal Company regarding the Fresh Water Canal and the formulation of these engagements in a Convention of 1863.[120] The Contracting Parties also reserved the rights of the Ottoman Empire as the territorial Power [121] and emphasised that the engagements resulting from the Convention were not limited by the duration of the concession agreement between the Ottoman Empire and the Suez Canal Company.[122]

In the discussions following the nationalisation of the Suez Canal Company, British, French and United States spokesmen and the Company itself fell back on these references in the Suez Canal Convention to the Company and the international functions fulfilled by the Company under the Convention.[123] They attempted to infer in this way a legal link between the Suez Canal Convention and the concessions granted to the Suez Canal Company, in particular a transnational status of the Company which made it immune from unilateral interference by the territorial sovereign. The subjection, for some purposes, of the Company to French law,[124] the use of the word " universal " in the Company's name and the overwhelmingly foreign ownership of its share capital were employed to similar ends.[125]

119 Article 16 (*loc. cit.* in note 116 above, *The Suez Canal*, p. 38) and van der Mensbrugghe, *loc. cit.* in note 118 above, p. 189 *et seq.*

120 Article II (*loc. cit.* in note 116 above, *The Suez Canal*, pp. 49–50).

121 Article XII (*ibid.*, p. 52).

By general consent, Egypt (and the United Arab Republic) is treated as successor to the rights and duties of the Ottoman Empire under the Convention and was invited in this capacity to the First London Conference of August, 1956 (Cmd. 9853 (1956), p. 4). See also, D. P. O'Connell, *State Succession in Municipal Law and International Law* (1967), Vol. II, p. 271.

122 Article XIV (*loc. cit.* in note 116 above, *The Suez Canal*, p. 52).

123 See, for instance, the Statement issued on August 3, 1956, by the British, French and United States Governments; Mr. Selwyn Lloyd's speech at the first London Conference, August 22, 1956 (Cmd. 9853 (1956), p. 16) and the Letter of August 14, 1956, from the Chairman of the Board of Directors of the Suez Canal Company to the Chairman of the First London Conference of 1956 (*The Suez Canal Company and the Decision taken by the Egyptian Government on 26th July, 1956*, published by the Company, Part I (1956), pp. 10 and 60. See also *ibid.*, p. 20).

On opinions by G. Gidel and G. Sauser-Hall on the status of the Suez Canal Company, taken in 1947 by the Suez Canal Company, when the Egyptian Government attempted for the first time to enforce automatically Egyptian legislation on the Company (actually a Companies Act), see Lord Kilmuir's speech in the House of Lords, September 12, 1956 (H.L.Deb., Vol. 199, cols. 708–709).

124 See above, p. 85.

125 See, for instance, G. Scelle, 2 *Annuaire français* (1956), p. 12; Obieta, *loc. cit.* above, p. 85, note 118, p. 99 *et seq.*; P. de Visscher, *loc. cit.* above, p. 85, note 116, p. 429, and the Suez Canal Company, *loc. cit.* above, note 123, p. 10.

On the discriminatory character of the Egyptian Nationalisation Law, see R. Delson, 57 *Col.L. Review* (1957), p. 767 *et seq.*, and on other singular features of this Law, Anthony Eden, *The Full Circle. Memoirs*, Vol. II (1960), pp. 425, 438–439 and 474–475.

In view of the clear affirmation of the Company's Egyptian nationality in the Concession Agreement of 1866,[126] these arguments were too sophisticated to carry conviction. The most that could be said was that, in view of the nationalisation and dissolution of the Suez Company—at least for purposes of Egyptian law—by the Egyptian Nationalisation Law of 1956,[127] the almost complete foreign ownership of the Company's share capital became relevant in a different way. It entitled in equity the two Governments most directly concerned—France and the United Kingdom—to grant diplomatic protection to their nationals who were shareholders or, as with the Government of the United Kingdom, to claim respect for its own rights as a major shareholder in the Company.[128]

(5) *Extraterritorial Effects of the Nationalisation Law.* By the Egyptian Nationalisation Law of July 26, 1956, the Suez Canal Company as such was nationalised, and not merely the Company's share capital. It also emerges from other provisions of this Law that the Company was treated as having been dissolved by the creation of a new legal entity, charged with the management of traffic in the Suez Canal.[129]

By a further Article, the assets of the nationalised company " in Egypt and abroad " were frozen, and banks, organisations and individuals abroad were prohibited from disposing of these assets in any manner, except by order of the board of the newly created body.[130] Any contravention of this Article was made punishable with imprisonment and a fine of three times the value of the amounts involved.[131] Short of recognition or acquiescence by other States, any attempt actually made by Egypt to exercise such extraterritorial jurisdiction would have been contrary to international customary law.[132]

(6) *Compensation.* Under the Egyptian Nationalisation Law of 1956, the Company's shareholders and holders of foundation bonds were to be compensated at the value of the shares and bonds at the close of the Paris Bourse on the day before nationalisation, but only " after completion of the handover by the State of all the funds and property of the nationalised company," that is, including the Company's funds held abroad.[133] Subsequently, the Egyptian Government made alternative offers of either paying

126 See above, p. 85, note 118.

127 *Loc. cit.* in note 116 above, *The Suez Canal*, p. 41.

128 At the time of nationalisation, 44 per cent. of the Company's share-capital was owned by the Government of the United Kingdom, and four-fifths of the rest by French nationals (*The Suez Canal Company*, etc., *loc. cit.* above, p. 86, note 123, p. 64).
See also above, p. 27, and below, pp. 112 and 156 *et seq.*

129 Article II (*loc. cit.* in note 116 above, *The Suez Canal*, p. 42).

130 Article III (*ibid.*, p. 43).

131 Article V (*ibid.*, p. 43—for Article II in this translation, read Article III. See, for instance, Rauschning, *loc. cit.* above, p. 84, note 112, p. 156).

132 See, further, Vol. II, p. 331 *et seq.*; Rauschning, *loc. cit.* above, p. 84, note 112, p. XXV *et seq.*, and M. Domke, 4 *New York Law Forum* (1958), p. 47 *et seq.*

133 Article I (*loc. cit.* above, p. 85, note 116, *The Suez Canal*, p. 42).
See also Article 16 of the Concession Agreement of 1856 (*loc. cit.* above, p. 86, note 123, *The Suez Canal*, p. 8) and B. Broms, *The Legal Status of the Suez Canal* (1961), p. 168, n. 6.

an average price, calculated on the basis of stock exchange prices during the preceding five years, or submission of the issue to arbitration.

While, at its face value, the second alternative offer was unexceptionable, the other two offers appear to fall short of the requirements of international customary law. Stock exchange prices of shares tend to minimise unduly long-range expectations of *lucrum cessans*, which forms part of full or adequate compensation.[134] The fact that, for instance, in the Eighteen-Power Declaration of August 1956, "just and equitable" compensation of the Company's shareholders was suggested [135] does not necessarily imply a more relaxed view of the applicable rules of international law.

It may be argued that nothing short of full or adequate compensation is just and equitable, and that if the State concerned lacks the means of complying with this rule—itself a product of international *jus aequum*—it would be more just and equitable to refrain from such unilateral action.

Even if this were otherwise, package deals such as those proposed by the eighteen Powers are not quasi-judicial pronouncements nor reliable evidence of attitudes to international law by the States concerned. They embody joint views of feasible compromise solutions for potentially dangerous international conflicts.

(7) *The Settlement*. The settlement ultimately reached between the United Arab Republic [136] and the Suez Canal Company—the Heads of Agreement of April 29, 1958, between the United Arab Republic and Representatives of the Stockholders of the Suez Canal Company and the Final Agreement of July 13, 1958, between the United Arab Republic and the Compagnie Financière de Suez [137]—reflected the realities of the situation. It was made in the aftermath of the unsuccessful British-French-Israeli intervention of 1956 and the temporary estrangement between the United States of America and her two West European allies. Moreover, provided Egypt respected the right of freedom of passage through the Suez Canal of the other major users of the Canal, these were not unduly concerned with the issues of principle involved in the nationalisation of the Suez Canal Company or the compensation of its shareholders.

Against this background, a rough and ready solution suggested itself. Again, the International Bank for Reconstruction and Development lent a helping hand in reaching agreement. By and large, each side kept what it held and renounced what was beyond its reach. The Company gave up its claims to any of its assets in Egypt, and Egypt did likewise regarding any of the Company's assets elsewhere. Liabilities were correspondingly treated.

[134] See also above, pp. 10–11, below, pp. 122 and 164, and Th. T. F. Huang, 51 A.J.I.L. (1957), p. 303 *et seq.*
[135] See above, p. 85.
[136] So styled since February 21, 1958.
[137] E. Lauterpacht (ed.), *The Suez Canal Settlement* (1960), p. 3 *et seq.*

In a more technical terminology, the settlement is based on the principle of the territoriality of nationalisation and the non-recognition of any extraterritorial effects of the Egyptian Nationalisation Law.

In addition, Egypt undertook to pay in seven instalments twenty-eight million Egyptian Pounds to the Compagnie Financière de Suez.

Any assessment of the Agreement in financial terms is unavoidably subjective. Yet consensus appears to exist on the merely partial character of the compensation paid by Egypt.[138] Moreover, what is apparent is that the compromise actually reached was based on considerations as pragmatic[139] as those productive of the settlement of the Anglo-Iranian Oil Dispute.

[138] See, for instance, L. Focsaneanu, 5 *Annuaire français* (1959), p. 191 *et seq.*
See, in this context, also the Letter of August 4, 1956, from the Chairman of the Board of Directors of the Suez Canal Company to the French Minister of Foreign Affairs (*The Suez Canal Company*, etc., *loc. cit.* above, p. 86, note 123, p. 8), the Company's Memorandum of August 7, 1956, in which it was estimated that the Company's net profits amounted to one-third of its transit receipts (*ibid.*, p. 26), and the statement made by the Financial Secretary to the Treasury in the House of Commons (H.C.Deb., Vol. 587, col. 82 (Written Answers—May 5, 1958), or *Contemporary Practice*, 7 I.C.L.Q. (1958), p. 552.

[139] For a perceptive analysis of the operative factors, see Matthews, *loc. cit.* above, p. 84, note 109, p. 95 *et seq.*, and, on the relevance of the blocking of Egyptian accounts abroad in connection with the settlement reached, Focsaneanu, *loc. cit.* above, note 138, p. 203.

Chapter 7

EVALUATION:

II—FURTHER CHALLENGES

A connection can be traced between the post-1945 measures of nationalisation in Eastern Europe and the Iranian oil nationalisation.[1] Similarly, it is reasonable to assume that the Egyptian action regarding the Suez Canal Company was encouraged by the ease with which these earlier acts of interference with foreign investments had been accomplished.

Successes of this type were more likely to weigh with the operators of precarious political regimes than the self-restraint shown by the United Kingdom in 1949 in connection with the first nationalisation of the British steel industry. On that occasion, the only foreign interest involved—the United States-owned Ford Works at Dagenham—was exempted from the operation of the Iron and Steel Act 1949,[2] and Ford remained equally unaffected by the subsequent re-nationalisation of British Steel.

It would have been surprising if, in more recent years, other hard-pressed governments had not tried to emulate the examples set by the earlier essays in nationalising foreign investments in Eastern Europe, the Near East and the Middle East. Even if some of these imitators did not consider it advisable to go all the way, they at least tried their hands on more piecemeal encroachments on foreign property rights. From their point of view, creeping nationalisation had the additional merit that, at every stage, the reaction—or lack of reaction—of the foreign interests and governments concerned could be tested. If necessary, these experimentalists could retrace their steps without undue loss of face or, if the other side proved unexpectedly pliable, they were free to increase the pressure.

1—Cross-Checks

A few sketches in alphabetical order of some of the more recent challenges to the safety of British overseas investments will convey an impression of the scale and variety of these interferences. It should, however, be

[1] Direct evidence for the connection between a statement made by the United Kingdom Foreign Secretary in the House of Commons on nationalisation in Burma and the Iranian policy of nationalisation is provided by Premier Musaddiq's speech at the meeting of the Majlis on December 17, 1950 (*Informations Iraniennes*, Paris, June 1, 1951, No. 60, p. 4).

[2] The Company was omitted from Schedule 3 as one of the companies liable to be nationalised. See also Mr. G. R. Strauss, Minister of Supply, in the Standing Committee of the House of Commons, *The Times* (London), January 28 and February 2, 1949, and, further, E. H. Scammell, 5 C.L.P. (1952), p. 30 *et seq.*

emphasised that this catalogue is not intended to be exhaustive. Moreover, in view of the current and unevenly documented character of these interventions, the summaries which follow are unavoidably fragmentary.

(a) Argentina

In 1963, the Argentine Government contemplated a proposal of exclusive access by firms in Argentinian hands to working capital from a fund to which Argentina and foreign companies in the Argentinian meat trade were liable to contribute.

According to a reply given by the Lord Privy Seal in the House of Commons, the Government of the United Kingdom had made representation to that of Argentina, pointing out the discriminatory character of the proposal.[3]

Actually, this scheme was merely a variation of one introduced by the Government of the Belgian Congo in 1931 during the economic depression. It gave rise to the *Oscar Chinn* case (1934) between Belgium and the United Kingdom before the Permanent Court of International Justice.[4]

It is doubtful whether, in the absence of specific treaty obligations, that is, under the governing rules of international customary law, the discrimination implied in measures of this type is illegal.[5] Actually, the contemplated Argentinian measure was incompatible with the spirit, and probably also with the letter, of the Treaty of Amity, Commerce and Navigation of May 12, 1825, between the United Province of Rio de la Plata, subsequently Argentina, and the United Kingdom.[6] It ran counter

[3] H.C.Deb., Vol. 681, cols. 18–19 (July 15, 1963) or B.P.I.L. 1963 (II), p. 125.

On the Settlement Agreement of November 8, 1965, between Argentina and Yacimientos Petroliferos Fiscales (Y.P.F.) and Shell regarding the dispute over Argentina's annulment of oil production contracts under Decree No. 744 of 1963, see 6 I.L.M. (1967), p. 19 *et seq.*

[4] Series A/B 63, and, further, Vol. I, p. 232 *et seq.*

[5] At least, in the view of the majority of the Court in the *Oscar Chinn* case, this was not the case.

See also below, pp. 120 and 163 *et seq.*, and further, *D. Schindler, Gleichberechtigung von Individuen als Problem des Völkerrechts* (1957), and J. H. W. Verzijl, *The Jurisprudence of the World Court* (1965), Vol. I, p. 383 *et seq.*

[6] United Kingdom, Foreign Office. *Handbook of Commercial Treaties* (1931), p. 15 *et seq.*

The Treaty was concluded for an indefinite period and never terminated.

Under Article 10 of the Agreement of December 1, 1936, on Trade and Commerce between Argentina and the United Kingdom, " nothing in the present Agreement shall be deemed to affect the rights and obligations arising out of the Treaty of Commerce and Navigation signed at Buenos Aires on the 2nd February 1825 " (Cmd. 5324—1936).

The 1936 Agreement was brought into force provisionally by a Protocol of Signature which also provided for termination of the provisional application of the Agreement on three months' notice. After notice of termination of the 1936 Agreement had been given by the Argentine Government in 1945 (Cmd. 7016—1946), the provisional application of the 1936 Agreement was indefinitely prolonged, subject to denunciation at any time by simple communication from the Parties (Cmd. 7123—1947).

A reference to the 1936 Agreement and, thus, by implication, to the 1825 Treaty, will also be found in Paragraph 8 of the Exchange of Notes of April 15, 1964, between Argentina and the United Kingdom (Cmnd. 2383—1964).

On the 1825 Treaty, see, further, *Principles of I.E.L.*, p. 80 *et seq.*

to the liberal formulation in this Treaty of the standard of national treatment accorded to nationals of the Contracting Parties.[7]

(b) Burma

In 1964, a question was asked in the House of Commons on the effective percentage rates of the taxation levied by the Burmese Government on the profits of British companies regarding their operations in Burma.

The Financial Secretary to the Treasury replied that such profits were taxed at rates rising to 99 per cent. on profits exceeding the equivalent of £22,500. He concurred with the view that such taxation was excessive and constituted *de facto* confiscation.[8]

The difficulty is where to draw the line. In principle, taxation is a matter within the exclusive jurisdiction of any sovereign State. Yet, at one point, ruinous taxation becomes indistinguishable from confiscation of the capital or income affected. A relevant criterion of distinction between severe taxation and confiscation is whether, in fact, such taxation applies to foreign enterprises alone. If this is the case, confiscation in disguise may well be suspected.[9]

(c) Ceylon

In connection with the nationalisation in 1961 of the import, distribution and marketing of oil in Ceylon, the Under-Secretary of State for Commonwealth Relations stated in the House of Commons that, at various times, the Government of the United Kingdom had made clear to the Ceylonese Government the importance it attached to the Shell Oil Company—one of

[7] An *a fortiori* argument from, for instance, Article 9 would suggest this (*ibid.*, p. 17).

[8] H.C.Deb., Vol. 704, col. 1036 (December 22, 1964) or B.P.I.L. 1964 (II), p. 202.

During a visit to Rangoon, Lord Carrington, Minister without Portfolio, informed the Burmese Government that while the Government of the United Kingdom did not complain about the quantum of compensation offered for nationalised British properties, it was concerned about the delays in such payments: "Very little has been paid so far" (*The Daily Telegraph* (London), April 10, 1964).

For the Burmese Industries Nationalisation Law of 1963, see 3 I.L.M. (1964), p. 13. In accordance with section 1 (2), this Law, which was adopted on October 19, 1963, applied retrospectively from August 16, 1963 onwards (*ibid.*, p. 13).

See, further, *The Financial Times* (London), October 21, 1963.

In 1963, the Burmese Government had offered to repay within three months all foreign-subscribed capital in the original currency and compensation for the loss of buildings and other installations (*Keesing's Archives*, January 12–19, 1963, p. 19192 B).

On the nationalisation in 1965 of the Burma Corporation (1951), a silver and mining corporation owned jointly by British interests and the Burmese Government, see *The Times* (London), January 19, 1965, and on the nationalisation of Burma Unilever, another such joint venture, *ibid.*, January 30, 1965.

See also W. Friedmann and R. Kalmanoff (eds.), *Joint International Business Ventures* (1961), pp. 60–61.

[9] See also A. Albrecht, 29 B.Y.I.L. (1952), p. 172; G. C. Christie, 38 *ibid.* (1962), p. 331 *et seq.*; E. Lauterpacht's note in B.P.I.L. 1964 (II), p. 202 *et seq.*; and C. F. Amerasinghe, *State Responsibility for Injury to Aliens* (1967), p. 137.

the three foreign companies affected—receiving "prompt, adequate and effective compensation."[10]

Under the Ceylon Petroleum Corporation Act 1961, the foreign oil companies concerned were permitted to continue their activities to a limited extent. In 1963, however, the distribution of oil in Ceylon was assigned exclusively to the Ceylon Petroleum Corporation. This legislation was to apply "notwithstanding anything to the contrary . . . in any undertaking, express or implied, given by or on behalf of the Government or the Corporation relating to the business of importing, exporting, selling, supplying or distributing petroleum."[11]

This section of the 1963 Act recalls a passage in *The Amphitrite* case (1921) in which Rowlatt J. had held that it was "not competent for the Government to fetter its future executive action, which must necessarily be determined by the needs of the community when the question arises. It cannot . . . hamper its freedom of action in matters which concern the welfare of the State."[12] Little doubt exists that, if the non-fulfilment by the United Kingdom of the executive contract involved had been tested on the international level, the United Kingdom would have incurred international liability.[13]

It also emerged from a further ministerial reply in the House of Commons that, under the 1963 Ceylonese legislation, the payment of compensation was precluded regarding property which the Ceylon Petroleum Corporation did not acquire, but which would be useless if the Shell Company was excluded from the internal Ceylonese market.

In this context, the Secretary of State for Commonwealth Relations reiterated that the Government of the United Kingdom "did not contest the right of any Government to nationalise undertakings in its territory," but expected that, in that event, "prompt, adequate and effective compensation in accordance with the principles of international law" would be paid to the British interests affected.[14]

[10] H.C.Deb., Vol. 672, col. 618 (February 21, 1963) or B.P.I.L. 1963 (II), p. 122. See also the Written Answer by the Secretary of State for Commonwealth Relations to a question in the House of Commons, H.C.Deb., Vol. 681, col. 231, July 26, 1963 or 2 I.L.M. (1962), p. 962, and the Joint Statement issued in Ceylon, July 29, 1963, by Esso, Caltex and Shell, *ibid.*, p. 967.

For Ceylon Petroleum Corporation Act, May 29, 1961, see I.L.M. (1962), p. 126.

[11] Section 10 of the Ceylon Petroleum Corporation (Amendment) Act 1963, 2 I.L.M. (1963), p. 951 at p. 960.

[12] [1921] 3 K.B. 500 at p. 503.

See, further, J. D. B. Mitchell, *The Contracts of Public Authorities* (1954), pp. 24 *et seq.*, 55 and 228; Sir David Hughes Parry, *The Sanctity of Contracts* (1959), p. 64 *et seq.*, and S. A. de Smith, *Judicial Review of Administrative Action* (1968), pp. 19 and 299.

[13] See above, p. 5 *et seq.*

[14] H.C.Deb., Vol. 681, cols. 231–232 (Written Answers—July 26, 1963) or B.P.I.L. 1963 (II), p. 123.

For the Compensation Agreements of June 22, 1965, between Ceylon and Caltex, Esso and Shell, see 4 I.L.M. (1965), p. 1074 *et seq.* See also 1 *ibid.* (1962), p. 126 *et seq.* and, for differences in the estimates of the quantum of compensation due, *Keesing's Archives*, July 10–17, 1966, p. 20851 A.

The Ceylon Petroleum (Foreign Claims) Compensation Act of December 18, 1965,

(*ctd. overleaf*)

In reply to questions on Ceylonese taxation in the House of Commons in 1964, the Minister of State for Commonwealth Relations informed the House that the rate of taxation levied in Ceylon on British companies depended on whether such companies held immovable property there. If they did, the total tax payable was 80 per cent. and, otherwise, between 72 and 74 per cent. These rates applied irrespective of the amount of profits earned.

The Minister conceded that taxation in Ceylon was "very high," but this did not preclude "British companies from continuing to operate at a profit." [15]

It also became clear from this reply and an earlier answer by the Under-Secretary of State for Commonwealth Relations that, since the Ceylonese budget of July, 1964, the remittance of interests, profits and dividends from Ceylon had been suspended and other measures damaging to British and other foreign investments introduced. The Government of Ceylon insisted, however, that these measures were intended primarily to safeguard Ceylon's foreign exchange reserves and were taken against all foreign property on a footing of complete non-discrimination.[16]

(d) India

Attention was drawn in the House of Commons to a section in the Indian Estate Duty Act of 1953. According to this provision, a non-Indian Company was not only deemed to have become resident in India if more than half of its total income was derived from India, but also incurred liability for estate duties of non-resident shareholders for Indian estate duty regarding the shares of non-resident shareholders who had died abroad.

Actually, before the Bill became law, the Government of the United Kingdom had made representations to the Indian Government against this charge on companies and emphasised that the contemplated tax was "essentially extraterritorial taxation, for neither the owner of the property nor the property is in India and, on accepted principles, this property being in the jurisdiction of this country, should not be charged with Indian

(*Note 14 ctd.*)
5 I.L.M. (1965), p. 224 *et seq.*, excels by a generous use of legal fictions for the purpose of putting some of the earlier legislation in reverse.

One illustration must suffice: "The Compensation Tribunal established or constituted under the provisions of the Ceylon Petroleum Corporation Act shall be deemed, at all times, not to have had, and not to have, any power or authority or jurisdiction to hear or determine any claim for compensation in respect of any assets which are a subject-matter of such agreement, and any such claim shall be deemed, for all purposes, to have abated on the relevant date" (section 2 (1) (*a*)—*ibid.*, p. 225).

See also Amerasinghe, *loc. cit.* above, p. 92, note 9, pp. 134, 143 and 159.

15 H.C.Deb., Vol. 706, col. 173 (February 9, 1965) or B.P.I.L. 1965 (I), p. 46.

16 H.L.Deb., Vol. 262, col. 92 (December 9, 1964) or B.P.I.L. 1964 (II), p. 201.

Between November, 1965, and March, 1968, the Government of the United Kingdom gave six interest-free loans, amounting to £10½ million, to that of Ceylon. All these loans are repayable over 25 years, with a three years' period of grace. The loans are given for the purchase from the United Kingdom of commodities and implements and are intended to maintain and develop Ceylon's economy. See, further, Cmnd. 2736 (1965) and Cmnd. 3180 (1967).

Estate Duty." Yet, the Indian Government was not prepared to modify its policy, and the Bill became law, containing this "unusual provision." [17]

The United Kingdom accepted this far-reaching exercise of extra-territorial jurisdiction by becoming a party to the Anglo-Indian Double Taxation Agreement of April 3, 1956. It is there expressly provided that "nothing in the present Agreement shall affect any provision of the law of India imposing duty on shares in, or debentures of a company incorporated outside India which carries on business in India and which has been treated for the purposes of the Indian Income Tax Act 1922 (XI of 1922) as resident in India for two out of the three completed assessments immediately preceding the death; nor shall anything in the present Agreement be considered to confer a right to a credit against duty so imposed for any duty imposed in Great Britain on any such debenture." [18]

(e) Indonesia

During the Sukarno regime, Indonesia had developed the technique of creeping nationalisation of foreign investments into a fine art. It had first applied these measures to Netherlands property and, subsequently, extended them to British, United States and other foreign investments. The key-words of this policy of official and unofficial harassment, practised by Indonesian government departments and trade unions, were intimidation, interference and supervision, falling short of formal confiscation. In 1963, this policy culminated in the burning of the British Embassy in Djakarta during officially tolerated riots, with widespread losses, damage and injury inflicted on British nationals.[19]

By a presidential decree of November 26, 1964, the isolated actions previously taken were "integrated" (to use the terminology of the Decree). All British-owned enterprises in Indonesia were brought under "full and direct control and management of the Central Government." [20] The Indonesian action was justified as being "in accordance with the policy of confrontation of the so-called puppet State of 'Malaysia,' which has to be pursued by the Government to consummate the Indonesian Revolution at the moment." [21]

[17] H.C.Deb., Vol. 553, col. 813 (June 4, 1956) or *Contemporary Practice* (II), 6 I.C.L.Q., p. 131.

[18] Article III (2) *U.N. International Tax Agreements*, Vol. 7 (1958), p. 307.

[19] Replies by the Foreign Secretary in the House of Commons, H.C.Deb., Vol. 685, cols. 12–13 (November 25, 1963) or B.P.I.L. 1963 (II), p. 120, and H.C.Deb., Vol. 696, cols. 123–124 (Written Answers—June 15, 1964) or B.P.I.L. 1964 (I), p. 66; Sir Francis Vallat, *International Law and the Practitioner* (1966), p. 123 *et seq.*, and *Inductive Approach*, pp. 172–173.

For the Heads of Agreement of June 1, 1963, between the Indonesian Government and the Caltex Pacific Oil Company, Stanvac Indonesia and Shell Indonesia, see 3 I.L.M. (1964), p. 81 *et seq.* See also *ibid.*, p. 243 *et seq.*, for one of the subsequently concluded working contracts, especially Article 25 on the Settlement of Disputes (*ibid.*, p. 280).

[20] Article 1 (B.P.I.L. 1964 (II), p. 197).

[21] Preamble under (a) (*ibid.*, p. 196).

In its Note of December 1, 1964, the Government of the United Kingdom stated that the measures taken against British commercial interests in Indonesia were a "*de facto* dispossession and expropriation and thereby gave rise to an obligation to provide compensation in accordance with international law." [22]

In a further Note of July 20, 1965, the Embassy of the United Kingdom in Djakarta reminded the Indonesian Department of Foreign Affairs that, so far, no reply had been received to the Note of December 1, 1964, nor to a further Note of February 24, 1965. Moreover, "in view of the complete inability of British enterprises and plantations to exercise and enjoy any of their rights of ownership in relation to their property in Indonesia," the Government of the United Kingdom considered this situation to amount to an expropriation of these properties. The Embassy was, therefore, instructed to request the Indonesian Government "either to restore this property promptly to the British owners or to acknowledge their obligation, in accordance with international law, to provide prompt, adequate and effective compensation." [23]

After the liquidation of the Sukarno regime, it required a massive international rescue operation to cope with the most urgent problems of Indonesia's international insolvency, described by the British Foreign Secretary as an "appalling economic situation." [24]

(f) Iraq

Under Law No. 80 of 1961, defining the exploitation areas for the oil companies, the Iraq Government was authorised to free lands other than those defined in a schedule attached to the Law of all rights acquired under concessions which had been granted to the Iraq Petroleum Company, the Basrah Petroleum Company and the Mosul Petroleum Company.

Actually, this meant that the three companies were deprived, so far without compensation, of 99½ per cent. of their combined concession areas. The Iraq Government justified this legislation on the ground that in the areas covered by the Law, especially in North Rumaila, the Iraq Petroleum Company had failed to develop large oil fields it had discovered.

[22] B.P.I.L. 1964 (II), p. 198.
For further Indonesian Decrees of the same type, see 4 I.L.M. (1965), p. 435 *et seq.*

[23] *Ibid.*, pp. 199–200.

[24] This formulation is to be found only in the Parliamentary Report of *The Times* (London), April 30, 1966, but is not contained in *Hansard*, H.C.Deb., Vol. 727. cols. 1111–1114 (April 29, 1966).
See also *ibid.*, Vol. 748, col. 123 (Written Answer by the Secretary of State for Foreign Affairs—June 15, 1967) and Vol. 751, col. 26 (Written Answer by the Secretary of State for Foreign Affairs—July 24, 1967).
On the Indonesian Decrees returning foreign enterprises to former owners (December 12, 1966) and ending Government control of foreign oil companies (December 30, 1966), see 6 I.L.M. (1967), p. 221 *et seq.* The latter Decree does not affect the Agreement of December 30, 1965, between the Indonesian Government and Shell for the sale of the assets of P. T. Shell Indonesia to the Indonesian Government (5 *ibid.* (1966), p. 1136). See also 4 *ibid.* (1965), p. 435.
See also above, p. 57.

Under the concession agreements, the Companies nominated Lord McNair as their arbitrator and requested the Iraq Government to nominate its arbitrator.[25] These requests received the support of the Governments of the United Kingdom, where the three companies are registered, have their head offices and more than half of their share capital is held, and of the United States of America, intervening on behalf of a substantial United States minority interest.[26]

So far, the Iraq Government has refused to comply with its duties under the concession agreements to appoint its own arbitrator and arbitrate the issues raised for years by the three oil companies. Actually, on April 10, 1968, the Iraq Government announced that its own Iraq National Oil Company was to develop the North Rumaila oil field.[27]

(g) El Salvador

In 1962, the Lord Privy Seal was asked in the House of Commons about the ultimatum issued by the Government of El Salvador to seize the British-owned El Salvador Railway Company whose concession had been granted until 1974.

[25] *The Times* (London), January 5, 1962, or *Contemporary Practice* (1962—I), p. 57.

The original concession of the Iraq Petroleum Company was embodied in a convention of March 14, 1925, between the Government of Iraq and the Turkish Petroleum Company (since the Amending Agreement of 1931 styled the Iraq Petroleum Company), as subsequently amended (published in the Iraq *Official Gazette*).

See, further, for instance, Article 3 (area) and Article 40 (arbitration) of the concession of the Iraq Petroleum Company: "If, at any time during or after the currency of this Convention, any doubt, difference or dispute shall arise between the Government and the Company concerning the interpretation or execution hereof, or anything herein contained, or in connection herewith, or the rights and liabilities of either party hereunder, or if the parties shall fail to agree upon any matter required to be settled by agreement, the same shall, failing any agreement to settle it in another way, be referred to two arbitrators, one of whom shall be chosen by each party, and a referee who shall be chosen by the arbitrators before proceeding to arbitration.

Each party shall nominate its arbitrator within thirty days of being requested in writing by the other party to do so. In the event of the arbitrators failing to agree upon a referee, the Government and the Company shall, in agreement, appoint a referee, and in the event of their failing to agree, they shall request the President of the International Court of Justice to appoint a referee.

The decision of the arbitrators, or in the case of a difference of opinion between them, the decision of the referee shall be final.

The place of arbitration shall be such as may be agreed by the parties, and in default of agreement shall be Baghdad."

Under Article 43 of the 1925 Convention and corresponding provisions of subsequent amending agreements, in case of any discrepancy between the meanings of the English and Arabic texts of these agreements, the English text prevails.

[26] *The Times* (London), January 8, 1962, and *Contemporary Practice* (1962—I), p. 57.

[27] *The Times* (London), April 11, 1968. See also *ibid.*, July 18 and August 5, 1968.

On Iraq Law No. 80 of 1961, see *ibid.*, December 13, 1961; on the Iraq Laws of July 14, 1964, on nationalisation and regulation of companies, see 3 I.L.M. (1964), p. 928 *et seq.*; on the Iraq Law of August 6, 1967, concerning allocation of oil exploitation areas, see 6 *ibid.* (1967), p. 1162; on the service agreement of November 23, 1967, between the Iraq National Oil Company and the French State-Owned Group ERAP, see 7 *ibid.* (1968), p. 233, and on the Iraq-U.S.S.R. Oil Agreement of December 24, 1967, *ibid.*, p. 307.

On the Syrian Decree of March 4, 1965, nationalising the oil companies, see 4 *ibid.*, p. 456 *et seq.*

In reply, it was stated that the Company was in touch with the Government of El Salvador about "fair and adequate" compensation. Representations by the Government of the United Kingdom to that of El Salvador on a governmental level were not considered "appropriate or useful at this stage," but it was stated that the British Ambassador in San Salvador maintained close contact with the parties concerned.[28]

(h) Somali Republic

In 1961, it was agreed between the Somali Republic and the United Kingdom that the Somali Republic should be responsible for the payment of pensions to retired overseas civil servants of the former Somaliland Protectorate who were then resident outside the Somali Republic. Actually, the special account set up for the purpose was financed from the grant-in-aid which the Government of the United Kingdom had agreed to make to the Somali Government.[29]

In 1963, the Somali Republic broke off diplomatic relations with the United Kingdom (resumed in January, 1968) and requested that payment of the grant-in-aid should cease. As a matter of principle, the Government of the United Kingdom held that the Somali Republic was responsible for this liability, but saw to it that the pensioners did not suffer.[30]

(i) Tanzania

In an article published in 1967 the day before President Nyerere assented to the nationalisation legislation then before him, he explained the Tanzanian policy of nationalisation of banks, insurance companies, and firms engaged in processing foods and other enterprises constituting key-industries. He added: "In all these cases we have stated quite clearly and categorically that we shall pay full and fair compensation for the assets acquired, and that we shall honour all existing commitments."[31]

Each of the Nationalisation Acts of 1967 contains the promised "full and fair" compensation clause.[32] Under this legislation, the key-person

[28] H.C.Deb., Vol. 666, cols. 20–21 (Written Answers—November 5, 1962) or *Contemporary Practice* 1962 (II), p. 216.

[29] Cmnd. 1101 (1960).

[30] H.C.Deb., Vol. 678, cols. 119–120 (Written Answers—May 28, 1963) or B.P.I.L. 1963 (I), pp. 51–52, and D. P. O'Connell, *State Succession in Municipal Law and International Law*, Vol. I (1967), p. 475, n. 1.

For the reasons prompting the rupture of diplomatic relations in 1963 between the Somali Republic and the United Kingdom, see *Keesing's Archives*, May 25–June 1, 1963, p. 19432 A.

[31] TANU, *The Arusha Declaration and Tanu's Policy on Socialism and Self-Reliance* (Dar-es-Salaam—1967), p. 22.

On the revocation of leasehold rights of occupancy in the Arusha area of Tanganyika, see the reply by the Secretary of State in the House of Commons, H.C.Deb., Vol. 703, col. 217 (December 1, 1964) or B.P.I.L. 1964 (II), p. 201.

[32] Section 10 (1) of the Act of February 15, 1967, on the National Bank of Commerce, 6 I.L.M. (1967), p. 1199; section 12 (1) of the Act of the same date on the State Trading Corporation, *ibid.*, p. 1207; section 17 (1) of the Act of February 16, 1967, on the National Agricultural Products Board, *ibid.*, p. 1217; section 6 (1) of the Act

(*ctd. overleaf*)

in fixing the compensation due is the Minister of Finance, who decides on the cases in which such compensation is due, and how it is to be determined.[33]

Some of the firms involved came to terms with the Government of Tanzania.[34] Others adopted a more eristic attitude. As described by the Tanzanian Minister of Finance in the Tanzanian National Assembly, three of the foreign banks affected withdrew their key staff and two of them—the Standard Bank and Barclays Bank—froze about 45 million (Tanzanian) Shillings which, at the time of nationalisation, were in the control of these Banks outside Tanzania.[35] According to the Tanzanian Minister of Finance, these funds belonged to Tanzanian depositors.

In the same speech, the Tanzanian Minister of Finance expressed the disquiet of his Government on the severe burdens imposed on the economy of the country by the Public Officers Agreements concluded by Tanganyika and Zanzibar with the United Kingdom and taken over by Tanzania.[36]

Under the Rhodesia Resolution adopted in December, 1965, by the Organisation of African Unity, Tanzania had severed diplomatic relations with the United Kingdom (resumed in July, 1968). The Tanzanian Government took it for granted, however, that its international obligations to the United Kingdom remained unaffected by this step. It, therefore, communicated its views on the " neither just nor equitable " character of the governing treaties, and its intention to " secure a new division of responsibility in which the Government of the United Kingdom assumes what we believe to be its proper share of the burden of making these payments " to the United Kingdom through the Canadian High Commission in Dar-es-Salaam.[37]

On June 20, 1968, the United Kingdom Minister of Overseas Development stated in a written reply to a question in the House of Commons that, from July 1 onwards, the Tanzanian Government would cease to meet most of its commitments under the Public Officers Agreements.

In these circumstances, the Government of the United Kingdom assumed in fact these Tanzanian responsibilities. Yet, " in making this arrangement, Her Majesty's Government do not regard themselves as relieving the Tanzanian Government of their liability in this matter." Moreover,

(*Note 32 ctd.*)
of the same date on the National Insurance Corporation, *ibid.*, p. 1222, and section 4 of the Act of the same date on certain Tanzanian Industrial Companies, *ibid.*, p. 1227.

33 See section 10 (3) of the Act on the National Bank of Commerce and the corresponding sections of the other Acts (*loc. cit.* above, note 32).

34 See, further, Section 49 of the speech made on June 14, 1967, by Mr. A. Jamal, the Minister for Finance, in the Tanzanian National Assembly, and Tanzanian Ministry of Information, *Press Releases* of May 20, 1967, August 31, 1967, December 21, 1967, January 17, 1968, February 12, 1968, April 15, 1968, and April 24, 1968.

35 Mr. Jamal's speech, *loc. cit.* above, note 34, Section 55.
Tanzania maintained the par value of her currency (T.Sh.) after the devaluation of the Pound Sterling in November, 1967 (T.Sh. 7 = U.S.$ 1; T.Sh. 17 = £1).

36 See also O'Connell, *loc. cit.* above, p. 98, note 30, Vol. I, p. 475, n. 1.

37 Mr. Jamal's speech, *loc cit.* above, note 34, Sections 160–161.

the whole aid programme of the United Kingdom for Tanzania was terminated.[38]

(j) United Arab Republic

Some of the interferences by Egypt (since 1958, the United Arab Republic) with British property were considered in other contexts.[39] It remains to deal with others which were completely unconnected with any direct conflict between the two countries.

In 1961, the Egyptian Government took further measures of sequestration and nationalisation. They affected about 600 people, 31 of whom were then known to be British subjects.

In the light of these figures, the Joint Under-Secretary of State for Foreign Affairs absolved the Egyptian Government of the charge of discrimination against British subjects, but treated these measures as matters of U.A.R. domestic policy. The Government of the United Kingdom merely informed the Government of the U.A.R. that it expected the assessment of compensation and the manner of its payment to "conform to the generally accepted principles of international law," and reserved its rights in the matter.[40]

By March, 1964, numerous inquiries in Cairo and representations there and at the U.A.R. Embassy in London had merely elicited that the U.A.R. Government accepted the "principle of compensation for that part of the property which is not returned to its owners," but not yet "how and when the compensation is to be paid and when the remainder of the property is to be released." [41]

Shortly after, the U.A.R. Government published a Decree Law, under which the property of natural persons sequestrated in 1961 devolved on the State, and compensation was to be paid in State bonds, up to a limit of £ (Egyptian) 30,000. On receiving this news, the United Kingdom Embassy in Cairo reserved all British rights in the matter and sought clarification on whether the Decree was to be applied to British subjects. Meanwhile, the number of British subjects known to have been affected by the 1961 sequestrations had grown to 135.[42]

All that further emerged by the end of 1964 was that the United Arab Republic intended to retain the greater part of the British properties,

[38] Statement by the Ministry for Overseas Development, H.C.Deb., Vol. 766, col. 174 (Written Answers—June 20, 1968).

[39] See above, pp. 54 and 84 *et seq.*

[40] H.C.Deb., Vol. 649, col. 637 (November 15, 1961) or *Contemporary Practice* 1962 (I), p. 58.

[41] H.C.Deb., Vol. 692, col. 8 (March 23, 1964) or B.P.I.L. 1964 (I), pp. 65–66.

[42] H.C.Deb., Vol. 696, col. 121 (Written Answers—June 15, 1964) or B.P.I.L. 1964 (I), p. 66.

resequestrated in 1961.[43] Actually, it took until the end of 1967 to settle these claims by an inter-governmental agreement.[44]

During the Arab-Israel War of 1967, several British ships were blocked in the Suez Canal. The refusal of the Egyptian authorities to take the measures required to release these ships or allow these measures to be taken by third parties is estimated to have involved losses of £500,000 in earnings during the first year of the enforced idleness of these ships.

To at least one member of the House of Commons it looked as if, in this way, a further ransom was being exacted from the United Kingdom to make it concur in a major loan Egypt hoped to obtain. The Foreign Secretary mildly dissented from this assessment: "I do not think it should be put entirely in that way." [45]

(k) Venezuela

The shape of things to come in oil-exporting States strong enough to adopt such a policy is indicated by the *bases minimas* formulated by C.V.P., the Venezuelan State Oil Company. They are the minimum conditions on which foreign oil companies are invited to submit exploration proposals. Actually, these *bases minimas* would be more accurately described as the starting points of negotiations.

In the past, oil concessions included the right of exploration, production and sale of the oil under the land inside the areas of such concessions. What Venezuela offered in 1968 were service agreements on the pattern of those concluded by Iran and Iraq with Italian and French oil companies.[46]

Under such service agreements, the Venezuelan State Oil Company would retain all rights over the land and the oil under it. The tasks of the foreign oil companies as its agents would be limited to the discovery and production of oil.

The most risky feature of the service agreements under discussion are the stringent relinquishment clauses regarding the land to be explored

[43] H.C.Deb., Vol. 704, col. 18 (December 18, 1964) or B.P.I.L. 1964 (II), p. 206.

[44] Cmnd. 3476 (1967), and, for a further governmental assurance that the negotiations regarding compensation for British property sequestrated in 1961 were in their concluding stages, H.C.Deb., Vol. 754, cols. 899–900 (November 20, 1967).

See also above, p. 54 *et seq.*

[45] H.C.Deb. (Daily Report), Vol. 765, col. 11 (May 20, 1968).

For figures of grants made by the United Kingdom to the United Arab Republic (and other Near Eastern States), see H.C.Deb., Vol. 748, cols. 357–358 (Written Answers by the Minister for Overseas Development—June 23, 1967). See also *The Times* (London), July 31, 1968.

[46] For the *bases minimas* of March 13, 1968, laid down by Corporacion Venecolana del Petroleo for service contracts in the southern part of Lake Maracaibo, see *El Nacional* (Caracas), March 25, 1968.

See also the Venezuelan Law of Partial Reform of the Law of Hydrocarbons, 1955 (*Official Gazette*, Extraordinary Number 471, October 13, 1955—English transl. by G. G. Cover—Caracas—no date).

by the foreign companies,[47] the high charges made to the oil companies, the onerous productivity formulas, constituting in effect an excess profit tax, and the rights reserved by the Venezuelan State Oil Company to approve the production and pricing policies of the contracting oil companies.[48]

So long as the Venezuelan principal of these foreign oil companies is willing to interpret such clauses as *jus aequum*, foreign service contractors accept a calculable risk. Should this assumption prove unjustified, investments made by the oil companies on the footing of the *bases minimas* would assume the character of risk capital to a greater degree than, in any case, is unavoidable if such assets are situated in politically volatile foreign States.[49]

(l) Zambia

Appropriately, this survey ends with President Kaunda's announcement of April 19, 1968. In it, he forecast large-scale control of key industries, with the State taking a 51 per cent. interest in the companies concerned. While banks, insurance companies and oil companies are to be excluded from these measures, a new royalty formula for the copper-mining industry is to be worked out and the remission abroad of profits from the copper industry is to be limited to 50 per cent.

It remains to be seen how the value of the shares to be transferred to Zambia will be fixed and how free the consent of the companies in the process of being transferred into joint ventures will be.[50]

2—Necessary Qualifications

In drawing a balance sheet of the significance of the bilateral British treaty programme on the protection of investments abroad in the post–1945 period, the test cases and cross-checks offered above require two qualifications:

(1) It would be misleading to read into these lists any specific indictment of " developing " countries as such.[51] Their performance must be viewed in the wider context of capital-importing States, most of which,

[47] On the development of relinquishment clauses, first incorporated in Article 6 of the 1925 Concession of the Turkish Petroleum Company (see above, p. 97, note 25), see H. Cattan, *The Evolution of Oil Concessions in the Middle East and North Africa* (1967), p. 11 *et seq.*

[48] See, further, J. Roeber, *Venezuelan Squeeze on the Oil Firms*, *The Times* (London), April 30, 1968, and *The Economist*, April 20, 1968, p. 91.

[49] See also above, p. 9, and below, p. 185 *et seq.*

[50] *The Times* (London), April 20, 1968, and *The Economist*, April 27, 1958, p. 60.
In the financial year 1967–68, Zambia received £3,800,000 aid from the United Kingdom excluding defence aid and contingency planning assistance (Minister for Overseas Development, H.C.Deb., Vol. 746, cols. 713–714—May 4, 1967).
On the trend to limit economic opportunities in Tanzania to Tanzanian nationals, including naturalised citizens, see *The Times* (London), April 25, 1968 and section 17 of the Trades Licensing Act 1968 (so far, Bill of August 17, 1968).

[51] See above, p. 15 *et seq.*

at one time or another, defaulted on their obligations under international customary law or consensual engagements. In particular, the breaches of their undertakings by most of the capital-importing States of earlier periods in the Balkans and Latin America [52] and policies of confiscation of foreign-owned property adopted by the Soviet Union and her Communist allies in Europe as well as Communist China [53] should be recalled.

(2) It is only fair to recall the existence of capital-importing States which, in any of the relevant periods, have distinguished themselves by their absence from the sombre debt histories and lengthy loan tables of the Annual Reports of the Council of the Corporation of Foreign Bondholders, London.[54]

3—The Bilateral Experience:

A Balance Sheet

In any comparison of the present with glories of the past, it is advisable to remember the twin bases of the success story of the classical type of British treaties of friendship, commerce and navigation: the conclusion of such treaties as a *de facto* condition of access to the money market of the City of London and the effective presence of the British Navy on the seven oceans of the world.[55]

It is also advisable to recall how, after an impressive start, the United States programme of post-1945 treaties on the earlier British model gradually ground to a halt.[56]

It is true that Switzerland and, even more so, Western Germany concluded a respectable number of bilateral investment treaties.[57] Yet, the willingness of their partners to become parties to such agreements corresponded to the expectation of substantial influxes of capital resulting from such an accommodating attitude.

The corresponding French treaties are in a class of their own.[58] Although not exclusively designed for the purpose, they form part of a limited, but effective programme of continuing French colonialism by other means.

If anything could have prevented the United Kingdom from adopting a similar course, it was the fear of any interpretation of the intentions or effects of corresponding investment treaties in terms of neo-imperialism.[59]

52 See above, p. 21, and below, p. 185.

53 See above, p. 40 *et seq.*
For illustrations of almost perverse infringements of the minimum standards of international law, even in relation to personal liberty and dignity by the authorities of Communist China, see *The Times* (London), July 19 and 20, and August 3, 1968.

54 Published since 1874.
See, for instance, the 94th *Annual Report* for 1967, pp. 37 and 257 *et seq.*

55 See above, p. 24.

56 See above, p. 32, and below, p. 109.

57 See above, p. 32.

58 See above, pp. 16 and 32.

59 See above, p. 16.

In the view of those responsible for the direction of United Kingdom treaty policy, such treaties might well have spoilt the image of the new multi-racial Commonwealth in its formative stage.[60] Moreover, as with more comprehensive treaties of commerce, the scarcity of qualified manpower for the constitution of the teams, required for the negotiation of a considerable number of bilateral investment treaties, was another powerful disincentive.

Post-colonial inhibitions in the United Kingdom coincided with anxieties among the leaders of the newly emancipated States. They could not afford to appear to be tied too closely to their former imperial or colonial Power nor to be associated, however indirectly, with one of the two sides in the Cold War.

Thus, these countries and the United Kingdom had reasons of their own to fight shy of traditional types of treaties of commerce or politically suspect bilateral investment treaties.[61] In any case, since the advent of GATT, the former had lost much of their significance. In some cases, more specialised and "technical," as distinct from "political," treaties such as double taxation agreements, conventions on technical assistance and pensions and long-term agreements regarding the export to the United Kingdom of selected agricultural products formed acceptable substitutes.

Perhaps the most inhibiting factor was the nagging doubt in the United Kingdom whether, under the system of the Charter of the United Nations,[62] bilateral investment treaties constituted any more effective form of protection of foreign investments than the obligations incumbent in any case on capital-importing States under international customary law or the general principles of law recognised by civilised nations. If anything, bilateral investment treaties might have the opposite effect. They might lead to these obligations, actually or apparently, being whittled down.

In any case, the failure of the Suez venture of 1956 drove home a double lesson. It was understood before that the threat or use of armed force otherwise than in self-defence or collective defence against armed force was contrary to the Charter of the United Nations.[63] Yet another lesson had still to be learnt: it was one thing to consider that the conditions of the exercise of these rights were fulfilled, and another—in the

[60] See, further, *Power Politics*, p. 75 *et seq.*

[61] See also above, p. 32 *et seq.*

On bilateral long-term agreements, concluded during and after the Second World War between the United Kingdom and members of the Commonwealth, regarding the import to the United Kingdom of selected agricultural products, see P. Vellas, *Droit International Economique et Social*, Vol. I: *Droit International Agricole* (1965), pp. 330, 391 and 433 *et seq.*, and *Annuaire français* (1957), p. 134 *et seq.*

[62] See above, pp. 26 and 57, and below, p. 186.

In exceptional situations, such as in the Persian Gulf, the threat of the *withdrawal* of British military presence, while it lasted, could also serve as an effective means of ensuring law-abidingness by the Gulf sheiks. See, further, Ch. Douglas-Home, *The Times* (London), November 14, 1967, p. 11.

According to official British estimates, Gulf oil produces nearly £200 million *p.a.* in foreign exchange (after deducting the costs of stationing troops there) and the value of the capital invested there is estimated at £900 million. The annual defence costs involved were £20 million (Douglas-Home, *ibid.*).

[63] See, further, 13 Y.B.W.A. (1959), p. 236 *et seq.*

environment of a divided world—to exercise these rights without the consent, or in the face of the disapproval, of one's hegemonial Power.[64]

This left economic retorsion and reprisals as more freely available sanctions. Whether they would work was, however, rather fortuitous. In the case of the Iranian oil nationalisation they proved to be more effective than in that of the nationalisation of the Suez Canal Company.[65]

In these circumstances, the bilateral possibilities in the field of the protection of British investments overseas appeared increasingly unattractive. The United Kingdom was ready for new experiments: the protection of foreign investments on a multilateral basis.

[64] See above, p. 66 *et seq.*

[65] See above, p. 84 *et seq.*

On the value of economic sanctions, applied and non-applied, in post-1945 British practice, see, further, Drucker, *loc. cit.* above, p. 45, note 38 (1950), p. 101 *et seq.*; Wortley, *loc. cit.* above, p. 5, note 7 (1959), p. 154 *et seq.*; D. Focsaneanu, 5 *Annuaire français* (1959), p. 203 (Section 59 (No. 7)); G. A. Christenson, 55 A.J.I.L. (1961), p. 622; Lillich (1962), pp. 107–108, and (1967), p. 129 *et seq.*

On refutations of the view that force in Article 2 (4) of the Charter of the United Nations means pressure other than the application of physical force, see the United Kingdom Proposal submitted in September, 1964, to the United Nations Special Committee on Principles of International Law concerning Friendly Relations and Co-operation among States and the comments made in the Committee by the United Kingdom representative, B.P.I.L. 1964 (II), p. 271 *et seq.*

PART TWO

MULTILATERAL APPROACHES

CHAPTER 8

THE ABS-SHAWCROSS DRAFT CONVENTION ON INVESTMENTS ABROAD

CAPITAL export since 1945 has primarily taken the forms of foreign aid and government loans. International institutions have also played a minor but significant role.[1] Yet, a large demand for more capital remains unsatisfied.[2] If the Western world desires to meet this need at least in part, a considerable portion of the capital required must come from private sources. Understandably, the private investor is hesitant to see history repeat itself at his expense.[3]

A growing number of countries interested in capital import have tried to tempt potential investors by means of reassuring national legislation.[4] Capital-exporting countries also have sought to encourage private investors by foreign investment guarantees, insurance schemes and tax concessions.[5] In addition, the United States of America and a number of European States [6] have reformulated in various types of bilateral treaties the rules of international customary law on the protection of foreign property. Even so, a considerable measure of doubt remains. The pertinent Resolutions adopted by the General Assembly of the United Nations on Permanent Sovereignty over Natural Resources have done little to alleviate this uncertainty. Thus, there is still plenty of scope for realistic and constructive thinking.

In the late Fifties, the interests primarily concerned in Western Europe with capital export—banking, oil and other forms of primary production—increasingly favoured concerted action on the basis of an international investment code, embodied in a multilateral convention.[7] A number of

[1] See above, p. 13, and below, p. 194.
[2] See below, p. 200; *GATT Report 1967*, p. 225 *et seq.*; W. Friedmann and Others, *International Financial Aid* (1967), and above, p. 13. See also United Nations Secretariat, Report on the *Financing of Economic Development and Promotion of Private Foreign Investment in Developing Countries* (1968).
[3] See above, p. 40 *et seq.*, and below, p. 185 *et seq.*
[4] See below, p. 188 *et seq.*, and, further, H. W. Baade, *Gesetzgebung zur Förderung ausländischer Kapitalanlagen* (1957); W. Friedmann and R. C. Pugh (editors), *Legal Aspects of Foreign Investment* (1959); A. A. Fatouros, *Government Guarantees to Foreign Investors* (1962), p. 120 *et seq.*, and United Nations, *Investment Laws and Regulations in Africa*, 1965.
A convenient collection of relevant provisions in constitutions and investment laws is contained in Appendix II to the Brief for the American Bar Association as *amicus curiae* in *Banco Nacional de Cuba* v. *F. S. Farr and Others*, compiled by G. W. Haight (1960).
[5] See, further, below, p. 170 *et seq.*
[6] See above, p. 32.
[7] See also below, pp. 153 and 189 *et seq.*
On earlier drafts, see M. Brandon, 9 J.P.L. (1960), p. 125 *et seq.*; A. S. Miller, 53 A.J.I.L. (1959), p. 371 *et seq.*, and S. D. Metzger, 9 J.P.L. (1960), p. 133 *et seq.*, and, further, L. B. Sohn and R. R. Baxter, 55 A.J.I.L. (1961), p. 545 *et seq.*, the
(*ctd. overleaf*)

earlier efforts coalesced into a draft *Convention on Investments Abroad*, the work of a committee under the direction of Dr. Abs, Director-General of the *Deutsche Bank*, and Lord Shawcross.[8] It still deserves critical examination on its own merits. Beyond this, the Draft Convention became the basis of subsequent draft conventions,[9] and today stands for a distinct pattern of the protection of foreign investments.[10]

As the text of the Abs-Shawcross Draft Convention is not easily available, it is probably fairest to provide a critique in the form of a commentary on the Articles which, where necessary, have been regrouped.[11]

1—Objects and Assumptions

The Preamble of the Draft Convention runs as follows:

> "The High Contracting Parties:
>
> believing that peace, security and progress in the world can only be attained and ensured by fruitful co-operation between all peoples on a basis of international law and mutual confidence; appreciating also the importance of encouraging commercial relations and promoting the flow of capital for economic activity and development;
>
> and considering the contribution which may be made towards these ends by a restatement of principles of conduct relating to foreign investments;
>
> have resolved for this purpose to conclude the present Convention."

The first two paragraphs of the Preamble are unnecessarily circuitous.

In spite of all experiences which might have advised them to the contrary, the banking interests concerned are still ready to export surplus capital to countries which can offer investors more attractive yields than can be obtained at home or in any of the other industrialised countries. Most of the oil and other fixed interests involved are even more inescapably linked with the countries which are the source of a considerable, if not the greater, part of their revenues. Thus, both groups try to improve by way of a multilateral convention what, in the light of Western experiences since the First World War, has become an increasingly dubious expectation:

(*Note 7 ctd.*)
accompanying Harvard Draft Convention on the International Responsibility of States for Injuries to Aliens (*ibid.*, p. 548 *et seq.*) and American Law Institute, *Restatement of the Law—Second: Foreign Relations Law of the United States* (1965), p. 551 *et seq.*

8 The Abs-Shawcross Draft Convention (subsequently so abbreviated) is dated April, 1959. References are to the text and Commentary published in 9 J.P.L. (1960), p. 116 *et seq.*

9 See below, p. 153 *et seq.*

10 See below, pp. 134 and 189 *et seq.*

11 Points made in an earlier version of this Chapter, but less relevant now, have been abbreviated or eliminated. See 9 J.P.L. (1960), p. 147 *et seq.*, or 14 C.L.P. (1961), p. 213 *et seq.*

See also Lord Shawcross, *The Protection of Foreign Private Investments in Trade and Industry* (Karachi), December 1960, p. 1 *et seq.*, and 102 Hague *Recueil* (1961), p. 339 *et seq.*

effective legal protection against default on their obligations by capital-importing States and grantors of concessions.

The capital-importing countries, in their turn, have reasons of their own to welcome such co-operation. They may have attained " sovereign equality " in the meaning of the Charter of the United Nations. Yet, in a divided and strongly hierarchical international society, cogent reasons readily come to mind why, compared with financial assistance in most other forms, private foreign investors may well be the lesser evil.

At least potentially, a measure of common ground exists: willingness to invest and willingness to accept foreign investments.[12] The rest is a matter of attitudes. Each side has reasons to be suspicious of the other. Capital-importing countries are afraid of private foreign investment which amounts to little more than a continuation of economic imperialism and colonialism by new and subtler means. On their part, capital-exporting countries may harbour doubts on the trustworthiness of promises profusely made before receipt of the golden eggs.

Clearly, the overriding object of agreements on the lines of the Abs-Shawcross Draft Convention is to drive home that they are not conceived in the antagonistic spirit of past ages, but that the interests involved are viewed as complementary and are adjusted on a footing of substantive reciprocity and good neighbourliness. Admittedly, some of these ideas find expression in subsequent Articles.[13] Yet, if Preambles such as that of this Draft were drafted on such more concrete and, perhaps, more realistic lines, they might gain in usefulness as guides to the intentions of the parties on the objects of such Conventions.

In the third paragraph of the Preamble of the Abs-Shawcross Draft Convention, the claim is advanced that it contains a " restatement of principles of conduct relating to foreign investments." It is not clear from this text whether these principles of conduct are supposed to be restatements of principles of business practice, ethical imperatives or rules of international law. As emerges only from the Commentary attached to the Abs-Shawcross Draft Convention,[14] the Articles of the Abs-Shawcross Draft Convention are intended to give expression to " the fundamental principles of international law regarding the treatment of the property, rights and interests of aliens."

If this is the object of the exercise, it should be stated unequivocally in the text. If not, it would perhaps be advisable to avoid the impression of evasiveness on so important a matter. Be this as it may, it will be the primary purpose of this Chapter to explore the extent to which the claim is acceptable that the Abs-Shawcross Draft Convention is essentially a restatement of *lex lata* in the form of a multilateral convention.

12 On this assumption, see, further, Miller, *loc. cit.* above, p. 109, note 7, pp. 375–376. See also A. Larson, 9 J.P.L. (1960), p. 172 *et seq.*
See also below, p. 185 *et seq.*

13 See below, p. 112 *et seq.*

14 *Loc. cit.* in note 8 above, p. 119.

2.—The Scope and Standards of Protection

In Article I, the scope and standards of protection granted to foreign property are formulated as follows:

> "Each Party shall at all times ensure fair and equitable treatment to the property of the nationals of the other Parties. Such property shall be accorded the most constant protection and security within the territories of the other Parties and the management, use and enjoyment thereof shall not in any way be impaired by unreasonable or discriminatory measures."

This Article calls for a number of comments.

(a) The Beneficiaries

The personal scope of protection is determined by the test of nationality. In paragraph (a) of Article IX, nationals are defined as including in relation to a Party to the Convention.

> "(i) companies which under the municipal law of that Party are considered national companies of that Party and (ii) companies in which nationals of that Party have directly or indirectly a controlling interest. 'Companies' includes both juridical persons recognised as such by the law of a Party and associations even if they do not possess legal personality."

A minor point of drafting may be mentioned in passing. It would probably be an improvement to speak of "nationals" rather than "national companies."

If the object of the Draft Convention is to attain the maximum of protection for nationals abroad, the net has to be widely cast. Even so, three points require discussion: (1) Does the formulation chosen keep within the limits of existing international law? (2) How far does this formulation diminish the risk that a national remains unprotected on the ground of dual or multiple nationality? (3) Is this formulation wide enough *de lege ferenda* to cover all cases worthy of protection?

(1) *The Declaratory Character of Article IX* (*a*). At least since the *Nottebohm* judgment of the International Court of Justice,[15] it is questionable whether, for purposes of diplomatic protection, a claimant State is wise in taking for granted that it is any longer entitled to protect automatically every national who, under its own municipal law, is regarded as possessing its nationality.

(2) *Problems arising from Dual Nationality.* Assuming that the difficulties arising from the *Nottebohm* case could be ignored, the problems connected with dual and multiple nationality would remain. It may be hoped that whenever the question should arise before a tribunal established

15 *I.C.J. Reports 1955*, p. 4. See, further, Vol. I, pp. 132, 140–141 and 354 *et seq.*, and the literature cited *ibid.*, p. 753 *et seq.*

under a convention on the lines of the Abs-Shawcross Draft Convention, the tribunal would settle such a preliminary issue regarding its jurisdiction by reference to the test of overriding nationality. As yet, it would hardly be safe to rely on this.[16]

The uncertainties inherent in the control test if formulated as vaguely as is done in Article IX (a) (ii) are apparent. Moreover, so long as a company is a going concern,[17] a defendant State is hardly bound under international customary law to consider a company registered in its own territory as a national of a claimant State simply because nationals of the latter State have "directly or indirectly a controlling interest" in the company.

In British and United States practice, intervention is normally limited in such cases to interposition on behalf of the individual beneficial owners who are British or United States nationals, as distinct from the company itself. Moreover, such intercession is limited to cases in which substantial injustice would otherwise be done to the interests of the nationals concerned.[18]

In any case, the potential extension of nationality for purposes of international protection to associations lacking legal personality constitutes an innovation.[19]

(3) *Critique de lege ferenda.* If the maximum of protection for investors is to be attained, two further points call for consideration.

In international judicial practice, the minimum period during which nationality must be continuous in order to entitle a State to commence or continue diplomatic intervention is yet unsettled. Even if, as is suggested in the Abs-Shawcross Draft Convention, nationals of Parties to the Convention were entitled to institute arbitral proceedings on their own, problems of *dies a quo* and *dies ad quem* would arise. Would an individual who became a national of a Party to the Convention subsequent to the act complained of be entitled to the protection of the Convention, and what would be the position of heirs who are not nationals of a Contracting Party? [20]

It may also be worth considering whether, in a subsidiary way, domicile in the territory of a Party should be made a connecting link between a claimant State and an individual. This would enable a Contracting Party with which a stateless person or refugee is connected more closely than with any other Party to espouse his claim.[21]

16 For the balance of opinion in international judicial practice, see *ibid.*, p. 362 *et seq.*

17 See *ibid.*, p. 387 *et seq.* See also below, p. 156.

18 See above, p. 27.

19 See, for instance, the decisions of the British-German Mixed Arbitral Tribunal in *Hyman* v. *Wydra* (1921) 1 M.A.T., p. 291 at pp. 293–294, and of the Franco-German M.A.T. in *Mercier et Cie* v. *Germany* (1923) 3 M.A.T., p. 686 at pp. 688–689.

20 See, further, Vol. I, p. 596 *et seq.*

21 See Ph. C. Jessup, *A Modern Law of Nations* (1948), p. 70.
See also above, p. 28, and below, p. 176.

(b) Property

This is defined in paragraph (b) of Article IX as including "all property, rights and interests, whether held directly or indirectly. A member of a company shall be deemed to have an interest in the property of the company."

This wide formulation in the Abs-Shawcross Draft Convention of property rights as including proprietary interests is in conformity with international customary law [22] and international law as applied on the international judicial level.[23]

(c) The Primary Standard Adopted

In order to assess the appropriateness of the primary standard adopted in the Abs-Shawcross Draft Convention, it is advisable to recall the seven optional standards which, in addition to the minimum standard applicable to foreigners under international customary law, are at the disposal of Contracting Parties: the standards of identical, national, most-favoured-nation, equitable and preferential treatment as well as the more recent additions of the standards of the open door and good neighbourliness.[24]

Article I presents an imaginative attempt to combine the minimum standard with the standard of equitable treatment. This decision is well justified on two grounds. The experiences of the last forty years suggest that whenever, in fact, an agreed settlement has been reached, the creditors and investors concerned have consented to temper the application of the minimum standard by the introduction of an equitable element in the form of considerable concessions on their part.[25] Thus, it appears wise to anticipate—and limit—such contingencies. Moreover, in relations between heterogeneous communities—in varying stages of technological advancement, social structure and political organisation—and in an age of rapid change, the standard of equitable treatment provides equality on a footing of commendable elasticity. Inevitably, it suffers from the drawbacks of its virtues: a corresponding measure of vagueness and subjectivity.

In this way, the beneficiaries of the Draft Convention would obtain three tangible advantages:

(1) The benefits of the minimum standard, embodied in the Draft Convention in the form of a positive obligation to ensure the "most constant protection and security" for property covered by the Convention.

(2) Treatment in accordance with the requirements of *jus aequum*: fairness and reasonableness [26]—for it would be difficult to imagine any

22 See above, p. 17.

23 See above, p. 7 *et seq.*, and Vol. I, p. 200 *et seq.*

24 See, further, Vol. I, p. 229 *et seq.*; *The Frontiers*, p. 219 *et seq.* and *Principles of I.E.L.*, p. 66 *et seq.*

25 See, for instance, above, p. 40 *et seq.*, and Wortley, *loc. cit.* above, p. 5, note 7, p. 58 *et seq.*

26 See, further, below, p. 158 *et seq.*, and Vol. I, p. 53 and Index *sub nomine: Jus Aequum.*

differentiation on the footing of either foreign or inland parity which would not be discriminatory, unfair or unreasonable.

(3) Substantially, the equality of treatment they would obtain from the cumulative application of the most-favoured-nation and national standards.[27]

The emphasis in Article I of the Draft Convention on protection and security of foreign property being " most constant " and being granted " at all times " does not appear to add any undue rigidity to the obligations expected to be undertaken by capital-importing States. What is promised at all times is merely the grant of equitable treatment.

Moreover, in Article V, a number of circumstances are enumerated which explicity exonerate Contracting Parties:

> " No Party may take measures derogating from the present Convention unless it is involved in war, hostilities or other public emergency which threatens its life; and such measures shall be limited in extent and duration to those strictly required by the exigencies of the situation. Nothing in this Article shall be construed as superseding the generally accepted laws of war."

In its objects, this Article is sensible enough. Yet, it may be questioned whether the formulation chosen allows for more novel forms of *status mixtus*—intermediate situations between states of peace and war—to be taken adequately into account. For instance, if the Arab States and Israel were to become Parties to the Convention, would the state of war existing between them entitle them to take against the property of one another's nationals discriminatory measures which they consider " strictly required by the exigencies of the situation " ?

Similarly, if the Security Council decided to apply economic sanctions under Chapter VII of the Charter of the United Nations—or if, under the Uniting for Peace Resolution of 1950, the General Assembly recommended member States to take such steps—would action of this kind be covered by Article V? If not, at least in the case of action under Chapter VII of the Charter, the position would be clear in the *inter se* relations between member States of the United Nations; for the members of the United Nations are bound to comply with decisions of the Security Council, and their duties under the Charter take priority over other incompatible commitments.[28]

In spite of the claims made in Article 2 (6) of the Charter of the United Nations, non-member States are not necessarily under any corresponding obligation.[29] Moreover, whenever member States should decide to apply economic sanctions in voluntary compliance with a resolution of the General Assembly, it could hardly be argued that member States were fulfilling any legal duty incumbent on them under the Charter.

27 See, further, *loc. cit.* above, p. 114, note 24.
28 Articles 25 and 103 of the United Nations Charter.
29 See, further, *Inductive Approach*, p. 112, and 18 C.L.P. (1965), p. 209.

Thus, from the point of view of drafting, Article V in its present formulation does not yet appear to be the last word. Similarly, Article I would perhaps benefit from further care being bestowed on its wording. "Ensure" is probably an overstatement of legal duties in situations which do not appear to call for more than a *grant* of the treatment set out in the Article. If, however, the object in using the word "ensure" is to cover also action by State-owned or State-controlled agencies, it would be advisable to say so in so many words. "Fair and equitable" appears to suffer from a proclivity to redundancy. The juxtaposition of "fair and reasonable" would probably bring out more clearly the essence of *jus aequum*.

Finally, the most important issue in relation to the application of so subjective a standard as that of equitable treatment must at least be raised at this stage.[30] Who is to decide whether a Contracting Party has complied with its obligations under the Convention?

3—The Observance of Undertakings

In accordance with Article II,

> "Each Party shall at all times ensure the observance of any undertakings which it may have given in relation to investments made by nationals of any other Party."

This Article covers undertakings by Contracting Parties to subjects and objects of international law. In so far as relations between subjects are concerned, the Article does not add anything to the binding character of such undertakings. Even if unilateral in form, they are as binding as other consensual undertakings. Nevertheless, even in these relations, the incorporation of such a promise has its value. If a breach of an undertaking is alleged, and this is not covered by Article V of the Convention,[31] any such act or omission may amount to a breach of the Convention and, thus, constitute an arbitrable dispute under the Convention.[32]

The main significance of the Article lies in a different direction. In effect, obligations towards objects of international law, which as such are beyond the pale of international law, are transformed by this Article into obligations under international law. For this purpose, it does not matter whether public contracts are treated as falling under any particular system of municipal law, under legal rules abstracted from a number of such legal systems, or are allocated to a separate legal system of quasi-international law.[33] Whichever of these solutions is preferred, it is clear that these relations are not *as such* governed by international law. By Article II, any undertaking relating to investments, and given by a Party to nationals

[30] See below, pp. 123 and 165 *et seq.*
[31] See above, p. 115.
[32] See below, p. 123.
[33] See above, p. 5.

of any other Party, would be paralleled by corresponding obligations between the Parties.

Under international customary law any breach of an undertaking between a sovereign State and a foreign national becomes the concern of the latter's home government only if it can show the requisite legal interest. This presupposes either a denial or delay of justice, or one of the exceptional situations in which there is no chance of any justice being administered and, therefore, the denial of justice is apparent without any need for the injured national to go through the motions of procedures falling below the minimum standard of international law.[34] In other words, a State must normally first be given the opportunity to remedy the alleged breach of any relevant standard imposed by international law.

Article II is so worded as to make it doubtful whether it is necessary for a national first to seek justice on the levels of the municipal law of a capital-importing State (or a State granting a concession) or the law specifically stipulated in a particular public contract. Whenever one of the Contracting Parties should claim that another Contracting Party had failed to ensure the observance of an undertaking "given in relation to investments made" by one of its nationals, it could be alleged that this other Contracting Party was in breach of the Convention.

This would be a far-reaching departure from the law as it stands and would tilt the balance too far in favour of the investor. Where non-international procedures and remedies for alleged breaches of non-international obligations exist, they should first be fully exhausted.

4—The Limits of Lawful Expropriation

In Article III of the Abs-Shawcross Draft Convention, the line between lawful expropriation and illegal confiscation is drawn as follows:

> "No Party shall take any measures against nationals of another Party to deprive them directly or indirectly of their property except under due process of law and provided that such measures are not discriminatory or contrary to undertakings given by that Party and are accompanied by the payment of just and effective compensation. Adequate provision shall have been made at or prior to the time of deprivation for the prompt determination and payment of such compensation, which shall represent the genuine value of the property affected, be made in transferable form and be paid without undue delay."

Existence of an adequate public interest and full compensation are two generally accepted conditions on which, under international customary law, depends the legality of expropriation of private foreign property.[35]

[34] See, further, Vol. I, p. 602 *et seq.*
See also below, p. 167.

[35] See above, p. 4.

The treatment which these and other requirements stipulated in Article III of the Abs-Shawcross Draft Convention have received calls for discussion.

(a) Public Interest

The omission of this constitutive element of lawful expropriation from Article III is surprising. According to the Commentary attached, this Article is meant to follow closely a provision uniform in recent United States treaties of friendship and commerce.[36] Yet, even in those treaties in which these words have been omitted, the "public interest" clause is implied in phrases such as the "full protection and security required by international law." In a number of these treaties it has, however, been considered advisable expressly to stipulate that the property of nationals and companies of either Party shall not be taken within the territories of the other Party "except for a public purpose."[37]

It is arguable that it is wiser not to press compliance with so subjective a factor, the absence of which is normally hard to prove. Yet, both State practice and international judicial practice know of cases in which the complete absence of a public interest in purported acts of expropriation has been clearly established. In such extreme cases, it is convenient to be relieved of the necessity to consider any other grounds which may give the action taken its confiscatory character.[38] It is also possible that the element of public interest is to be inferred from other terms employed in Article III. Yet, why infer what, without apparent difficulty, can be stated unequivocally in a few words?[39]

(b) Protection against Indirect Deprivation of Property

It is difficult to determine where indirect deprivation of property ends and, for instance, taxation, planning legislation or property law reform begins. While it is impossible to lay down a hard and fast rule on the dividing line, it is all to the good that, in Article III, an attempt is made to cover surreptitious forms of confiscation. Whenever this is the real object, the label of the ostensible action taken is of little consequence.[40]

Whether an act of State belongs to one or the other category and, thus, constitutes an illegal interference with property rather than an unchallengeable exercise of State power largely depends on the purpose of the measure. Thus, again, the evaluation of objects and motives cannot be avoided. Moreover, any judgment on matters of this kind is itself

[36] *Loc. cit.* above, p. 110, note 8, p. 121. See also Wilson, *loc. cit.* above, p. 32, note 15, pp. 120–121.

[37] Art. VI (4) of the Pakistan-United States Treaty of Friendship and Commerce of November 12, 1959. See also the F.C.N. Treaties with Greece (Art. VII (3)—August 3, 1951, TIAS 3057) and Israel (Art. VI (3)—August 23, 1951, TIAS 2948).

[38] For illustrations, see Lord McNair, 6 *Netherlands R.I.L.* (1959), pp. 222–223, and the present writer, 42 *Grotius Transactions* (1956), pp. 154–155.

[39] See also below, p. 162.

[40] See above, pp. 4 and 95, and below, p. 162.

greatly influenced by non-legal considerations. Under the Abs-Shawcross Draft Convention, the last word would be with the umpire of the arbitral tribunal.[41]

(c) Due Process of Law

On the face of it, this term is capable of a number of interpretations. It may mean compliance with such legal procedures as the law of the land—*lex terrae* of Magna Carta—provides. In this case, the clause would offer protection against arbitrary action by an executive which was in disregard of even the national law of the Contracting Party concerned. The "due process" clause may also be intended to suggest complete immunity from any interference unless certain minimum requirements of judicial review are met. This would be in accordance with a widespread Continental—liberal and nineteenth-century—view of the legality of expropriation.[42] Beyond this, any "due process" clause evokes memories of the naturalist interpretations accorded to the Fifth and Fourteenth Amendments by the United States Supreme Court.

It is a generally accepted rule of treaty interpretation that terms must not be given a meaning attached to them by only one or some of the Contracting Parties.[43] Nevertheless, it would be arguable that, in this context, the *travaux préparatoires* lead to a different conclusion. The "due process" clause has been employed in a number of United States treaties of commerce and navigation since 1919 and from there found its way into the Abs-Shawcross Draft Convention. On this dubious foundation extravagant claims could easily be based. If, by any chance, the umpire of an arbitral tribunal under the Convention were swayed by this argument, a minority view on this issue, however sensible, might well be overruled. Considering the extent to which, in United States constitutional practice, the "due process" clause has been used as a vehicle for the incorporation in *lex lata* of natural law claims of "inalienable" property rights,[44] such apprehensions cannot be easily dismissed.

If this is what the sponsors of conventions on the pattern of the Abs-Shawcross Draft Convention have in mind, they ought to say so. If not, they should guard themselves against the suspicion, however unjustified, of keeping a "secret weapon" in reserve. All that is needed is a definition of "due process" and its addition to the other definitions assembled in Article IX.

41 See below, p. 123 *et seq.*

42 See above, p. 22, and below, p. 163, and, further, Wilson, *loc. cit.* above, p. 32, note 15, p. 114 *et seq.*

43 See, further, Vol. I, p. 70. See also R. R. Wilson, *The International Law Standard in Treaties of the United States* (1953), pp. 51–52 and 101.

44 See, for instance, C. G. Haynes, *The Revival of Natural Law Concepts* (1930), p. 104 *et seq.*, and W. B. Cowles, *Treaties and Constitutional Law, Property Interference and Due Process of Law* (1941).

(d) Non-Discrimination

The prohibition of discriminatory measures in the Abs-Shawcross Draft Convention is formulated in sweeping terms. Inevitably, a number of questions arise.

What is meant by discrimination? Does it cover any kind of unequal treatment or is it limited to arbitrary differentiation? Does every privileged treatment of some constitute discrimination against others? What is *tertium comparationis*—the nationals of the States taking the measures in question, the nationals of other Contracting Parties, foreigners at large, or all these categories together?

It is widely accepted that, at least in the field of expropriation, non-discrimination is an absolute condition of lawful expropriation.[45] On closer examination the picture becomes more complicated. Extracts from State practice and judicial pronouncements which are based on treaties and others in which reliance is placed on international customary law are not always kept sufficiently apart. Moore's careful distinction between just and unjust forms of discrimination is not always remembered.[46] Evidence of rules prohibiting discrimination between foreigners and nationals in the application of municipal law and between foreigners according to criteria such as race or religion tends to be treated as proof of the illegality of *all* forms of discrimination.[47]

In practice, the requirements of the minimum standard of international law in favour of foreigners and their property are stricter than those of the municipal laws of more backward States.[48] Thus, as a rule of thumb, it is correct to consider as illegal any discrimination between nationals and foreigners to the latter's disadvantage. Yet, what really matters is not whether the treatment of foreigners is better or worse than that accorded to a State's own nationals or is equal to their treatment, but whether it measures up to the minimum standard of international law.

A relevant dictum which deserves to be recalled will be found in the Award of the British-United States Arbitral Tribunal (under the Special Agreement of August 18, 1910) in the *Eastern Extension, Australasia and China Telegraph Company* case (1923). In this case, which was concerned with the property claims of neutral nationals, it was held that "it is perfectly legitimate for a government, in the absence of any special agreement to the contrary, to afford to subjects of any particular government treatment which is refused to the subjects of other governments, or to reserve to its own subjects treatment which is not afforded to foreigners.

[45] See, for instance, the Opinions by Lord McNair, Rolin and Verdross, *loc. cit.* above, p. 118, note 38, pp. 243, 247, 269 and 284. See also below, p. 163.

[46] *Digest of International Law*, Vol. VI (1906), p. 698 *et seq.*

[47] For a balanced treatment, see D. Schindler, *Gleichberechtigung von Individuen als Problem des Völkerrechts* (1957).

On the need for further research on this and related issues, see 87 Hague *Recueil* (1955), pp. 315–316. See also above, pp. 86 and 91.

[48] See, further, J. Charpentier, 9 *Annuaire français* (1963), p. 35 *et seq.*, and Vol. I, p. 200 *et seq.*

Some political motive, some service rendered, some traditional bond of friendship, some reciprocal treatment in the past or in the present, may furnish the ground for discrimination." [49]

This dictum appears to be too wide and does not sufficiently allow for situations in which discrimination between foreigners and nationals may well be the first indication of a breach of the minimum standard. Yet, even with these reservations, awareness of this award probably assists in arriving at a more balanced view of the matter.

If the duty of non-discrimination under Article III of the Abs-Shawcross Draft Convention were absolute, this would lead to a remarkable extension of the immunity of foreign private property; for a further exception clause in this Article excludes from lawful interference measures contrary to undertakings given by a Contracting Party. Thus, if a Contracting Party granted to one oil company permanent or temporary immunity from expropriation, not only all other oil companies which are nationals of the same Contracting Party, but also those of the nationality of all other Contracting Parties, might consider themselves entitled to the same privileged treatment, and they might well claim that to treat them otherwise would amount to discrimination. Similarly, if the prohibition of discrimination were absolute, any reprisals against the property of nationals of Contracting Parties—another aspect of the matter which appears to call for further consideration—would also be excluded.[50]

It is possible that such an extreme view of the matter accurately reflects the intentions of the sponsors of the Abs-Shawcross Draft Convention. It is also possible that these high-powered operators are all sweet reasonableness and, by discriminatory measures, understand merely arbitrary or unreasonable differentiation. In any case, the matter is sufficiently obscure to call for clarification in an interpretative definition of discriminatory measures.

(e) The Sanctity of Undertakings

If nationals of Contracting Parties have received undertakings exempting their property from any particular kind of interference, expropriation, however unobjectionable it may be otherwise, is precluded by the Abs-Shawcross Draft Convention.

Whenever the breach of an undertaking given to a foreign national involves an act of bad faith on the part of the State taking such measures,

[49] 6 R.I.A.A., p. 112 at p. 117.
See, further, Vol. II, p. 412 *et seq.*

[50] While, in this context, the celebrated Report of the British Law Officers of January 18, 1753 (B.F.S.P., Vol. 20, p. 889 *et seq.*) is relevant, its authors did not maintain that, under international customary law, private property of foreigners was immune from reprisals in all circumstances.
See also the Judgment of the O.L.G. Bremen in *N. V. Verenigde Deli-Maatschappijen and Another* v. *Deutsch-Indonesische Tabak-Handelsgesellschaft* (Oberlandesgericht Bremen—1959), 28 I.L.R., p. 16, at pp. 36–38, and *Bank Indonesia* v. *Senembah Maatschappij and Twentsche Bank* (Court of Appeal, Amsterdam—1959), 30 *ibid.*, p. 28 *et seq.*, and below, p. 129.

the minimum standard of international law has been contravened.[51] To this extent, the clause in Article III on the sanctity of undertakings is merely declaratory of international customary law.

In aiming at so high a degree of sacrosanctity of foreign investments in this clause and in Article II of the Abs-Shawcross Draft Convention,[52] the draftsmen may have erred on the side of freezing the *status quo*. This question is hardly answered by recitation of the maxim: *Pacta sunt servanda*. Actually, this is merely a *petitio principii*, for, as usual, a relevant counter-maxim is available: *Omnis conventio intellegitur rebus sic stantibus*.

Thus, the question arises whether, in the Draft Convention, enough safety valves are provided to allow for the dynamics of events in mid-twentieth-century world society. A capital-importing State or a State granting a concession would remain free to insist on reservations in favour of its own national *ordre public* being incorporated in the original undertaking.

Moreover, whatever the legal system to which an undertaking under Articles II and III were subject,[53] it would be likely to provide a number of grounds of temporary or permanent liberation from undertakings given. In such cases, measures taken on either of these grounds would be compatible with such an undertaking. In addition, within narrow confines, the Abs-Shawcross Draft Convention itself allows for measures derogating from the Convention.[54]

Finally, it is always possible to modify a pledge with the consent of the other party concerned, and the history of foreign investments over the last half-century appears to disprove the legend of the all-powerful and ruthless foreign investor. It illustrates more readily the inherent vulnerability of economic as compared with political and military power, so vividly depicted by Bertrand Russell.[55] Thus, on closer examination, the Abs-Shawcross Draft Convention leaves more scope for changing conditions than is apparent at first sight.

(f) Compensation

Under Article II of the Abs-Shawcross Draft Convention, lawful expropriation calls for the payment of " just and effective " compensation. To be just, compensation must be determined at, or prior to, the time of deprivation of the property and represent its " genuine value " (full or

[51] See above, p. 4 *et seq.*

See, however, the discussion in *Institut de Droit International*, 44 (II) *Annuaire* (1952), p. 305 *et seq.*, in particular p. 318, when a draft resolution on this very point was lost by 20 votes to 16 votes, with 22 abstentions, and the Arbitral Award in *Alsing Trading Company, etc.* v. *Greece* (1954) I.L.R. 1956, p. 633 at p. 636.

[52] See also above, p. 4, and below, p. 164 *et seq.*

[53] See above, p. 5, and below, p. 143 *et seq.*

[54] See above, p. 115.

[55] *Power* (1938), for instance, p. 126.

See also above, p. 66 *et seq.*, and below, p. 190, note 22.

adequate compensation). To be effective, it must usually, but not necessarily, be paid in a transferable currency with a recognised exchange value and, in any case, without undue delay.

Subject to the reservation that, in some cases, payment in the local currency may constitute effective compensation, the formulation of the last of the constituent elements of lawful expropriation in the Abs-Shawcross Draft Convention conforms with international customary law. While illegal confiscation primarily calls for restitution, lawful expropriation requires merely full compensation. If sufficient reasons of national public policy for interference with foreign property exist, to this extent international law relaxes the duty of a State under the minimum standard to protect—and itself not to interfere with—the property of foreign nationals. Nonetheless, in accordance with the liberal views of the nineteenth century when these rules crystallised, any State interference with private property, even in such extenuating circumstances, remains inherently suspect. It is for the State concerned to prove its law-abidingness by doing, at the earliest moment, the next best thing to leaving the property unmolested: paying full or adequate, prompt and effective compensation.[56]

5—" Without Prejudice "

By Article VI of the Abs-Shawcross Draft Convention, " the provisions of this Convention shall not prejudice the application of any present or future treaty or municipal law under which more favourable treatment is accorded to nationals of any of the Parties."

The object of this Article is to prevent what are intended as minimum standards in the field of private foreign investment from being interpreted as constituting an upper ceiling for the treatment of foreign nationals.

This leaves unaffected the complementary issue raised above.[57] The grant of more favourable treatment than is prescribed by the Draft Convention to nationals of one Contracting Party, to the exclusion of others, may be viewed by the latter as amounting to discriminatory measures under Articles I and III of the Draft Convention.

6—The Settlement of Disputes

In accordance with Article VII of the Abs-Shawcross Draft Convention,

> " 1. Any dispute as to the interpretation or application of the present Convention may, with the consent of the interested Parties, be submitted to an Arbitral Tribunal set up in accordance with the provisions of the Annex to this Convention. Such consent may take the form of specific agreements or of unilateral declarations. In the

[56] See, further, above, p. 4 *et seq.*, and Vol. I, p. 654 *et seq.*
[57] See above, p. 120, and below, p. 163 *et seq.*

absence of such consent or of agreement for settlement by other specific means, the dispute may be submitted by either Party to the International Court of Justice.

2. A national of one of the Parties claiming that he has been injured by measures in breach of this Convention may institute proceedings against the Party responsible for such measures before the Arbitral Tribunal referred to in paragraph 1 of this Article, provided that the Party against which the claim is made has declared that it accepts the jurisdiction of the said Arbitral Tribunal in respect of claims by nationals of one or more Parties, including the Party concerned."

(a) Scope and Character of the Arbitral and Judicial Jurisdiction

The arbitral, as distinct from the judicial, settlement of any dispute between the Contracting Parties regarding the interpretation or application of the Abs-Shawcross Draft Convention would be optional. Provision is, however, made for the " compulsory " or, rather, automatic jurisdiction of the International Court of Justice in the last resort. By way of contrast, extension of jurisdiction of the tribunals to disputes between Contracting Parties and nationals of other Contracting Parties who allege that they have been injured by measures in breach of the Convention remains optional and limited to the arbitral level. Even if the draftsmen had wished otherwise, they would have been barred by Article 34 of the Statute of the International Court of Justice from securing so extensive a jurisdiction on the level of the World Court.

It is not likely that any Contracting Party would lightly make a general declaration under paragraph 2 of Article VII. Neither in Article VII nor in the Annex on the Arbitral Tribunal is any provision made for checking frivolous claims by nationals of Contracting Parties, other than by use of the general power granted to the tribunal to settle all matters relating to costs or, under its freedom in matters of procedure, to insist on adequate security for costs being given in advance.

The solution in classical international law of leaving the government concerned with exclusive responsibility for submitting claims of its nationals to arbitral or judicial settlement may not constitute an absolute guarantee against undeserving cases coming before an international judicial organ. It may also mean that deserving cases never reach this stage. Yet, even this eventuality appears a lesser evil than the solution favoured by the authors of the Abs-Shawcross Draft Convention.[58]

(b) Constitution of the Arbitral Tribunal

Under Section 1 of the Annex to the Draft Convention,

"The Arbitral Tribunal referred to in Article VII of the Convention shall consist of three persons appointed as follows: one arbitrator

[58] See also below, p. 167.

shall be appointed by each of the parties to the arbitration proceedings and a third arbitrator (hereinafter sometimes called 'the Umpire') shall be appointed by agreement of the parties or, if they shall not agree, by the President of the International Court of Justice, or, failing appointment by him, by the Secretary-General of the United Nations. If either of the parties shall fail to appoint an arbitrator, such arbitrator shall be appointed by the Umpire. In case any arbitrator appointed in accordance with this Article shall resign, die or become unable to act, a successor arbitrator shall be appointed in the same manner as herein prescribed for the appointment of the original arbitrator and such successor shall have all the powers and duties of such arbitrator."

This Section is drafted with an eye on the unfortunate experiences with the ex-satellite Powers of the Hitler-Mussolini Axis, the hardly encouraging opinion of the International Court of Justice on *Interpretation of Peace Treaties* (*Second Phase*—1950) and the major flaw in the Anglo-Iranian Concession Agreement of 1933.[59]

It would perhaps be advisable to avoid the numbering of the umpire as a "third" arbitrator. This invites the kind of mechanical thinking displayed in the majority opinion of the International Court on the *Interpretation of Peace Treaties* (*Second Phase*). Nevertheless, the express provision made in Section 1 of the Annex for the umpire to appoint a national arbitrator in default of appointment by the Party concerned should constitute an adequate safeguard against a repetition of this particular experience. Similarly, the cumulative provision made for persons competent to appoint an umpire in the case of disagreement between the Parties disposes of one of the potential difficulties under the pattern of the Anglo-Iranian Concession Agreement.

Further provision is made in Sections 2 and 3 of the Annex to forestall other forms of possible obstruction to the constitution of the arbitral tribunal and the initiation of proceedings before it. These may be taken to be self-explanatory:

"2. Arbitration proceedings may be instituted upon notice by the Party instituting such proceedings (whether a Party to the Convention or a national of a Party to the Convention, as the case may be) to the other Party. Such notice shall contain a statement setting forth the nature of the relief sought, and the name of the arbitrator appointed by the Party instituting such proceedings. Within 30 days after the giving of such notice, the adverse Party shall notify the Party

[59] See above, p. 71 *et seq.*; below, p. 145 *et seq.*; K. S. Carlston, 44 A.J.I.L. (1950), p. 728 *et seq.*; D. H. N. Johnson, 30 B.Y.I.L. (1953), p. 152 *et seq.*; Hersch Lauterpacht, *The Development of International Law by the International Court* (1958), p. 284 *et seq.*; 4 C.L.P. (1951), p. 11 *et seq.*, and Vol. I, pp. 450 *et seq.* and 523 *et seq.* See also below, p. 167.

instituting proceedings of the name of the arbitrator appointed by such adverse Party.

3. If, within 60 days after the giving of such notice, instituting the arbitration proceedings, the Parties shall not have agreed upon an Umpire, either Party may request the appointment of an Umpire as provided in Article 1 of this Annex."

7—Breaches of the Convention, Including Non-Compliance with Awards

In accordance with Article IV of the Abs-Shawcross Draft Convention,

> "Any breach of this Convention shall entail the obligation to make full reparation. The Parties shall not recognise or enforce within their territories any measures conflicting with the principles of this Convention and affecting the property of nationals of any of the Parties until reparation is made or secured."

Moreover, it is stipulated in Article VIII that

> "If a Party against which a judgment or award is given fails to comply with the terms thereof, the other Parties shall be entitled, individually or collectively, to take such measures as are strictly required to give effect to that judgment or award."

(a) Reparation

The breach of the rules underlying the principle of consent brings into operation those on international responsibility, and one of the primary rules under this heading is the duty to make full reparation.[60] Thus, the first sentence of Article IV may claim to be merely declaratory of international customary law.

(b) A New International Quasi-Order

In mature systems of municipal law, the legal effects of tortious and criminal acts are regulated by rules of *jus cogens*, *ordre public* or public policy. International customary law lacks any corresponding public order.[61] In unorganised international society, the legal effects of international torts are, therefore, necessarily limited to the *inter se* relations between the tortfeasor and the injured party. In other words, on this level of loose social integration, the principle of the relativity of torts reigns supreme.

(1) *The Relativity of International Torts.* Attempts have been made, and are relied on in the Commentary on the Abs-Shawcross Draft Convention,[62] to supply the missing rule—transforming a relative wrong into

[60] See, further, Vol. I, pp. 562 and 653 *et seq.*
[61] See, further, *loc. cit.* above, p. 115, note 29.
[62] See *loc. cit.* above, p. 110, note 8, p. 122.

an absolute wrong, *i.e.*, one which everybody must treat as such—in the form of a general principle of law recognised by civilised nations and epitomised in the maxim: *Ex injuria jus non oritur.* In this formulation, the maxim is a fairly recent addition to the legal vocabulary. It is, however, well established both in Anglo-American and in Continental laws of tort, but with one significant difference. It is known there as *Ex delicto jus non oritur.*

As is so often the case, legal experiences to the opposite effect are telescoped into a counter-maxim: *Ex facto jus oritur.* Both maxims summarise some of the relevant rules in a number of legal systems of civilised nations. It, therefore, remains to be established whether the alleged general principle of law is based on one or the other maxim or where between the two extremes it is supposed to lie.[63]

Actually, the substitution of *injuria* (injury) for *delictum* (tortious act) is an instructive illustration of a legal *petitio principii.*

If *injuria* means any injury, irrespective of whether it is recognised by law, proper evidence has to be furnished for the proposition that international law recognises so wide a notion of international torts.

If *injuria* is used in any narrower sense, it is synonymous with *delictum*, and the maxim leaves matters where they were before its invocation. Thus, the confiscation of property in violation of promises made constitutes a breach of the pledged word and of good faith. If the nationals of a foreign State are the objects of such action, an international tort against their home State has been committed.[64] In these relations, the *ex delicto* maxim applies but is redundant.[65]

If the tortfeasor State disposed abroad of the confiscated property or of produce from confiscated mines or estates, this would amount to a further tortious act against the home State of the nationals so affected. Yet what evidence is there of a legal rule that every tort against State X obliges State Y to treat such an act as a more serious contravention than an international tort committed against itself?

State Y is always free to condone a tort committed against itself. If, however, the alleged general principle of law applied, State Y would have no choice but to apply this rule as one of international *jus cogens.*

At this point, the function of the *ex injuria* maxim becomes plain. It is to serve as an apparently self-evident substitute for a rule which would produce the desired result. In fact, this effort amounts to an astounding exercise in surreptitious law-making.[66]

This is far from saying that the principle of the relativity of international torts is either desirable *de lege ferenda,* or that international law lacks legitimate means of avoiding so asocial, or anti-social, a result. Thus, the assertion that the *ex injuria* maxim expresses an "important" legal

63 See Vol. I, p. 473 *et seq.*
64 See above, p. 17.
65 See, further, Vol. I, p. 627 *et seq.*
66 See, further, *Inductive Approach*, p. 48 *et seq.*

principle of existing international customary law [67] would gain from more convincing attempts than have been made so far to discharge the burden of proof for this proposition.

(2) *The Governing Rules.* In the absence of other operative rules of international customary law, treaties or general principles of law recognised by civilised nations, the matter is regulated by the rules of international law governing the principle of sovereignty. In other words, States may please themselves whether they desire to recognise or apply foreign laws—or titles based on such laws—which are alleged to be tainted by breaches of international law against themselves or third States. This must be so; for, in the absence of treaty obligations, a legal duty to apply *any* foreign municipal law or to recognise *any* title derived from such law exists only in two exceptional cases.

In the first place, this would be so if the non-application or non-recognition of foreign law would lead to a miscarriage of justice of such magnitude as to amount to a breach of the rule on the minimum standard of international law in favour of foreign nationals.[68] Secondly, in the few cases in which the application of specific rules of international customary law presupposes reliance on a system of municipal law—as, for instance, determination of the nationality of an individual [69]—the non-recognition of foreign public acts may be incompatible with a State's fulfilment in good faith of its duties under international law.

In all other cases, the recognition and application of any foreign system of municipal law is still regulated by considerations of justice, comity and reciprocal interest. As such, none of these is a substitute for one of the three forms in which alone rules of international law can be generated.[70]

Thus, in the relations between members of the United Nations, the principle of good neighbourliness requires the recognition and application of foreign municipal law also in cases in which common justice demands this, and no grounds of national public policy militate against such a co-operative attitude.[71]

In this respect, English judicial practice is instructive. Subject to significant reservations regarding the supremacy of statute law, English courts apply international law as part of the law of the land. Nonetheless, they steadfastly refuse to examine the compatibility of the law of other States with international law in situations in which the English rules on the conflict of laws refer to such foreign law. Even when British subjects are the objects of measures as objectionable as illegal confiscation of property, no exception to the above rule is thought permissible.[72]

[67] *Loc. cit.* above, p. 110, note 8, p. 122.
[68] See, further, Vol. I, p. 200 *et seq.*, and Vol. II, p. 331 *et seq.*
[69] See, further, Vol. I, p. 354 *et seq.*
[70] Vol. I, p. 25 *et seq.*
[71] See, further, Vol. I, pp. 50–51 and 218, and *Inductive Approach*, p. 95.
[72] For the relevant case law *prior* to the Anglo-Iranian Oil Dispute, see, for instance, Sir Arnold McNair, *Legal Effects of War* (1948), p. 361; K. Lipstein, 35 *Grotius Transactions* (1949), pp. 187–188; J. H. C. Morris, *Cases on Private International Law* (*ctd. overleaf*)

It is arguable that, in taking this position, English courts mean to apply international law. They may be thought to show an absolute, and perhaps unnecessary, respect for foreign territorial sovereignty, even in circumstances in which good faith and the sanctity of the pledged word should counsel a different course.[73] Yet, the very basis of this argument is of doubtful validity. On settled grounds of public policy, English courts are free to refuse to apply any foreign law even if this is not tainted in any way by an alleged breach of international law.

In these circumstances it would be difficult to prove that their regard for territorial sovereignty in the *Luther* v. *Sagor* type of situation[74] is the result of the application of international law rather than of considerations of a more pragmatic character, such as international comity, reciprocity and practical convenience.

Moreover, assuming that a third State or its nationals are the objects of an alleged breach of international law, can it really be said that, on the level of international customary law, any such act, even if constituting a breach of international law in relation to such a third State, amounts to a breach of international law *vis-à-vis* the United Kingdom?

The most that can be conceded is that, as international customary law lacks any relevant prohibitory rule, English courts are free—*sub specie juris gentium*—to minimise the relativity of international torts.

This is how, in recent and directly relevant cases, German,[75] Italian[76] and Japanese[77] courts approached the issue. While the question before the German court concerned the ownership in tobacco shipped from Indonesia to Germany after the nationalisation of tobacco concessions which had formerly been operated in Indonesia by Netherlands subjects, that before the Italian and Japanese courts was the legality of the titles

(*Note 72 ctd.*)
(1951), p. 25; E. D. Re, *Foreign Confiscation in Anglo-American Law* (1951), p. 128 *et seq.*; F. Morgenstern, 4 I.L.Q. (1951), p. 326 *et seq.*, and G. A. van Hecke, *ibid.*, p. 345 *et seq.* See also below, p. 130, note 79.

The addition of the words "as are not contrary to International Law" to Rule 6 in the 1955 ed. of Oppenheim's *International Law* (ed. H. Lauterpacht, Vol. I, Sect. 75, pp. 138–139), as compared with the 1948 ed. (ed. H. Lauterpacht—Sect. 75, p. 133) should also be noted. Similar adjustments were made in Sect. 115aa (1955 ed.) p. 267 (as compared with the 1948 ed., p. 42). See also H. Lauterpacht, *Recognition in International Law* (1947), p. 285, and the note on the *Rose Mary*, *Cambridge L.J.* (1954), p. 20.

73 If such a self-delusion had been an operative factor, it would have deserved the strictures made in an animated contribution to this topic (J. H. W. Verzijl in *Makarov Festgabe* (1958), p. 547). See also McNair, *loc. cit.* above, p. 128, note 72, p. 322, and L. A. E. Hjerner, 2 *Scandinavian Studies in Law* (1959), pp. 202–203.

74 [1921] 3 K.B. 532. See also M. Zander, 53 A.J.I.L. (1959), p. 826 et seq., and W. H. Reeves, 54 *ibid.* (1960), p. 141 *et seq.*

75 See above, p. 121, note 50; M. Domke, 54 A.J.I.L. (1960), p. 305 *et seq.*, and H. W. Baade, *ibid.* 54 (1960), p. 801 *et seq.*

76 *Anglo-Iranian Oil Co.* v. *S.U.P.O.R. Co.* (*The Miriella*), I.L.R. 1955, pp. 19 and 23. For the special meaning of international public policy in Article 31 of the Preliminary Rules of the Italian Civil Code, see *ibid.*, p. 38.

77 *Anglo-Iranian Oil Co.* v. *Idemitsu Kosan Kabushiki Kaisha*, *ibid.* 1953, p. 305. See also I. Seidl-Hohenveldern, *Internationales Konfiskations- und Enteignungsrecht* (1952), p. 47 *et seq.*, and W. Niederer, 11 *Annuaire suisse* (1954), p. 91 *et seq.*

to oil shipped from Iran after the nationalisation of the oil-producing industry in Iran.

Each of these courts considered the alleged incompatibility of the titles of the defendants with international law in the light of its own municipal public policy. As they all found that the acts of nationalisation at issue had not been contrary to international law, they could avoid concerning themselves, otherwise than *en passant*, with the problem whether, under international law, they were bound to refuse recognition to titles which, in relation to the United Kingdom, constituted breaches of international law.

In the *Rose Mary*[78] before the Supreme Court of Aden, Campbell J. chose to reinterpret *Luther* v. *Sagor* so as to restrict its *ratio decidendi* to acts of confiscation inside the confiscating country against nationals of the confiscating State, as distinct from foreign nationals. In this way, he attempted to restore to the English judiciary an otherwise lost discretionary power. Concern that this distinction was incompatible with the whole weight of applicable precedents probably accounts, at least in part, for the reserve with which this judgment of a British colonial court has been received even in the United Kingdom.[79]

It is extremely doubtful whether this judgment should be viewed as a lance broken in the cause of the supremacy of international law over municipal law. It is perhaps more realistic to view it as an effort to reassert a freedom to refuse recognition of foreign municipal law as a means of judicial retaliation. This may involve the application of international law, but only because a national legislature or judiciary chooses to temper its discretionary powers by applying this test in deciding whether its public policy requires such action.

If States desire to find a substitute for the shortcomings of the principle of the relativity of international torts, they are not condemned to rely on any spurious general principle of law. They are free to achieve this object above board, that is, by means of a treaty. If the Abs-Shawcross Draft Convention ever came into force, the second sentence of Article IV would produce this result. Until reparation was made or secured, it would

[78] *Anglo-Iranian Oil Co. Ltd.* v. *Jaffrate and Others* (*The Rose Mary*) [1953] 1 W.L.R. 246.

[79] See, for instance, *Re Helbert Wagg & Co. Ltd.* [1956] 1 Ch. 323 at 346–349; D. P. O'Connell, 4 I.C.L.Q. (1955), p. 276 *et seq.*; E. J. Cohn in *Janssen Festschrift* (1958), p. 61 *et seq.*; J. S. Ziegel, 6 *McGill L.J.* (1959), p. 1 *et seq.*; J. H. C. Morris, *Cases on Private International Law* (1960), p. 348; P. R. H. Webb and D. J. L. Brown, *A Casebook on the Conflict of Laws* (1960), pp. 448–449 and 453–454; G. C. Cheshire, *Private International Law* (1965), pp. 126–127; R. H. Graveson, *The Conflict of Laws* (1965), p. 578; Lord McNair and A. D. Watts, *The Legal Effects of War* (1966), p. 429, n. 2, and Dicey and Morris, *Conflict of Laws* (1967), pp. 76 and 649–650.

See also the survey of practice and literature in W. Birke, *Die Konfiskation ausländischen Privatvermögens, etc.* (1960), p. 136 *et seq.*, and the case notes on the *Rose Mary* case by H. W. Baade, 3 *Jahrbuch für Internationales Recht* (1954), p. 132 *et seq.*, on *Re Helbert Wagg* by M. Mann and E. Lauterpacht, 5 I.C.L.Q. (1956), p. 295 *et seq.*, and Hjerner, *loc. cit.* above, p. 129, note 73, p. 186.

prevent Contracting Parties from recognising or enforcing measures conflicting with the " principles " of the Convention and affecting the property of nationals of the Contracting Parties.

It is conceivable that, on the level of international integration to be attained by this Draft Convention, the clause would be merely declaratory of otherwise implied intentions of the Contracting Parties to the same effect. Yet, even in the *inter se* relations of the Parties to this Convention, it would be inadvisable to take for granted so large a measure of inter-capitalist solidarity. Neither the Preamble nor the other provisions of the Abs-Shawcross Draft Convention provide sufficient clues to justify such an inference.

In any case, it would strengthen Article IV and corresponding provisions of other drafts if the words " the principles of " were deleted from the second sentence. They invite unnecessary controversy on possible distinctions between principles and mere detail. If, however, the object of these words is to create an obligation for Parties not to recognise or enforce measures taken by non-Parties, this intention should be more articulately expressed. It would probably also be advisable not to make any bones about the constitutive character of this sentence and to explain frankly the need for this addition to the growing body of rules of the contemporary international quasi-order, *i.e.*, rules of international public policy created by way of multilateral treaties.[80]

(c) The Enforcement of Awards

In Section 6 of the Annex to the Abs-Shawcross Draft Convention, it is stipulated that " any such award rendered in accordance with the provisions of this Annex shall be final and binding upon the parties and shall be published. Each party shall abide by and comply with any such award rendered by the Arbitral Tribunal."

The reference to the Annex in Article VII of the Draft Convention [81] suggests that the Annex is to be regarded as an integral part of the Convention. Thus, in the absence of any special clause on the subject in the Draft Convention or the Annex, any failure to comply with an award would amount to a breach of the Convention and would bring Article IV into operation.[82] Any interested party would also be entitled to bring a dispute regarding the alleged non-compliance of another Contracting Party before an arbitral tribunal under Article VII.

As it is, no Contracting Party need consult any organ on the issue whether another Contracting Party has actually failed to give effect to the award of an arbitral tribunal under the Convention or to a judgment of the International Court of Justice under Article VII of the Draft Convention. It is provided in Article VIII that a Contracting Party, alone or

[80] See, further, *loc. cit.* above, p. 115, note 29, above, p. 126, and below, under (c).
[81] See above, p. 123, *et seq.*
[82] See above, p. 126.

together with other Contracting Parties, may " take such measures as are strictly required to give effect to that judgment or award." At this point, we are back in a state of auto-interpretation of rights and duties as in the international customary law of old.

It may be thought that, once an award or judgment is available, the danger of any error regarding the alleged non-compliance of a party with an award or judgment is considerably diminished. Whenever the issue is one of the payment of a liquidated sum, this is true. In cases in which reparation has to be made in kind or the judgment is of a declaratory character, the position may well be different.

Even in the case of a monetary award or judgment, the freedom to proceed against a defaulter under Article VII is of alarming liberality. On the face of it, the measures he can take are not limited to steps of an economic or administrative character, but may include even the application of force.

This raises the compatibility of Article VIII of the Abs-Shawcross Draft Convention with the Charter of the United Nations. Under Article 2 (4) of the Charter, members must refrain in their international relations " from the threat or use of force against the territorial integrity or political independence of any State, or in any other manner inconsistent with the Purposes of the United Nations."

In the wider and probably better construction of this Paragraph, it rules out any threat or use of force other than in self-defence or collective defence against armed aggression under Article 51, or action under Articles 106 and 107 of the Charter of the United Nations.[83] It is, however, also possible to hold the view that the use of force for the purpose of executing an award or judgment can be squared, at least in spirit, with the Purposes of the United Nations, for one of these Purposes—actually the first and foremost mentioned in Article 1 of the Charter—is to maintain international peace and security, and to that end, *inter alia*, to bring about " by peaceful means, and in conformity with the principles of justice and international law, adjustment or settlement of international disputes or situations which may lead to a breach of the peace." If a State fails to carry out an award or decision of an international judicial institution, it may be considered to have acted contrary to this Purpose of the United Nations. Then, subject to the ultimate control by the Security Council under Chapter VII of the Charter, the use of force by an aggrieved Party may be viewed as a vindication of this Purpose of the United Nations. Yet, even so, it would be difficult to maintain that a State acting in this way keeps within the bounds of " peaceful means."

In substance, this argument comes near to that advanced by the United Kingdom in the *Corfu Channel* (*Merits*) case in justification of its

[83] See, further, Vol. II, p. 50 *et seq.*

" judicial " intervention to secure decisive evidence. It has, however, been unequivocally rejected by the International Court of Justice.[84]

The rationale of Article 2 (4) of the Charter offers an additional argument against any lax interpretation. Subject to the reservations stated above, the purpose of this Paragraph is to eliminate the threat or use of force on the level of the auto-interpretation of international rights and obligations. While couched in a form complying with the letter of the Charter, any attempt to justify the use of force by individual States in other contingencies runs counter to the spirit of the United Nations Charter.[85]

In this context, Article 94 (2) of the Charter of the United Nations also calls for consideration. If a party to a case fails to perform its obligations under a judgment of the International Court of Justice, all that the other party is entitled to do is to appeal to the Security Council. It is then entirely left to the Council whether to make recommendations or decide upon measures to be taken to give effect to the judgment. This is the limit of what, under the Charter, members of the United Nations may do if, in their view, another party has failed to comply with a judgment of the World Court.[86] Thus, *a fortiori*, they are not meant to be free to resort to armed self-help for the purpose of enforcing an award of a mere arbitral tribunal or a judgment of the World Court by leave of a treaty between some member States.

One difficulty remains. If, on a treaty basis, States consent in advance to measures including the application of force against them in stipulated contingencies, it is arguable that the application of such force is outside the range of Article 2 (4) of the Charter. This paragraph, it may be thought, is limited to force applied *ad invitum.*

The closest analogy to this type of situation which, so far, has arisen in United Nations practice is intervention by consent in the case of the Anglo-American intervention of 1958 in the Lebanon and Jordan and the interventions by a number of States on the invitation of rival governments and puppet regimes.[87] To judge by these experiences, the sovereign equality of members of the United Nations—one of the Principles on which, in accordance with Article 2 of the Charter, the Organisation is based—is compatible with any amount of limitation of this status by consent, provided that such a dependence is not successfully challenged by other member States in any of the United Nations organs. Thus, by consent, an otherwise illegal intervention may be legalised.

The use of force by consent given in advance under a treaty can be similarly justified. Acceptance of this argument has, however, far-reaching implications. It provides powerful Contracting Parties to any

[84] See, further, *I.C.J. Reports 1949*, p. 35, and *loc. cit.* above, p. 132, note 83.
[85] See, for a further reservation which, however, applies only if a State refuses to submit disputes to any form of peaceful settlement, *Fundamental Principles*, p. 354.
[86] See also above, p. 73 *et seq.*
[87] See, further, *Fundamental Principles*, p. 176.

such convention with handy grounds for justifying the use of force in circumstances in which this may be far from uncontroversial.

It is likely that any draft convention on the protection of foreign investments which is so incalculably open-ended will merely have a deterrent effect.[88]

8—Evaluation

Much is to be said for the view that to safeguard foreign nationals effectively against unreasonable interference with their investments by the host State, the Abs-Shawcross Draft Convention constitutes the minimum of protection that is required.

It may even be argued that clear and strict rules on the subject are in the best interest of capital-importing States themselves. Otherwise, they are likely to drive away more respectable—and, probably less exacting—investors and, at best, attract more speculative capitalists, out for the maximum of short-term profit at the highest obtainable risk rates.

Yet, the fact has to be faced that even moderate governments of capital-importing countries find it impossible to pay the political price involved in becoming parties to conventions on the Abs-Shawcross lines.

Realisation of these difficulties has led to a number of further attempts at solving the problem on a multilateral basis: concentration on the procedural aspects of the protection of foreign property,[89] efforts at the more cautious reformulation of the substantive rules of international law on the subject[90] and schemes for multilateral insurance as a last line of defence of foreign investments.[91]

88 See, further, below, p. 153 *et seq.*
89 See below, p. 135 *et seq.*
90 See below, p. 153 *et seq.*
91 See below, p. 170 *et seq.*

CHAPTER 9

THE I.B.R.D. CONVENTION ON THE SETTLEMENT OF INVESTMENT DISPUTES

THE Convention on the Settlement of Investment Disputes between States and Nationals of other States was sponsored and signed by the International Bank for Reconstruction and Development in 1965. The signatures on behalf of the Bank by its President and General Council served to indicate that the Bank was prepared to fulfil the functions with which it was charged under the Convention. Thirty days after the deposit of the twentieth instrument of ratification, the Convention came into force on October 14, 1966.[1]

Of all the attempts made in the post-1945 period to protect investments abroad on a multilateral and, potentially, universal scale,[2] this was the first and, so far, the only one to get beyond the drafting stage. This fact alone would justify closer analysis of an apparent success story.

1—THE BACKGROUND

The rules of classical international law on the protection of property abroad were largely clarified in diplomatic practice, bilateral treaties—frequently linked *de facto* by most-favoured-nation clauses—and the awards of *ad hoc* arbitration tribunals.[3] In the post-1919 period, the Permanent Court of International Justice and the Mixed Arbitral Tribunals established under the Peace Treaties of 1919 contributed to the further elaboration of these rules.

In the post-1945 era, the emphasis in the law relating to the protection of property was on diplomatic and lump-sum settlements. Beyond this, the United States and, to a minor extent, the United Kingdom and other West European countries attempted to stem the trend towards the erosion of the traditional law by restating these rules in bilateral treaties. A number of these treaties contain arbitration clauses.[4]

[1] Article 67 (Cmnd. 2745 (1965), p. 30).
See also below, p. 151 *et seq.*

[2] On the relevant activities of the Council of Europe, see above, p. 58.
On possible conflicts between obligations under the I.B.R.D. Convention and the First Protocol to the European Convention on Human Rights, see E. Lauterpacht in *Mélanges Guggenheim*, p. 657, n. 34.

[3] See above, p. 21 *et seq.*

[4] See above, pp. 32 and 109 *et seq.*
In this context, the arbitration clauses in United States investment guarantee agreements and in the loan and guarantee agreements of the International Bank for Reconstruction and Development should also be mentioned.
See, further, A. Broches, 98 Hague *Recueil* (1959), p. 370 *et seq.*, and, generally, M. Domke, 7 *Arbitration Journal* (N.S.—1952), p. 73 *et seq.*; 17 *ibid.* (1962), p. 129 *et seq.*; 12 *Business Lawyer* (1957), p. 264 *et seq.*, Yale Law School, *International* (*ctd. overleaf*)

It is symptomatic that, during this period, the International Court of Justice and bilateral arbitration tribunals had few opportunities of concerning themselves with the peacetime protection of property abroad. In relation to wartime measures taken against enemy property, international judicial institutions—significantly misnamed conciliation commissions—under the Peace Treaties of 1947 and the Peace Treaty of 1951 with Japan made minor contributions to the elucidation of the law within their purview.[5] Even if, in any such assessment, the national claims commissions, established under the municipal law of countries such as the United States and the United Kingdom, were included, this would affect but little the overall picture.[6] It is one of decline of the arbitration pattern in the post-1945, period, though less marked in International Economic Law than in other branches of Public International Law.

Actually, in the field of investment disputes, four major attempts, on a multilateral basis were made to reverse this trend.

The first of these efforts to inject new life into the arbitration pattern[7] was made in the *Havana Charter on Trade and Employment* (1948). The problem was treated as one of both substance and procedure. In a rule which fell considerably short of the minimum standard of international customary law on the protection of foreign property, member States of the envisaged International Trade Organisation were enjoined not to take "unreasonable or unjustifiable action" within their territories, "injurious to the rights or interests of nationals of other members in the enterprise, skills, capital, arts or technology which they have supplied." The Organisation was also authorised to make recommendations for, and promote, bilateral or multilateral agreements or measures designed to "assure just and equitable treatment for the enterprise, skills, capital, arts and technology brought from one member country to another."[8]

Differences regarding these and other obligations under the Havana Charter were to be settled by procedures in which the emphasis was put on the non-judicial organs of the Organisation. In this scheme, arbitration between individual members and requests for advisory opinions of the International Court of Justice were allocated merely subordinate places. The draftsmen of the Havana Charter placed little more trust in the

(*Note 4 ctd.*)
Financing and Investment (1964), p. 525 *et seq.*, and *The Law and Practice of Commercial Arbitration* (1968); A. Verdross, 18 Z.A.Ö.R.V.R. (1957–58), p. 635 *et seq.*, E. Snyder, 40 *North Carolina L.Rev.* (1962), p. 665 *et seq.*, R. Preiswerk, *La Protection des investissements privés dans les traités bilatéraux* (1963), p. 125 *et seq.*; I. Seidl-Hohenveldern, *Investitionen in Entwicklungsländern und das Völkerrecht* (1963), p. 43 *et seq.*, and *Mélanges Séfériadès* (1961), Vol. I, p. 251 *et seq.*; Ch. M. Spofford, 113 Hague *Recueil* (1964), p. 121 *et seq.*; K.-H. Boeckstiegel, 59 A.J.I.L. (1965), p. 579 *et seq.*, and I. Szássy, *International Civil Procedure* (1967), p. 588 *et seq.*

5 See, further, Vol. II, p. 758 *et seq.*

6 See above, p. 42 *et seq.*

7 Unless otherwise stated, the term as used in this Chapter includes internationally created arbitral tribunals accessible to private investors as well as international adjudication by permanent international judicial institutions.

8 Article 11 (Cmd. 7375 (1948), pp. 12–13).

arbitration pattern than had those of the Bretton Woods Agreements of 1944.

The governments of the independent capital-importing States which existed at the time of the Havana Conference viewed with considerable suspicion even these meagre provisions on the protection of foreign investments in the draft Charter. If anything, the fact that they had been so carefully hidden among other and, apparently, more respectable activities, served to rouse further misgivings. It was only fear of losing eagerly awaited Dollar-injections which, so long as the United States appeared to be keen on the Havana Charter, made these countries toe the line.

Once the United States had decided to abandon the Havana project, the governments of capital-importing States swiftly withdrew into politically safer exercises, such as draft resolutions on permanent sovereignty over natural wealth and resources, coupled with the expression of a sincere desire to attract foreign capital on trust in their good intentions.[9]

The second attempt was on tougher creditors' lines. This was the *Abs-Shawcross Draft Convention on Investments Abroad* (1959). In this Draft Convention it was attempted to link the minimum and equitable standards regarding the protection of property abroad and strengthen unobtrusively these rules by devices some of which, by their very subtleness, exposed their authors to the charge of having been less than frank.[10]

In this Draft Convention, extensive use was made of the arbitration pattern. The arbitral, as distinct from the judicial, settlement of any dispute between Contracting Parties regarding the interpretation or application of the Convention remained optional. Provision was, however, made in the last resort for the "compulsory" or, rather, automatic jurisdiction of the International Court of Justice.

In contrast, any extension of the arbitral pattern to disputes between Contracting Parties and nationals of other Contracting Parties, who had been injured by measures in breach of the Convention, remained optional.

The provisions made for the enforcement of awards were so vague and far-reaching as to give rise to doubts on their compatibility with the duties of Contracting Parties under the Charter of the United Nations. They also lent themselves to the interpretation of serving sinister ends of Western "neo-imperialism."[11]

These features sufficed to ensure burial with, at least, second-class honours for the Abs-Shawcross Draft Convention. A last-ditch attempt to save it in a more innocuous version was made within the framework of the Organisation for European Economic Co-operation and the Organisation for Economic Co-operation and Development.

9 See above, p. 59, and below, p. 188 *et seq.*
10 See above, p. 109 *et seq.*
11 See above, pp. 16 and 126 *et seq.*, and below, p. 198 *et seq.*

In two versions of a *Draft Convention on the Protection of Foreign Property* (1962 and 1967) the substantive provisions of the Abs-Shawcross Convention were toned down. The automatic jurisdiction contemplated for the International Court of Justice in disputes between Contracting Parties was entrusted to an arbitral tribunal. More important, all the provisions on the enforcement of awards were eliminated.[12]

In its earlier version of 1962, the Draft Convention failed to attract interest in capital-importing States. What had started as a united-capitalist-front effort, became a half-way house, too weak to serve its original purpose and too suspect in its antecedents to be acceptable to the overwhelming majority of capital-importing States.

After these abortive efforts, the International Bank for Reconstruction and Development took over and tried its hand in a field in which so many others had failed.

2—The Drafting of the Convention

The reasons which, in 1962, prompted the International Bank for Reconstruction and Development to step into the breach are set out in the Report of the Bank's Executive Directors on the *Convention on the Settlement of Investment Disputes between States and Nationals of other States* (1965).[13]

In particular, it was hoped that clear-cut facilities for conciliation and arbitration in capital-importing States would " provide additional inducement and stimulate a larger flow of private international investment "[14] into countries in need of such capital.

At the same time, the draftsmen tried hard to avoid the risk of their work becoming identified with any exclusive interests of capital-exporters. Thus, the drafting of the Convention took place in a series of regional meetings in which lawyers of capital-importing States preponderated. The object-in-chief of these meetings was to attain a " careful balance between the interests of investors and those of host States."[15]

3—The Mechanics of the Convention

The organisational framework is provided by the International Centre for Settlement of Investment Disputes.[16]

[12] See below, p. 153 *et seq.*

[13] Cmnd. 2745 (1965), Paras. 9–13 (p. 5). See also A. Broches, *Proceedings of the American Society of International Law 1965*, p. 35 *et seq.*, and in *Domke Symposium*, pp. 12–13; G.-R. Delaume, 93 *Journal du Droit International* (1966), p. 1 *et seq.*, and, on the earlier literature on the Convention, *ibid.*, p. 20, n. 3, the Draft Statutes of the Arbitral Tribunal for Foreign Investments, proposed by the I.L.A. Committee on the Juridical Aspects of Nationalisation and Foreign Property, Brussels Report of the International Law Association (1962), p. 132 *et seq.*, and the bibliography, below, p. 219 *et seq.*

[14] Para. 12 (Cmnd. 2745 (1965), p. 5).

[15] Para. 13 (*ibid.*, p. 5).

The preparatory material of the Convention is scheduled for publication by the Secretariat of I.C.S.I.D. in four volumes in 1968–69.

[16] Article 1 (1), Cmnd. 2745 (1965), p. 13.

(a) Object

The object of the Centre is to provide facilities for conciliation and arbitration of investment disputes between Contracting States and nationals of other Contracting States.[17]

The term " investment " is not defined in the Convention. According to the Report of the Executive Directors on the Convention this was intentional. The idea was to leave it to the parties concerned to decide on the classes of disputes they wished to submit to the Centre.[18]

(b) Seat and Legal Personality

The seat of the Centre is, in principle, at the principal office of the International Bank for Reconstruction and Development. It may, however, be moved elsewhere by a decision of the Administrative Council of the Centre, adopted by a two-thirds majority of its members.[19]

The legal status of the Centre is defined as one of " full international legal personality," including the capacity to contract, acquire and dispose of movable and immovable property and institute legal proceedings.[20]

This formulation differs from that of the other Bretton Woods institutions, each of which was given " full juridical personality." [21] Yet, it means the same thing: independent international personality and legal personality under the municipal laws of all member States, with the additional privileges expressly granted in similar terms in each of the five conventions of the Bretton Woods organisations.

Thus, although closely linked with the International Bank for Reconstruction and Development,[22] the Centre has its own distinct legal personality.

(c) Membership

Membership of the Centre is limited to Contracting States. States which are eligible to become Contracting States are, in the first place, the members of the International Bank. In addition, the Convention is open for signature by any other State which is a party to the Statute of the International Court of Justice and which the Administrative Council, on a two-thirds majority of its members, invites to sign the Convention.[23]

(d) Organisation

The organs of the Centre are the Administrative Council and the Secretariat.

17 Article 1 (2) (*ibid.*, p. 14).
18 Section 27 (*ibid.*, p. 8).
See also below, p. 142 *et seq.*
19 Article 2 (Cmnd. 2745 (1965), p. 14).
20 Article 18 (*ibid.*, p. 17).
21 See, for instance, Article VII of the I.B.R.D. Agreement of December 27, 1945 (Cmd. 6885 (1946), p. 49).
22 See below under (c).
23 Article 67 (Cmnd. 2745 (1965), p. 30).

(1) *The Administrative Council* is the members' meeting. It is composed of one representative of each Contracting State or an alternate. In the absence of any other arrangement made by member States, these functions are fulfilled by the governors and alternate governors of the Bank, appointed by these States.[24] The President of the International Bank is *ex officio* Chairman of the Administrative Council, but without a vote.[25]

The Council is the governing body of the Centre. In particular, it adopts the administrative and financial regulations of the Centre (Administrative and Financial Regulations), the rules of procedure for the institution of conciliation and arbitration proceedings (Institution Rules) and the rules of procedure (Conciliation and Arbitration Rules). It also approves arrangements with the International Bank for the use of the Bank's administrative facilities and determines the conditions of service of the Secretary-General.[26]

Each member of the Council has one vote. In principle, decisions are made by a majority of the votes cast. The Chairman may ascertain the sense of the meeting in lieu of a formal vote, but must ask for a formal vote at the request of any member. Decisions on matters expressly specified in the Convention, including the various regulations mentioned above, have to be made by a two-thirds majority of the members of the Council.[27] A majority of the members of the Council constitutes a quorum.[28]

(2) *Secretariat.* The Secretary-General is the head of the staff of the Centre and is elected by the Administrative Council for a term not exceeding six years, but is eligible for re-election. He also acts as Secretary of the Council, performs the functions of the Registrar of the Centre and has the power to authenticate arbitral awards made under the Convention and issue certified copies of such awards.[29]

(e) The Panels of Conciliators and Arbitrators

The Centre maintains lists of qualified persons willing to serve as conciliators and arbitrators.

Each Contracting State may designate to each panel four persons who may, but need not be its nationals. The Chairman of the Administrative

[24] Article 4 (*ibid.*, p. 14).

[25] Article 5 (*ibid.*, p. 14).

[26] Article 6 (*ibid.*, pp. 14–15).

The Administrative Council adopted all these sets of Rules in a definite form, with effect from January 1, 1968 (ICSID/4 (1968)).

The Administrative and Financial Regulations and Institutional Rules are instructive illustrations of derivative *jus cogens* of a consensual character, from which the parties may derogate only within the limits provided in these rules.

In contrast, the Arbitration and Conciliation Rules are drafted as *jus dispositivum*, with the exception of those rules which merely repeat binding provisions of the Convention.

[27] Articles 6 (1) and 7 (2) (Cmnd. 2745 (1965), pp. 14–15) and Regulation 6 (1) of the Administrative and Financial Regulations (*loc. cit.*, above, note 26, pp. 10–11).

[28] Article 6 (3) (Cmnd. 2745 (1965), p. 15).

[29] Articles 10–11 (Cmnd. 2745 (1965), pp. 15–16) and Regulation 4 of the Administrative and Financial Regulations (*loc. cit.*, above, note 26, p. 10).

Council may designate ten more persons to each panel, but each of the persons so designated to either panel must have a different nationality.

The persons designated to serve on the panels " shall be persons of high moral character and recognised competence in the fields of law, commerce, industry or finance, who may be relied upon to exercise independent judgment." For reasons of incompatibility of functions, the members of the Centre's Secretariat are not eligible as members of either panel.[30] In the case of members of the Panel of Arbitrators, the modest requirement of competence in the field of law is expressly mentioned.

In exercising his own powers of designation, the Chairman of the Administrative Council must bear in mind the importance of assuring representation on both panels of the principal legal systems of the world and of the main forms of economic activity.[31]

Panel members are to serve for renewable periods of six years and may serve on both panels.

(f) Finance

In principle, the Centre is to finance itself out of charges for the use of its facilities. The excess of expenditure over income is borne by Contracting States which are members of the International Bank in proportion to their respective subscriptions to the Bank's capital stock, and by Contracting States which are not members of the Bank in accordance with rules adopted by the Administrative Council.[32]

(g) Disputes between Contracting States

In the absence of any other method of settlement between the States concerned, any dispute between Contracting States on the interpretation or application of the Convention shall be submitted to the International Court of Justice on the application of any party to such dispute.[33]

(h) Denunciation

Any Contracting State may denounce the Convention by written notice to the International Bank as the depositary of the Convention. The notice takes effect six months after receipt by the Centre. Yet, it leaves unaffected rights and obligations of that State or of any of its nationals arising out of consent to the jurisdiction of the Centre,[34] given before such notice was received by the depositary.[35]

[30] Article 14 (1) (Cmnd. 2745 (1965), p. 16) and Regulation 12 of the Administrative and Financial Regulations (*loc. cit.*, above, p. 140, note 26, p. 12).
[31] Article 14 (2) (Cmnd. 2745 (1965), p. 16).
[32] Article 17 (*ibid.*, p. 17).
[33] Article 64 (*ibid.*, p. 29).
[34] See below, p. 142 *et seq.*
[35] Articles 71–72 (Cmnd. 2745 (1965), pp. 30–31).

4—Jurisdiction of the Centre

The crucial question is the extent to which the draftsmen of the Convention considered it prudent to commit the governments of capital-importing States, without unduly rousing their susceptibilities as sovereign and equal members of the United Nations. They have come as near as is possible to the point of squaring this particular circle. With remarkable ingenuity, they have couched the minimum of legal commitments in a form which leaves everything on the level of optional undertakings, but attains as much as, in the present political climate, is likely to be attained for the protection of foreign investments through conciliation and arbitration.

It is possible to become a party to the Convention and, thus, acquire additional credit-worthiness without thereby accepting any obligation to submit any particular investment dispute to conciliation or arbitration. So that this attractive feature of the Convention cannot possibly be overlooked, it is spelled out in full in the last paragraph of the Preamble.

The potential jurisdiction of the Centre is limited to legal disputes "arising directly out of an investment" between a Contracting State (or any of the sub-divisions or agencies of that State designated to the Centre) and nationals of other Contracting Parties which the parties to such disputes consent in writing to submit to the Centre. With the exception of the term "national of another Contracting Party," none of these operative terms—"legal dispute," arising "directly" out of an "investment"—is defined in the Convention. Actually, all of them are sufficiently controversial to call for definitions in an interpretative section.[36] In particular this applies to a Convention intended for parties the great majority of which have but recently acquired a direct connection with international law.

The legal consequences of consent to arbitration are far-reaching. Unless a Contracting State has reserved its right to require the prior exhaustion of local administrative or judicial remedies, the issue is taken out of its own jurisdiction.[37] Correspondingly, the Contracting State whose national is involved in the dispute must refrain from giving diplomatic protection to its national (otherwise than by informal diplomatic exchanges for the sole purpose of facilitating a settlement of the dispute) or from bringing an international claim in the matter against the other Contracting Party. On the model of the Porter Convention,[38] this self-denying ordinance continues to apply until the other Contracting Party has failed to comply with the award.[39]

[36] The Report of the Executive Directors is hardly a commensurate substitute for this (see Sections 26–27, *ibid.*, p. 8).

The Secretariat of I.C.S.I.D. has prepared a number of model clauses to assist parties to investment arrangements in formulating their consent to the Centre's jurisdiction (I.C.S.I.D./5—1968).

[37] Article 26 (*ibid.*, p. 19).

[38] Article 1 (2) of Hague Convention II of 1907 on the Limitation of the Employment of Force for the Recovery of Contract Debts (J. B. Scott, *The Conventions and Declarations of 1899 and 1907* (1915), p. 89 *et seq.*).

[39] Art. 27 (I), (Cmnd. 2745 (1965), pp. 19–20).

5—The Applicable Law

In substance, such disputes are and remain primarily disputes under municipal law. While the parties remain free to agree on other rules, in the absence of such agreement the tribunal is enjoined to apply the law of the Contracting State party to the dispute, including its rules on the conflict of laws. In addition, the tribunal is to apply " such rules of international law as may be applicable." [40]

Like any other consensual engagement between a sovereign State and any subject or object of international law, agreements relating to investments between States and foreign nationals are subject to whichever legal system is acceptable to the parties concerned. This rule is codified in the first sentence of Article 42 (I).

Similarly, it is still good law that, in the absence of convincing evidence to the contrary, a sovereign State cannot be presumed to subject any contract to which it is a party with a foreign national or company to any law other than its own.[41] In the second sentence of Article 42 (I), this rule appears to be more rigidly formulated. Agreement may, however, be tacit as well as express. On this assumption, no substantial difference exists between the traditional presumption and the rule as formulated in the Convention.

Under the Convention the reference to the law of the Contracting State party to the dispute includes that party's rules on the conflict of laws. Thus, these rules are the test of any further reference to any other system of municipal law.

On the surface, this formulation appears to go further than *lex lata.* If the arbitration tribunals under the Convention were international tribunals, they would have to apply their own *lex fori,* which is international law. From this starting point, they would evolve their own rules for deciding issues of conflicting national laws.[42] Yet, to judge by the law which, under the Convention, the tribunals are primarily intended to apply, these tribunals are more akin to internationally postulated domestic tribunals than to international tribunals in the strict sense of the term.[43] Thus, it was necessary to settle whether the reference to the law of the Contracting State party to the dispute was limited to the substantive law of that State or included its law on the conflict of laws. The same reasons which counsel the one may well be thought to counsel the other. In any case, why should such tribunals be more closely tied to the law of Contracting States parties to disputes than the municipal courts of such States?

40 Article 42 (*ibid.*, p. 23).

41 See above, p. 5 *et seq.*

42 See, further, Vol. I, p. 74 *et seq.*, and K. Lipstein, 27 *Grotius Transactions* (1941), p. 142 *et seq.*, and 29 *ibid.* (1943), p. 51 *et seq.*

43 In para. 33 of the Report of the Executive Directors, the jurisdiction of the Centre is termed " international " (Cmnd. 2745 (1965), p. 9). In the formal sense that it rests on an international agreement, this is correct.

It is more difficult to ascertain the meaning of the words employed in Article 42 (I): " and such rules of international law as may be applicable." Let it be assumed that a Contracting State has notified the Centre of the classes of disputes it would consider submitting to the jurisdiction of the Centre and, on this basis, a foreign investment in the terms of the Convention has been made. Subsequently, a Contracting State passes legislation, under which the foreign investment involved is confiscated without compensation, ruinous taxation discriminating against foreign enterprises is imposed or the supremacy of its own national law over international law is asserted.

What would be the position of a foreign investor who is a national of another Contracting Party? In the first instance, he would find that the notification of the classes of disputes covering his own investment did " not constitute the consent required by Paragraph (I)." [44] Yet even if the Contracting State party to the dispute had given its consent in a binding form as, for instance, in a prior investment agreement or *ad hoc* after the above-mentioned legislation had been passed,[45] what law would the tribunal apply under Article 42 of the Convention?

Would it be the national law of the Contracting State party to the dispute, including the above-mentioned legislation, or this national law, but only to the extent to which it was compatible with international law, including the protection of foreign property under the minimum standard of international law?

No dogmatic answer to this question appears possible. The interpretation of Article 42 would have to be left with each individual arbitration tribunal. It, thus, becomes a matter of some importance to explore how these tribunals are constituted. In the last resort, each of the tribunals consists of three members. One of these is nominated by each party. The third, who shall be the president of the Tribunal, is agreed upon by the parties. If they cannot agree on his appointment, he is nominated from a panel of arbitrators by the Chairman of the Administrative Council of the Centre, *i.e.*, the President of the International Bank.[46] In the typical case, it would be the president of any such tribunal who would have the decisive voice on all these issues.

In these circumstances, can it be truly said of the facilities for arbitration to be provided by the Centre that they would be " carried out according to rules known and accepted in advance by the parties concerned."? [47]

[44] Para. 4 of Article 25 (*ibid.*, p. 19).

[45] For further illustrations of binding forms of consent, see para. 24 of the Report of the Executive Directors (*ibid.*, pp. 7–8).

[46] See Articles 5, 12, 14 and 37 (*ibid.*, pp. 14, 16 and 22–23), and above, p. 140.

[47] Para. 11 of the Report of the Executive Directors (*ibid.*, p. 5). See also N. S. Rodley, 4 *Canadian Yearbook of International Law* (1966), p. 57 *et seq.*, especially the analysis of the preparatory material, and E. Lauterpacht in *Mélanges Guggenheim*, p. 652 *et seq.*

On the drafting history of Article 42, see A. Broches, in *Domke Symposium*, p. 13 *et seq.*

On the substantive law applied in comparable cases prior to the Convention, see

(*ctd. overleaf*)

6—Procedure

Several of the rules applicable to conciliation and arbitration proceedings are substantially the same.

(a) Institution of Proceedings

Conciliation and arbitration proceedings are initiated by a Contracting State or one of its nationals by a written request, addressed to the Secretary-General of the Centre.

Unless the Secretary-General finds that, on the basis of the information contained in the request, the dispute is manifestly outside the jurisdiction of the Centre, he is bound to register the request and take the further steps required from him under the Convention to assist in getting the proceedings under way.[48]

(b) Constitution of the Conciliation Commission and Arbitral Tribunal

If the parties themselves do not constitute the Conciliation Commission or the Arbitral Tribunal as prescribed in the Convention,[49] the Chairman of the Centre's Administrative Council must intervene and, at the request of either party and after consulting both parties as far as possible, appoint the member or members of either body not yet appointed.[50]

After proceedings before a Commission or Tribunal have begun, in principle the composition of the organ must remain unchanged. The status of a member is not affected by the member ceasing to be a member of the panel. In the case of death, incapacity or resignation of a member, the resulting vacancy is filled in the same way as in the case of the original constitution of the organ concerned. However, if a conciliator or arbitrator appointed by a party resigns without the consent of the Commission or Tribunal of which he was a member, the Chairman of the Administrative Council shall appoint a person from the appropriate panel to fill the vacancy.

The Commission or Tribunal decides, primarily, itself on pleas to disqualify a member. If the members are equally divided or the allegation is directed against a sole conciliator or arbitrator or a majority of the conciliators or arbitrators, the Chairman of the Administrative Council of the Centre decides. If he considers the allegation to be well founded, the disqualified members are replaced in the same way as if the issue had

(*Note 47 ctd.*)
Petroleum Development (*Quatar*) *Ltd.* v. *Ruler of Quatar* (1950), I.L.R. 1951, p. 161; *Petroleum Development Ltd.* v. *Sheikh of Abu Dhabi* (1951), *ibid.* p. 144; *Ruler of Quatar* v. *International Marine Oil Company Ltd.* (1953), *ibid.* 1953, p. 534; *Alsing Trading Co. Ltd., etc.* v. *Greece* (1954), *ibid.* 1956, p. 633; *Société Européenne d'Études et d'Entreprises* v. *Yugoslavia* (1956), *ibid.* 1957, p. 761; *Saudi Arabia* v. *ARAMCO* (1959), 27 *ibid.* p. 117, and *Sapphire International Petroleum Ltd.* v. *National Iranian Oil Company* (1963), 35 *ibid.* p. 136.

48 Articles 28 (Cmnd. 2745 (1965), p. 20) and 36 (*ibid.*, p. 22). See, further, the Institution Rules (*loc. cit.* in note 26 above, p. 28 *et seq.*).

49 Articles 29 (Cmnd. 2745 (1965), p. 20) and 37 (*ibid.*, p. 22).

50 Articles 30 (*ibid.*, p. 21) and 38 (*ibid.*, p. 23).

arisen in the initial phase of the constitution of the Commission or Tribunal.[51]

(c) Challenges to Jurisdiction

The presumption that, in the absence of express provision to the contrary, international judicial institutions decide themselves on their own competence is formulated as a firm rule in relation to both the Commissions and Tribunals under the Convention.[52]

(d) Conciliation Procedure

Five procedural rules, peculiar to the conciliation procedure, must be mentioned:

(1) *Conciliation Rules.* In addition to the provisions of Section 3 of Chapter III of the Convention, Conciliation Commissions have to apply, except as the parties otherwise agree, the Conciliation Rules adopted by the Administrative Council of the Centre and in effect on the date on which the parties consented to such proceedings.[53]

(2) *Duty of Co-operation in Good Faith.* The duty *juris aequi*, which, in any case, would arise in the consensual nexus of a treaty, of the parties to co-operate in good faith with the Commission in order to enable it to carry out its functions has been expressly stated.[54]

(3) *Recommendations.* Similarly, the character of the findings of the Conciliation Commissions as mere recommendations, as distinct from binding decisions, has been reaffirmed.[55]

(4) *Without Prejudice.* As is customary in conventions providing for conciliation and, even more so, for conciliation and arbitration side by side, a "without prejudice" clause protects parties to conciliation proceedings under the Convention from being estopped in other proceedings—and not only in proceedings under the Convention—from going back on statements, admissions or offers of settlement. Similarly, the other party may not invoke or rely in subsequent proceedings on any report or recommendation made by the Commission.[56]

[51] Articles 56–58 (Cmnd. 2745 (1965), pp. 27–28). See, further, Chapter I of the Conciliation and Arbitration Rules (*loc. cit.* above, p. 140, note 26, pp. 41 and 75 *et seq.*).

[52] Articles 32 (1) (Cmnd. 2745 (1965), p. 21) and 41 (1) (*ibid.*, p. 23); Rule 30 of the Conciliation Rules (*loc. cit.* above, p. 140, note 26, p. 66) and Rule 41 of the Arbitration Rules (*ibid.*, p. 106).

[53] Article 33 (Cmnd. 2745 (1965), p. 21).

Definitive Rules of Conciliation, adopted by the Administrative Council on September 25, 1967, are in use as from January 1, 1968 (ICSID/4).

For comparable conciliation proceedings prior to the Convention, see *In re Imperial Japanese Government Loan of 1910* (1955) 29 I.L.R., p. 4, and *In re City of Tokyo 5 per cent. Loan of 1912* (1960), *ibid.*, p. 11.

[54] Article 34 (1) (Cmnd. 2745 (1965), p. 21), and Rule 23 of the Conciliation Rules (*loc. cit.* above, p. 140, note 26, p. 61).

[55] Article 34 (1) (Cmnd. 2745 (1965), p. 21), and Rule 33 of the Conciliation Rules (*loc. cit.* above, p. 140, note 26, p. 68).

[56] *Loc. cit.* in note 14 above, Article 35 (Cmnd. 2745 (1965), p. 22).

See also above, p. 123, and, further, Article 13 (5) of the Treaty of July 7, 1965, for Conciliation, Judicial Settlement and Arbitration between Switzerland and the United Kingdom, Cmnd. 3285 (1967), p. 8.

(5) *Costs and Expenses.* It is in the nature of proceedings before conciliation commissions that neither party wins or loses its case. Thus, each party is liable for an equal share of the costs of the Commission and bears exclusive responsibility for its own expenses. This rule is restated in the Convention.[57]

(e) Arbitration Procedure

Eleven rules relating to the procedural side of arbitration proceedings under the Convention call for attention:

(1) *Arbitration Rules.* In addition to the provisions of Section 3 of Chapter IV of the Convention, the Arbitration Tribunals have to apply, except as the parties otherwise agree, the Arbitration Rules adopted by the Administrative Council of the Centre and in force on the date when the parties consented to arbitration.

If a question of procedure arises which is not covered by the Convention, the Arbitration Rules or any agreement between the parties, it is to be decided by the Tribunal.[58]

(2) *Awards ex aequo et bono.* If the parties so agree, the Tribunals are authorised to decide disputes *ex aequo et bono.*[59]

(3) *Procedure on Default.* Failure of a party to appear or present its case shall not be deemed an admission of the other party's assertions. The latter may, however, request the Tribunal to deal with the questions submitted to it and to render an award. Before rendering such an award *in absentia*, the Tribunal must notify, and grant a period of grace to, the party failing to appear or to present its case, unless it is satisfied that the party in default does not intend to do so.[60]

(4) *Incidental Claims and Counter-Claims.* Unless the parties otherwise agree, the Tribunals must, if requested by a party, determine any incidental or additional claims or counter-claims arising directly out of the subject-matter of the dispute, provided that they are within the scope of the consent of the parties and are otherwise within the jurisdiction of the Centre.[61]

57 Article 57 (Cmnd. 2745 (1965), p. 28). See also Regulation 13 of the Administrative and Financial Regulations (*loc. cit.* above, p. 140, note 26, p. 13).

58 Article 44 (Cmnd. 2745 (1965), p. 24).
The Definitive Rules of Arbitration adopted by the Administrative Council on September 25, 1967, are in force as from January 1, 1968 (ICSID/4).

59 Article 42 (3) (Cmnd. 2745 (1965), p. 23).
See, for instance, Article 50 of the Long-Term Convention of Establishment and Implementation of July 19, 1967, between Mauritania and Société des Mines de Mauritanie (S.O.M.I.N.A.), 6 I.L.M. (1967), p. 1085.

60 Article 45 (Cmnd. 2745 (1965), p. 24) and Rule 42 of the Arbitration Rules (*loc. cit.* in note 26 above, p. 107).
On the drafting history, see A. Broches, *Domke Symposium*, p. 17 *et seq.*
In two recent cases—*Société Européenne d'Études et d'Entreprises* v. *Yugoslavia* (1956—*loc. cit.* above, p. 145, note 47) and *Sapphire International Petroleum Ltd.* v. *National Iranian Oil Company* (1963—*loc. cit.*, *ibid.*), the proceedings had to take place in the absence of the government parties concerned, and the awards were made *in absentia*. See also below, p. 189.

61 Article 46 (Cmnd. 2745 (1965), p. 24) and Rule 40 of the Arbitration Rules (*loc. cit.* above, p. 140, note 26, p. 105).

(5) *Interim Measures.* Unless the parties otherwise agree, the Tribunals may, in suitable circumstances, recommend provisional measures which should be taken to preserve the respective rights of either party. They may not, however, make decisions to this effect.[62]

(6) *Non Liquet.* In accordance with generally accepted legal doctrine and practice under municipal and international law, the Tribunals may not avoid a decision of the case before them on the ground of apparent silence or obscurity of the law.[63]

(7) *Award.* Following the practice of international courts and tribunals, the Tribunal decides questions by a majority of the votes of all its members. Under the Arbitration Rules, abstention is equated with a negative vote. In the award, the Tribunal must deal with every question submitted to it and state the reasons upon which the award is based.

Individual opinions by members of the Tribunal are permitted in the form of separate and dissenting opinions.

Provision is also made for the supplementation and rectification of the award. On the request of a party made within 45 days after the award is rendered, the Tribunal may, after notice to the other party, decide any question which it had omitted to decide and must rectify any clerical, arithmetical or similar error in the award. Such decisions become part of the award and must be notified to the parties in the same manner as the award.[64]

(8) *Interpretation and Revision of the Award.* If any dispute arises between the parties on the meaning or scope of the award, either party may request interpretation by a written application addressed to the Secretary-General of the Centre. If possible, the request is to be submitted to the Tribunal which rendered the award. Otherwise, a new tribunal must be constituted. Pending its decision,[65] the Tribunal has power to stay enforcement of the award.

Also by a written application addressed to the Secretary-General, either party may request revision of the award. The request must be based on the ground of discovery of some fact of such a nature as to affect the award decisively. In accordance with the two provisos usually made in instruments permitting the revision of awards and judgments, the fact relied on must have been unknown to the Tribunal and to the applicant at the time of the award, and the applicant's ignorance of the fact must not have been due to negligence. The application for revision must be made within

[62] Article 47 (Cmnd. 2745 (1965), p. 24) and Rule 39 of the Arbitration Rules (*loc. cit.* above, p. 140, note 26, p. 104).

[63] Article 42 (2) (Cmnd. 2745 (1965), p. 23).

[64] Articles 48–49 (*ibid.*, pp. 24–25) and Rule 16 and Chapter VI of the Arbitration Rules (*loc. cit.* above, p. 140, note 26, pp. 89 and 111 *et seq.*).

For an illustration of a controversial award, which, under the Convention might have been considered to have been inadequately reasoned or incompletely decided, see *Jordan Investments Ltd.* v. *All-Union Foreign Trade Corporation Moscow* (1958), 53 A.J.I.L. (1959), p. 800, and the comments by M. Domke, *ibid.*, p. 787 *et seq.*

[65] Article 50 (Cmnd. 2745 (1965), p. 25) and Chapter VII of the Arbitration Rules (*loc. cit.* above, p. 140, note 26, p. 114 *et seq.*).

ninety days after the discovery of such fact, and in any case, within three years after the date of the award. Again, if possible, the request is to be submitted to the same Tribunal which rendered the award. Otherwise, a new Tribunal must be constituted. The Tribunal may stay the enforcement of the award pending its decision.[66]

(9) *Annulment of the Award.* Either party may request annulment of the award in the same way as in interpretation or revision proceedings on one or more of the following five grounds: that the Tribunal was not properly constituted; that the Tribunal had manifestly exceeded its powers; that one or more members of the Tribunal had been corrupted; that there had been a serious departure from a fundamental rule of procedure, or that the reasons on which the award was based were not stated.

In all cases except that of corruption, the application has to be made within 120 days after the award. In the case of corruption it suffices that the application should be made within 120 days after discovery of the corruption and, in any case, within three years after the date of the award.

On receipt of the request, the Chairman of the Administrative Council must forthwith appoint an *ad hoc* Committee of three members from the Panel of Arbitrators. Several grounds of exclusion from membership of the *ad hoc* Committee are enumerated in the Convention: none of the members of the Committee shall have been a member of the Tribunal which rendered the award, shall be of the same nationality as any such member, shall be a national of the State party to the dispute or of the State whose national is a party to the dispute, shall have been designated to the Panel of Arbitrators by either of those States, or shall have acted as a conciliator in the same dispute.

The Committee may annul the whole or any part of the award on any one or more of the grounds set out above. If the award is annulled, either party may request that the dispute is referred to a new Tribunal, constituted in accordance with the normal rules applicable to the constitution of Tribunals under the Convention.[67]

(10) *Recognition and Enforcement of Awards.* Subject to the remedies mentioned under previous heads, awards, including decisions interpreting, revising or annulling such awards, are binding on the parties.

Each Contracting State has to recognise any such award and enforce the pecuniary obligations imposed by the award in its territories as if it were a final judgment of one of its own courts. A federal State fulfils its obligations as a Contracting State by enforcing the award in or through its federal courts and may provide that such courts shall treat the award as if it were a final judgment of one of the courts of a constituent State.

[66] Article 51 (Cmnd. 2745 (1965), p. 25).

[67] *Ibid.*, Article 52 (p. 26).

The abortive arbitration on the ***Buraimi Oasis***, broken up among accusations of corruption against members of the Tribunal established under the Arbitration Agreement of July 30, 1954, between Saudi Arabia and the United Kingdom (Cmd. 9272—1954) still awaits monographic treatment. See, further, J. B. Kelly, ***Eastern Arabian Frontiers*** (1964), pp. 172 and 199 *et seq.*

Execution of the award is governed by the laws on the execution of judgments in force in the State in whose territories such execution is sought.

These rules are not, however, intended to derogate from the law in force in any Contracting State relating to immunity of that State or of any foreign State from execution.

From a practical point of view, it is important that Contracting States have undertaken to designate competent courts or authorities to which, for purposes of recognition or enforcement, awards under the Convention may be handed.

It will be a small, but significant pointer to the efficiency and degree of earnestness with which the Contracting States treat their obligations under the Convention, to observe how soon and how many of these States notify such designations to the Centre as they promised to do.[68]

(11) *Costs and Expenses.* In arbitral proceedings the position differs from those in conciliation proceedings under the Convention.[69] Unless the parties agree otherwise, the Tribunal's judicial discretion is preserved to fix the costs and expenses as it sees fit. Any such decision forms part of the award.[70]

7—Revision of the Convention

Any Contracting State may propose amendments of the Convention. If, by a two-thirds majority of its members, the Administrative Council so decides, the proposed amendment is to be circulated to all Contracting States. If all Contracting States have ratified, accepted or approved the amendment, it enters into force thirty days after dispatch by the Centre of a notification to this effect to Contracting States. No such amendment affects the rights of any Contracting Party or national of such a State arising out of prior consent to the Centre's jurisdiction.[71]

The more successful the Centre will be, the more it may find its limitation of jurisdiction to legal disputes for purposes of even mere conciliation proceedings to be a serious handicap. Its helping hand may well be required in the renegotiation of existing investment conditions and agreements.[72]

If provision is made in the investment agreement for its revision, the facilities of the Centre are available. Especially in conciliation proceedings,

[68] Articles 53–55 (Cmnd. 2745 (1965), pp. 26–27).
See also Spofford, *loc. cit.* above, p. 136, note 4, p. 210 *et seq.*, and M. Domke in University of Illinois *Law Forum on International Trade, Investment and Organisation* (1965), p. 399 *et seq.*

[69] See above, p. 147.

[70] Article 61 (Cmnd. 2745 (1965), p. 28). See also Regulation 13 of the Administrative and Financial Regulations (*loc. cit.* above, p. 140, note 26, p. 13) and Rule 27 of the Arbitration Rules (*ibid.*, p. 96).

[71] Articles 65–66 (Cmnd. 2745 (1965), pp. 29–30).

[72] See, further, the Report by the United Nations Secretariat on *Financing of Economic Development—Promotion of Private Foreign Investment in Developing Countries* (preliminary text of Summary and Conclusions in U.N.Doc. E/4293—1967). See also below, p. 190, note 22.

it is unlikely that any hard and fast line will be drawn between legal and non-legal aspects of the dispute.

In this context, it is advisable to recall the relevant passage of Article 34 (1) of the Convention: " It shall be the duty of the Commission to clarify the issues in dispute between the parties and to endeavour to bring about agreement between them upon mutually acceptable terms. To that end, the Commission may at any stage of the proceedings and from time to time recommend terms of settlement to the parties." [73]

In the absence of a revision clause in the investment contract, the dispute would be non-legal and, therefore, outside the jurisdiction of the Centre. Thus, it might be worth considering whether an extension of the revisory functions of the Centre—aptly described by the Secretary-General of the Centre as a " rounding out " of the functions of the Centre [74]—would be acceptable to the Contracting State as a topic for the revision of the Convention.

8—Evaluation

By May 20, 1968, fifty-seven eligible States had signed the Convention and forty of these had ratified it.

Arranged according to continents, the forty States in relation to which the Convention is binding are in

(1) *Africa*: Cameroon, Central African Republic, Chad, Congo (Brazzaville), Dahomey, Gabon, Ghana, Ivory Coast, Kenya, Malagasy Republic, Malawi, Mauritania, Morocco, Niger, Nigeria, Senegal, Sierra Leone, the Somali Republic, Togo, Tunisia, Uganda and Upper Volta (22).

(2) *America*: Jamaica, Trinidad and Tobago, and the United States of America (3).

(3) *Asia*: Ceylon, Japan, Korea, Malaysia and Pakistan (5).

(4) *Europe*: Cyprus, Denmark, France, Iceland, the Netherlands, Norway, Sweden, Switzerland, the United Kingdom, and Yugoslavia (10).[75]

Among capital-importing States, significant absentees are Spain, Greece, Turkey, Ethiopia, Iran, India, Burma, Thailand, Indonesia, the Philippines and nearly all Latin American countries.[76]

[73] Cmnd. 2745 (1965), p. 21. See also Rule 33 of the Conciliation Rules (*loc. cit.* above, p. 140, note 26, p. 68).

[74] Speech at the First Annual Meeting of the ICSID Administrative Council, September 25, 1967. See also H. Brandon, 6 *Il Diritto* (1967), p. 409.

[75] ICSID/3/Rev. 4.

On the significant decision of the Saudi Arabian Cabinet regarding, *inter alia*, the arbitration of investment disputes, see 3 I.L.M. (1964), p. 45, and above, p. 5, note 8.

[76] The three official languages of the Convention are English, French and Spanish (Article 75—Cmnd. 2645 (1965), p. 31). In accordance with Regulation 34 of the Administrative and Financial Regulations, the initial official languages are English

(*ctd. overleaf*)

Even so, this essay in multilateral law-making is remarkable and, compared with other comparable attempts, astounding. Thus, it is apposite to analyse the reasons for this singular achievement.

Four factors appear to have played a major role:

(1) The general environment of the Bretton Woods institutions. They have succeeded in creating the atmosphere of a powerful and prestigious international partnership among the member States. As in most enterprises, there are senior and junior partners, but the smaller States are made to feel that they co-exist with their more powerful fellow-members on a footing of more than formal quality. If anything, the latter tend to fall over backwards not to press their points and become oppressive.

Other aspects of the Convention, such as the availability of procedures under the Convention to the host State *against* the investor and for disputes relating to investments in primarily capital-exporting States, tend to underline the reciprocity and equality aimed at in the Convention.[77]

(2) The techniques of drafting the Convention in a succession of regional meetings, and in close consultation with all member States of the International Bank, were well suited, from the start, to convey a sense of general participation in the formative stages of decision-making on the essential features of the Convention.[78]

The Bank's General Counsel and his colleagues deserve credit for their share in this model of psychologically and technically well-conducted staff work.

(3) The draftsmen were aware of one of the classic rules of legal planning: to aim at the minimum of legal restraint required or attainable in a particular historical situation. Thus, they have succeeded in achieving a compromise acceptable to a fair number of capital-importing States and considered far from negligible by those in charge of directing a substantial portion of the flow of capital exports.[79]

(4) Considering the allergies of capital-importing States to committing themselves to substantive rules on the protection of foreign property,[80] the emphasis throughout on the procedural aspects of the subject was a stroke of genius. If perhaps such an approach to the problem was more ingenious than ingenuous,[81] the explanation lies in the unavoidable relativity of the distinction between form and substance in the reality of law as in any other sphere of human endeavour.

(*Note 76 ctd.*)
and French. Spanish will be added "as soon as a Spanish-speaking State becomes a party to the Convention" (*loc. cit.* above, p. 140, note 26, p. 23).

On the position of Latin American States, see also the hearings of the U.S. Senate Committee on Foreign Relations, March 29, 1966, 5 I.L.M. (1966), pp. 23–24.

77 These points are rightly stressed by M. Brandon, *loc. cit.* above, p. 151, note 74, p. 403.

78 See above, p. 138.

79 See above, p. 138.

80 See above, pp. 109 and 135 *et seq.*, and below, p. 189 *et seq.*

81 See above, p. 143 *et seq.*

CHAPTER 10

THE O.E.C.D. DRAFT CONVENTION OF 1967 ON THE PROTECTION OF FOREIGN PROPERTY

IN a circuitous way, the I.B.R.D. Convention on Investment Disputes of 1965 led back to the issue the draftsmen of the I.B.R.D. Convention had tried hard to evade: the substantive rules of international law governing the protection of foreign property.[1] Thus, retrospectively, the Abs-Shawcross Draft Convention and its derivatives acquired a new topicality.[2]

The fate of the Abs-Shawcross Draft Convention had not been an easy one. The Bretton Woods Organisations were not prepared to touch the Draft Convention. The only international body conceivably willing to sponsor it was the Organisation for European Economic Co-operation, since 1960 the Organisation for Economic Co-operation and Development. Being predominantly under the influence of the Western capital-exporting States,[3] it was, for purposes of launching the project, merely a poor second-best.

Even so, it required considerable effort to find a member State willing to accept responsibility for the Draft Convention and submit it to the O.E.C.D. Council. Eventually, the German Government undertook this, subject to a number of modifications of the original draft. Largely under Swiss influence, the revised text was further pruned until, in 1962, a suitably toned-down Draft Convention on the Protection of Foreign Property emerged.[4] When it was published, the O.E.C.D. Council made it clear that it had not yet taken any decision on the " principle and content " of the Draft Convention and merely authorised member countries and the Secretary-General to make the text available for comment by non-member States and other interested circles.

In the years that followed, the draft was considered by the Committee for Invisible Transactions and the Payments Committee of O.E.C.D., and both the text and the commentary attached to it were further modified. In a Resolution, passed on October 12, 1967, the O.E.C.D. Council

1 See above, p. 135 *et seq.*

2 See above, p. 109 *et seq.*

3 The members are Austria, Belgium, Canada, Denmark, France, the Federal Republic of Germany, Greece, Iceland, Ireland, Italy, Japan, Luxembourg, the Netherlands, Norway, Portugal, Spain, Sweden, Switzerland, Turkey, the United Kingdom and the United States of America.

4 No. 15637.

See also the supporting Opinion No. 39 (1963) of the Consultative Assembly of the Council of Europe, 3 I.L.M. (1964), p. 133 *et seq.*, and M. J. van Emde Boas, 1 *Common Market Law Review* (1963–64), p. 265 *et seq.*

The first O.E.C.D. draft will be subsequently referred to as *Draft Convention 1962*.

associated itself with this draft and authorised it for publication.[5] In doing so, the Council invoked in the first place the provisions of the O.E.C.D. Convention, charging the Organisation with duties to promote economic expansion and assistance to developing countries.[6]

1—Objects

In the Resolution of October 12, 1967, the O.E.C.D. Council observed that the Draft Convention embodied "recognised principles relating to the protection of foreign property" and rules designed to "render more effective the application of these principles." It further considered that a "clear statement" of these principles would be a valuable contribution towards the strengthening of international economic co-operation "on a basis of international law and mutual confidence," and that a wider application of these principles in domestic legislation and international agreements would encourage foreign investments. Finally, it was pointed out that the Draft Convention would be a useful document in the preparation of other agreements on the protection of foreign property.

The Council used the opportunity of this Resolution to reaffirm the adherence of the member States of O.E.C.D. to the "principles of international law embodied in the Draft Convention" and commended the text as a basis for further extending and rendering more effective the application of these principles.[7]

In the Preamble of the Draft Convention, the objects outlined in the Council Resolution are more concretely related to that of promoting the flow of capital for "economic activity and development."[8] In addition, the future parties to the Convention are made to express the desire that "other States will join them in this endeavour by acceding to this Convention."[9]

No hint is given in the Draft Convention or the Commentary of the identity of the signatories-to-be. Nor is any information vouchsafed on the States eligible to become acceding States. Article 14 which is supposed to cover the subject is left blank.[10] In view of the political difficulties arising from the only partial recognition of some States and rival governments in others, it was probably considered prudent to leave these issues to a future diplomatic conference, concerned with the task of drafting the final text.

[5] No. 23081, p. 5.
The second O.E.C.D. draft will be subsequently referred to as *Draft Convention 1967*.

[6] See the Preamble and Articles 1–2 of the O.E.C.D. Convention (Cmnd. 1257 (1960), pp. 3–4).

[7] *Loc. cit.* above, note 5 (1967), p. 5.

[8] Para. 2 of the Preamble (*ibid.*, p. 13).

[9] Para. 3 of the Preamble (*ibid.*, p. 13).

[10] *Ibid.*, p. 57.

2—The Status of the Commentaries

Before proceeding to a closer analysis of the 1967 Draft Convention, it is advisable to consider the authority of the commentaries attached to the 1962 and 1967 O.E.C.D. Draft Conventions.

In Paragraph Three of the Resolution of the O.E.C.D. Council of October 12, 1967, the text of the Draft Convention on the Protection of Foreign Property and the " Notes and Comments constituting its interpretation " together are comprised in the definition provided in the Resolution of the words " Draft Convention." [11] Thus, it is possible to argue that when the Council reaffirmed the adherence of member States to the principles of international law embodied in the Draft Convention and in its other references to the Draft Convention,[12] it intended to include the Commentary in its endorsement of the Draft Convention.

The fact that, on a number of points, the 1967 Commentary has been reworded and passages from the 1962 Commentary have been deleted, further suggests that somebody has paid considerable attention to the drafting and redrafting of these Notes and Comments. It is not, however, stated anywhere whether the O.E.C.D. Committees concerned with the two drafts, the O.E.C.D. Secretariat or the Council accept responsibility for the Notes and Comments in their final version.

This matter is of some significance. Thus, for instance, in the Council Resolution of October 12, 1967, it is asserted that the Draft Convention embodies " recognised principles relating to the protection of foreign property." As in the Preamble to the Abs-Shawcross Convention,[13] the legal or metalegal character of these principles is left inarticulate. Yet, in the 1962 and 1967 Commentaries, one of these principles—the duty of a State to respect and protect the property of nationals of other States—emerges not only as a recognised rule of international customary law, which it is, but also as a " well-established general principle of international law," [14] which is perhaps overstating the case of one among a considerable number of rules of international law.[15]

A single discrepancy of such magnitude suffices to counsel caution. In analysing the Draft Convention, it will be necessary to watch whether the draftsmen of the Convention have fallen for the temptation of employing the less than frank technique of soft texts and hard commentaries, to be resurrected at a future date for the interpretation of these texts. However this may be, the status and significance of these Notes and Commentaries will have to be clarified at any diplomatic Conference concerned with the final scrutiny of this Draft Convention.

To facilitate comparison between the relevant Articles of the 1967 Draft Convention and the Abs-Shawcross Draft Convention, the system

11 *Ibid.*, p. 5.
12 See above, p. 154.
13 See above, p. 110.
14 *Loc. cit.* above, p. 153, note 4, p. 8, and p. 154, note 5, p. 14.
15 See, further, *Inductive Approach*, p. 72 *et seq.*

chosen in the analysis of the Abs-Shawcross Draft Convention [16] will be followed in this Chapter.

3—The Scope and Standards of Protection

In Article 1, the scope and standards of protection granted to foreign property are formulated as follows:

> " Each Party shall at all times ensure fair and equitable treatment to the property of the nationals of the other Parties. It shall accord with its territory the most constant protection and security to such property and shall not in any way impair the management, maintenance, use, enjoyment or disposal thereof by unreasonable or discriminatory measures. The fact that certain nationals of any State are accorded treatment more favourable than that provided for in this Convention shall not be regarded as discriminatory against nationals of a Party by reason only of the fact that such treatment is not accorded to the latter.
>
> The provisions of this Convention shall not affect the right of any Party to allow or prohibit the acquisition of property or the investment of capital within its territory by nationals of another Party."

(a) The Beneficiaries

As in the Abs-Shawcross Draft Convention,[17] the personal scope of protection is determined by the test of nationality, and nationals include both natural persons and companies.[18]

In the 1962 and 1967 Draft Conventions, companies are more narrowly defined than in the Abs-Shawcross Draft Convention.[19] They are limited to entities which, under the law of a Party, are recognised as legal persons or which have themselves, or through their members, the capacity to dispose of property or to institute legal proceedings.[20]

In the definition of companies in the Abs-Shawcross Draft Convention, companies in which nationals of a Party have directly or indirectly a controlling interest had formed a separate category.[21] In the O.E.C.D. Draft Convention, these equitable interests are mentioned only in the context of the definition of property.[22] In this respect, the 1962 and 1967 drafts conform more closely to the position under existing international customary law than the Abs-Shawcross Draft Convention.[23]

16 See above, p. 109 *et seq.*

17 See above, p. 112 *et seq.*

18 Article 9 (a) (*loc. cit.* above, p. 154, note 5, p. 45).

19 See above, p. 112 *et seq.*

20 Article 9 (b) (*loc. cit.* above, p. 154, note 5, p. 45).

21 See above, p. 112 *et seq.*

22 See above, p. 122 *et seq.*

23 See above, p. 27.

See also *ibid.*, p. 27 *et seq.*, on other points, also left unsettled in the 1962 and 1967 *Draft Conventions*, but discussed in the Commentaries (*loc. cit.* above, p. 153, note 4, p. 42 *et seq.*, and p. 154, note 5, p. 46 *et seq.*).

(b) Property

Again following the Abs-Shawcross Draft Convention,[24] property is defined widely as including " all property, rights and interests whether held directly or indirectly." [25] In the Commentaries, it is correctly pointed out that the term includes, but is not limited to, investments.[26] If used, as in the title of this book, the term " investments " is employed as *pars pro toto*.

It is further explained in the Commentaries that, to come within the provisions of the Draft Conventions, property must be *lawfully* acquired or invested by the foreign national or his predecessor in title.[27]

This means " lawful " by the standard of the municipal law of the country under whose law the property has been acquired or the investment has been made. In cases in which it is left to the State of a national to decide on the worthiness of such a claim to be taken up on the international level, a limitation of protected property to untainted property may be more readily taken for granted. If, however, as under the O.E.C.D. Draft Convention it is possible, in certain circumstances, for nationals to become auxiliary parties to arbitral proceedings,[28] the requisite standards of business ethics may call for more exact definition.

The question may arise in several typical situations. In some countries, for instance, bribery on all or most levels of government and administration may be customary or endemic. Thus, in the case of a national revival, a more puritan type of government may well consider it necessary to reopen proceedings regarding concessions granted or investments made in circumstances which it considers were and are contrary to public policy, *ordre public* or its national *jus cogens*.

It is possible to argue that it could be left with the tribunals provided in the Draft Convention to apply in appropriate cases the Equity maxim of " clean hands " or corresponding rules of estoppel under international procedural law.[29] Yet, this would leave the matter in a state of some uncertainty. It appears preferable to face the issue and add a suitably worded clause to the text of Article 9 (c) on the requirement of the *lawful* character of the property or investment concerned.

As in the Abs-Shawcross Draft Convention, a member of a company is " deemed " to have an interest in the property of the company.[30] It is,

24 See above, p. 114 *et seq.*
25 Article 9 (c) (*loc. cit.* above, p. 154, note 5, p. 45).
26 *Loc. cit.* above, p. 153, note 4, p. 43, and p. 154, note 5, p. 47.
27 *Loc. cit.* above, p. 153, note 4, pp. 8 and 43, and p. 154, note 5, pp. 14 and 47.
28 See above, p. 123 *et seq.*, and below, p. 165 *et seq.*
29 See, further, *Fundamental Principles*, p. 320 *et seq.*
30 See above, pp. 112 and 156.
In order to safeguard Spain's position on this point in the case against Belgium concerning the *Barcelona Traction, Light and Power Company* (*Merits*), pending before the International Court of Justice, the Spanish representative abstained from voting in favour of the O.E.C.D. Council Resolution of October 12, 1967 (see above, p. 153). For different reasons, which can only be surmised, Turkey also abstained.
See also *I.C.J. Reports 1964*, pp. 44–45, 48, 55 *et seq.* and 80 *et seq.*

however, expressly provided that, in two types of case, no claim shall be made under the Convention regarding such an interest:

(1) if the company is a *national of a Party other than* the Party which has taken the measures affecting the property of the company; or

(2) in the case of a company which is a *national of a Party by whose measures its property is affected*, if the interest of the member of the company does not arise out of and, at the time of such measures, does not represent either an investment made by him or his predecessor in title or an investment of compensation or damages paid under the Convention.[31]

In accordance with the *first* Proviso, the equitable exception from the rule of international customary law, limiting diplomatic protection by States to their own nationals, is restricted to cases in which the company concerned is a national of the State interfering with foreign property. Even so, the rule is extended beyond its present scope under international customary law.[32]

In accordance with the *second* Proviso, the equitable concession made by host States in Proviso 1 beyond existing international customary law is counterbalanced by considerations which limit it to cases of genuine investment of capital or compensation under the Convention.

The protection under the Convention covers property acquired before and after the date at which the Convention comes into force in relation to any Party. Yet, as distinct from other relevant rules of international customary law or general principles of law recognised by civilised nations, the Convention itself applies only to measures taken after the date mentioned above. The fact that such measures are based on legislative or administrative authority existing before this date is irrelevant.[33]

(c) The Standard of Equitable Treatment

The rule of fair and equitable treatment of foreign property, including the pleonasm criticised on an earlier occasion,[34] is almost literally borrowed from the Abs-Shawcross Draft Convention.[35] In the following sentence on constant protection and security to be granted to foreign property, the prohibition of the impairment of such property by unreasonable or discriminating measures is elaborated by the addition of maintenance and disposal of property to the forms of its unhampered enjoyment.[36]

In the formulation of Article I of the Abs-Shawcross Draft Convention it was merely implied that the Convention did not cover questions of

[31] *Loc. cit.* above, p. 154, note 5, p. 41.

[32] See above, p. 27, but, against this, Judge Wellington Koo's Separate Opinion in the case of the *Barcelona Traction, Light and Power Company* (*Preliminary Objections*), *I.C.J. Reports 1964*, p. 51, at p. 54 *et seq.*

[33] Article 12 (c) (*loc. cit.* above, p. 154, note 5, p. 49).

[34] See above, p. 116.

[35] See above, p. 114 *et seq.*

[36] See above, p. 156.

establishment. In Articles 1 (b) of both O.E.C.D. Draft Conventions, this is made explicit. It is expressly stated that the Convention leaves any Party free to allow or prohibit the acquisition of property or the investment of capital within its territory by nationals of another Party.[37]

It was one of the failings of the Abs-Shawcross Draft Convention that its authors did not try to distinguish between lawful and illegal forms of discrimination.[38] In the O.E.C.D. Draft Conventions, an attempt has been made to remedy this omission. Both in the 1962 and 1967 drafts, it is provided that the treatment of certain nationals of any State on a footing more favourable than that granted under the Conventions is not by itself discrimination in the meaning of these instruments.[39]

Exceptions from the application of the standard of equitable treatment under general international law, which do not require to be expressly stipulated, are of two kinds. Some, including the justification or excuse of non-performance of a treaty in the case of *vis major*,[40] follow from the *jus aequum* nexus of consensual engagements. Others are implied in economic and technical agreements at large, such as the reservation of freedom of action on grounds of national public policy.[41]

In an age in which the border lines between internal and international war, and between war and other armed conflicts, are becoming increasingly blurred,[42] it is advisable to provide expressly for such contingencies. In this respect, the formulation chosen in the 1967 Draft Convention compares favourably both with those of the Abs-Shawcross Draft Convention [43] and the O.E.C.D. Draft Convention of 1962.[44]

Under the 1967 draft, a Party may take measures in derogation of the Convention if it is " involved in war, hostilities or other grave national emergency due to force majeure or provoked by unforeseen circumstances or threatening its essential security interests." [45]

The Abs-Shawcross Convention also failed to allow for exceptions of international public policy under the complementary international quasi-orders of the Kellogg Pact and the Charter of the United Nations.[46] With the state of near-universality attained by the United Nations, this matter is less important now than it was in the past.[47] It is, however, preferable to have the point clearly settled. Thus, under the 1962 and 1967 Draft Conventions, a Party may also take measures in derogation of the Convention if such measures are " taken pursuant to decisions of the

[37] See above, p. 156.
On related conventions sponsored by the Council of Europe, see above, p. 58 *et seq.*
[38] See above, pp. 4 and 120.
[39] *Loc. cit.* above, p. 153, note 4, p. 7, and p. 154, note 5, p. 13. See also above, p. 156.
[40] See Vol. I, p. 641 *et seq.*
[41] See *Most-Favoured-Nation Standard*, p. 110.
[42] See, further, 21 C.L.P. (1968), p. 239 *et seq.*
[43] See above, p. 115.
[44] See *loc. cit.* above, p. 153, note 4, p. 29.
[45] See Article 6 (a) (*loc. cit.* above, p. 154, note 5, p. 33).
[46] See above, p. 115.
[47] See, further, *Inductive Approach*, p. 108 *et seq.*

Security Council of the United Nations or to recommendations of the Security Council or General Assembly of the United Nations relating to the maintenance or restoration of international peace and security." [48]

The most important issue remains, however, as open as it was in the Abs-Shawcross Draft Convention [49] and the 1962 O.E.C.D. Draft Convention: terms as wide as those employed in Article 1 and the exception clause of Article 6 (I) invite large-scale disagreement between individual Parties. Correspondingly, on the level of international adjudication, the settlement of such conflicts calls for the exercise of wider judicial discretion than the majority of "sovereign and equal" States are likely to accept.[50]

4—The Observance of Undertakings

For investors abroad, the undertaking given by Parties in Article II of the Abs-Shawcross Draft Convention to ensure the observance of *any* undertakings given in relation to foreign investments is probably the arch of the covenant.[51] This was to be the answer to the traumatic experience of an agreement armed with all the safeguards of the Anglo-Iranian oil concession of 1933 being promiscuously "musaddiked." [52]

If such an eventuality were to recur, a Party to the Abs-Shawcross Convention would no longer be able to assert successfully, as Iran had done before the International Court of Justice,[53] the difference between assurances given on the international and municipal levels. Moreover, in future, any alleged contravention of a pledge given to a national of another Party would enable that Party to invoke in its own right Article II of the Convention. The beauty of this formulation was that it would make unnecessary any prior exhaustion of local remedies by the national concerned.

With a minor reformulation—the replacement of the term "investments" by "property" [54]—this provision has been incorporated literally in Article 2 of the O.E.C.D. Draft Conventions of 1962 and 1967.

As Article 2 now stands, it is open to three major objections:

(1) It is one of the distinctive features of the O.E.C.D. Draft Convention of 1967 that, in relation to the settlement of disputes between Parties and nationals of other Parties, the rule of the need for the exhaustion of local remedies by such nationals has been reintroduced.[55] A corresponding reaffirmation in Article 2 of the rule in cases of alleged non-observance of undertakings given by a Party to a national of another Party would

[48] Article 6 (b) of the 1962 and 1967 Draft Conventions (*loc. cit.* above, p. 153, note 4, p. 29, and *loc. cit.* above, p. 154, note 4, p. 33).
[49] See above, p. 109 *et seq.*
[50] See above, p. 123 *et seq.*, and below, p. 165 *et seq.*
[51] See above, p. 116 *et seq.*
[52] See above, p. 66 *et seq.*
[53] See, further, above, p. 72 *et seq.*, and Vol. I, p. 147 *et seq.*
[54] *Loc. cit.* above, p. 153, note 4, p. 13, and above, p. 154, note 5, p. 19.
[55] See above, p. 116.

probably complete the process of the restoration of this, on balance, beneficial rule of international customary law.[56]

(2) In view of the apparently absolute character of the obligation imposed by Article 2 (Each Party shall at all times ensure . . .), a cross-reference in the text—or, at least, in some authentic form of preparatory material [57]—to the equitable defences for non-performance provided in Article 6 [58] appears desirable.

(3) Similarly, the relation between Article 2 and Article 3 (on the Taking of Property) calls for clarification.

Provided that the conditions of lawful expropriation under Article 3 are fulfilled,[59] this Article appears to cover any property of a national of another Party, including rights acquired under a public contract.[60]

It is uncertain whether this view is shared by the authors of the Notes and Comments [61] accompanying the O.E.C.D. Draft Convention of 1962 and 1967. The only reference there to relevant literature is to a lecture by Lord Shawcross on " The Problem of Foreign Investment in International Law " in which he very properly disclosed his " interest as Director of an International Oil Company." [62] In this lecture Lord Shawcross drew a sharp distinction, for purposes of expropriation, between public contracts and other property owned by foreign nationals. He did so on the ground that while, in the former case, the government itself had created the contractual rights, in the latter case the property rights of the foreign national had come into existence without any direct participation of the host government. Thus, in his view, such public contracts are immune from the normal right of expropriation.[63]

It is doubtful whether the dividing line can be drawn at the point Lord Shawcross considers desirable. It is more likely that the primary distinction must be drawn between public contracts which, according to the intention of the contracting parties, are subject to the law of the State party to it and others which are governed by the law of a third State, the general principles of law recognised by civilised nations or a regime of quasi-international law.[64] A secondary relevant distinction is whether the State party to such a contract has given specific undertakings regarding non-interference with

[56] See, further, above, pp. 23 and 117; Vol. I, p. 602 *et seq.*; Th. Haesler, *The Exhaustion of Local Remedies in the Case Law of International Courts and Tribunals* (1968), p. 150 *et seq.*, and C. F. Amerasinghe, 28 Z.A.Ö.R.V.R. (1968), p. 257 *et seq.*

[57] See above, p. 155.

[58] See above, p. 159.

[59] See above, p. 117, and below, p. 162.

[60] See, further, above, p. 5, and Vol. I, p. 146 *et seq.*

[61] See above, p. 155.

[62] Hague *Recueil*, Vol. 102 (1962), p. 339.

[63] *Ibid.*, pp. 352–353.

In the case of the *Serbian and Brazilian Loans* (1929), cited in the Commentaries on Article 2 (*loc. cit.* above, p. 153, note 4, p. 14, and p. 154, note 5, p. 20) as the only other authority, the chief issue of substance was not the right of the debtor States to modify the loan contracts, but the question whether the *French* Statute of August 5, 1914, was a case of *vis major* or created a relative impossibility of performance for Brazil and Yugoslavia. See, further, Vol. I, p. 540 *et seq.*

[64] See above, p. 5 *et seq.*

the contract which create an estoppel against any subsequent interference of a unilateral character with the contract.[65]

It is unnecessary to pursue this argument any further in this context. Yet, the doubts arising from this preliminary examination appear to suggest the need for a thorough re-examination of the relations between Articles 2 and 3 of the 1967 Draft Convention.

5—The Limits of Lawful Expropriation

Article 3 of the O.E.C.D. Draft Convention of 1967 deals with the core of the issue: the lawful taking of foreign property. If differs sufficiently from the corresponding Article III of the Abs-Shawcross Draft Convention [66] to deserve quotation in full:

> No Party shall take any measures depriving, directly or indirectly, of his property a national of another Party unless the following conditions are complied with:
>
> (i) The measures are taken in the public interest and under due process of law:
>
> (ii) The measures are not discriminatory; and
>
> (iii) The measures are accompanied by provision for the payment of just compensation. Such compensation shall represent the genuine value of the property affected, shall be paid without undue delay, and shall be transferable to the extent necessary to make it effective for the national entitled thereto.

(a) Public Interest

In contrast to the Abs-Shawcross Draft Convention, the existence of public interest as a traditional element of lawful expropriation has been restored in the texts of the O.E.C.D. Draft Conventions of 1962 and 1967.[67] For the reason given above,[68] this is to be welcomed.

(b) Protection against Indirect Deprivation of Property

Indirect deprivation of property is largely a matter of conjecture regarding undeclared motives. In the Commentaries, a number of illustrations of such " creeping nationalisation " are offered: excessive or arbitrary taxation; prohibition of dividend distribution, coupled with compulsory loans; imposition of administrators; prohibition of dismissal of staff and refusal of access to raw materials or of essential export or import licences.[69]

65 See above, pp. 6 and 116.

66 See above, p. 117.

67 *Loc. cit.* above, p. 153, note 4, p. 17, and p. 154, note 5, p. 23.

68 See above, p. 118.

69 *Loc. cit.* above, p. 153, note 4, p. 19, and p. 154, note 5, p. 25.

For illustrations from recent practice, see above, p. 90 *et seq.*, and, further, *Whiteman Digest*, Vol. 8, p. 980 *et seq.*

As in the Abs-Shawcross Draft Convention,[70] the ultimate arbiter on such matters under the O.E.C.D. Draft Convention would be the Chairman of the Arbitral Tribunal envisaged in the Convention.[71]

(c) Due Process of Law

For the reasons given in the Chapter on the Abs-Shawcross Draft Convention,[72] the meaning attached to the term " due process of law " should be clarified in an authoritative definition in the text of the Convention.[73]

This view is strengthened by the Commentaries attached to the Draft Conventions. In a circuitous way, they reintroduce the " principles of international law." [74] Thus, in fact, we are back again at the minimum standard regarding the protection of foreign property under international customary law which it is the object of Article 3 to codify. Since this standard embodies elements of the Rule of Law,[75] these requirements ought to be more clearly stated in the text of the Draft Convention than is conveyed by the term " due process of law."

(d) Absence of Discrimination

As mentioned earlier, the lack of distinction between justifiable and non-justifiable forms of discrimination was one of the objections against the prohibition of discriminatory measures under Article I of the Abs-Shawcross Draft Convention.[76] In relation to Article 1 of the O.E.C.D. Draft Conventions, this omission has been remedied by the addition of a qualifying clause: justifiable discrimination is limited to treatment more favourable than that provided for in the Draft Convention, and, for this reason alone, is not to be regarded as a prohibited form of discrimination.

This exception does not, however, apply to forms of discrimination prohibited in the Convention itself. In other words, the exception of Article 1 (a) does not apply to any discrimination in the taking of property which, otherwise, would be justifiable under Article 3. Any such discrimination would continue to constitute a breach of the Convention under Article 5.[77]

As explained in relation to the corresponding provision in the Abs-Shawcross Draft Convention, the prohibition of *all* forms of discrimination, as distinct from those of an arbitrary or unreasonable character, appears to go beyond the requirements of the minimum standard

[70] See above, p. 123 *et seq.*
[71] See below, p. 167.
[72] See above, p. 119.
[73] Article 9 (*loc. cit.* above, p. 154, note 5, p. 45).
[74] *Loc. cit.* above, p. 153, note 4, p. 20, and p. 154, note 5 above, p. 26.
[75] See, further, Vol. I, p. 200 *et seq.* and R. R. Wilson, *United States Commercial Treaties and International Law* (1960), p. 115.
[76] See above, p. 120.
[77] See below, p. 167.

of international customary law and the protection needed by foreign property.[78]

(e) The Sanctity of Undertakings

In the Abs-Shawcross Draft Convention, the general obligation under Article II to ensure the observance of any undertakings in relation to investments made by nationals of other Parties [79] was coupled with an absolute prohibition under Article III to take any measures of expropriation " contrary to undertakings given by that Party." [80]

In Article 3 of the O.E.C.D. Draft Convention of 1962, this prohibition was maintained. It is, however, deleted in the corresponding Article of the 1967 Draft.[81] In the 1967 Commentary, the story behind this deletion is covered with silence. There is, however, good reason to believe that the passage as it stood was not even acceptable to the government of the strongest capital-exporting State represented in the O.E.C.D. Council and considered by it as an unacceptable curtailment of its own right of eminent domain.[82]

(f) Compensation

The formulation of the compensation provision in the Abs-Shawcross Draft Convention represented merely a codification of the governing rule of international customary law on the subject.[83]

In the texts of the O.E.C.D. drafts of 1962 and 1967, the operative rule of international customary law is reformulated in ways which emphasise its character as *jus aequum*: The requirement of adequate provision, at or prior to the time of deprivation, for the prompt determination and payment of compensation is no longer expressly stated. Moreover, the requirement of effective compensation, that is, compensation in a freely transferable form, has been changed from a duty which can be objectively determined into one which varies according to the individual circumstances of the foreign national concerned. It applies to the extent necessary to make compensation effective for the national entitled to such compensation.

This limitation of the duty to pay effective compensation is equitable. For instance, in a case in which a foreign national or company is subject to the exchange regulations of a host State, it would be pointless first to oblige this State to make payment in a transferable form but permit the host State, under its foreign exchange legislation, to oblige the foreign national concerned to surrender the foreign currency or his permit to transfer national currency.[84]

[78] See above, p. 120, and, for a relevant illustration from post-1945 British nationalisation practice, above, p. 90.
[79] See above, p. 116.
[80] See above, p. 122.
[81] Compare the texts *loc. cit.* above, p. 153, note 4, p. 17, and *loc. cit.* above, p. 154, note 5, p. 23.
[82] See, further, Vol. I, p. 203, and E. D. Brown, 18 C.L.P. (1965), p. 169 *et seq.*
[83] See above, p. 122.
[84] See above, p. 11.

It is convenient to deal in this context with a " recommendation " on transfers, contained in Article 4. It reads as follows:

> " Each Party recognises, with respect to property in its territory owned by a national of another Party, the principle of the freedom of transfer of the current income from, and proceeds upon liquidation of, such property, to such national of a Party as is entitled to them. While this Recommendation does not contain any obligation in this respect, each Party will endeavour to grant the necessary authorisations for such transfers to the country of the residence of that national and in the currency thereof." [85]

The chief value of the Article is that it clarifies the compatibility of *bona fide* exchange restrictions with the duties of the Parties under the Convention.

It may be doubted whether the text of a Convention is the most suitable place for the recognition of a principle, which is followed by a denial of its legally binding character and the description of this pseudo-commitment as a mere recommendation. It would probably be preferable to relegate such a sub-legal rule to the more usual place of *voeux* in the Final Protocol of the diplomatic conference if and when this is to be held.

6—" Without Prejudice "

The provision of Article VI of the Abs-Shawcross Draft Convention, reserving more far-reaching rights of beneficiaries under other international treaties or municipal law,[86] has been reformulated and the reference to relevant rules of municipal law deleted.[87]

This deletion should not be interpreted as justifying any argument *a contrario*. In the interpretation of international conventions concluded in favour of nationals, it must always be presumed that Contracting Parties did not intend to detract from the rights they could claim in any case under the minimum standard of international customary law, and which their nationals could expect to enjoy automatically under the municipal law of the host State. The object of conventions of establishment, commerce and navigation is to clarify such rights and, if possible, improve on the position under international customary law and the existing municipal law of the host State.

Even so, the reference in the Abs-Shawcross Draft Convention to municipal law was helpful, and it is difficult to see why the words have been deleted. The Commentaries remain silent on the matter.

7—Disputes

In accordance with Article 7 of the O.E.C.D. Draft Convention of 1967,

[85] *Loc. cit.* above, p. 154, note 5, p. 29.
[86] See above, p. 123.
[87] *Loc. cit.* above, p. 154, note 5, p. 43.

"(a) Any dispute between Parties as to the interpretation or application of this Convention may be submitted by agreement between them either to an Arbitral Tribunal established in accordance with the provisions of the Annex to this Convention, which shall form an integral part thereof, or to any other international tribunal. If no agreement is reached for this purpose between the Parties within a period of sixty days from the date on which written notice of intention to institute proceedings is given, it is hereby agreed that an Arbitral Tribunal established in accordance with that Annex shall have jurisdiction.

(b) A national of a Party claiming that he has been injured by measures in breach of this Convention may, without prejudice to any right or obligation he may have to resort to another tribunal, national or international, institute proceedings against any other Party responsible for such measures before the Arbitral Tribunal referred to in paragraph (a), provided that:

(i) the Party against which the claim is made has accepted the jurisdiction of that Arbitral Tribunal by a declaration which covers that claim; and

(ii) the Party of which he is a national has indicated that it will not institute proceedings under paragraph (a) or, within six months of receiving a written request from its national for the institution of such proceedings, has not instituted them.

(c) The declaration referred to in paragraph (b) (i), whether general or particular, may be made or revoked at any time. In respect of claims arising out of or in connection with rights acquired during the period of the validity of such declaration, it shall continue to apply for a period of five years after its revocation.

(d) At any time after the expiry of the period of six months referred to in paragraph (b) (ii), the Party concerned may institute proceedings in accordance with paragraph (a). In this case proceedings instituted in accordance with paragraph (b) shall be suspended until the proceedings instituted in accordance with paragraph (a) are terminated." [88]

(a) Scope and Character of the Arbitral Jurisdiction

Article 7 differs from the corresponding Article of the Abs-Shawcross Draft Convention [89] in two major respects:

(1) elimination of the residuary jurisdiction of the International Court of Justice in disputes on the interpretation and application of the Convention and substitution for this purpose of an arbitral tribunal established in accordance with the Annex to the Convention [90];

[88] *Loc. cit.* above, p. 154, note 5, pp. 37–38.
[89] See above, p. 123 *et seq.*
[90] See below, under (b).

(2) restoration of the rule of prior exhaustion of local remedies [91] and greater emphasis on the auxiliary character of the optional adjudication of justiciable disputes between a host State and nationals of other Parties.

(b) Constitution of the Arbitral Tribunal

By and large, the constitution of the Arbitral Tribunal provided for in the Annex to the O.E.C.D. Draft Convention of 1967 follows the pattern laid down in the Abs-Shawcross Draft Convention.[92]

It is to be welcomed that, on a number of procedural points, especially for the protection of host States against frivolous claims by nationals of other Parties,[93] the inherent powers of any international judicial organs are articulately specified.[94]

8—Breaches of the Convention

In Article 5 of the O.E.C.D. Draft Convention of 1967, it is provided that "any breach of this Convention shall entail the obligation of the Party responsible therefor to make full reparation." [95]

A comparison with Articles IV and VIII of the Abs-Shawcross Draft Convention [96] and Article 5 of the O.E.C.D. Draft Convention of 1962 [97] shows how far the draftsmen of the 1967 text have gone to meet the criticism of earlier drafts.

These strictures were not directed against the codification of the duty of a Party to any treaty under international customary law to make full reparation for its breach in the same way as for the commission of any other international tort.[98] They had as their targets attempts to pass highly controversial proposals *de lege ferenda* as propositions *de lege lata* [99] and against a rather open-ended provision on the enforcement of awards under the Abs-Shawcross Draft Convention.[100]

In the O.E.C.D. Draft Convention of 1962, the Article in the Abs-Shawcross Draft Convention on the enforcement of awards had vanished, but a milder section on "regard" for the "principle" of non-recognition of measures contrary to the Convention had survived the other purges of the Abs-Shawcross Draft Convention. According to Article 5 (b) of the draft Article, as it stood in 1962, "each Party shall have regard to the principle that any measures taken by any State, whether or not a Party to this Convention, which are in conflict with the provisions of Article 2 or 3

91 See above, p. 117.
92 See above, p. 123 *et seq.*
93 See above, p. 124.
94 See, further, Article 6 of the Annex (*loc. cit.* above, p. 154, note 5, pp. 59–60).
95 *Ibid.*, p. 31.
96 See above, p. 126.
97 *Loc. cit.* above, p. 153, note 4, p. 25.
98 See above, p. 126.
99 See above, p. 127 *et seq.*
100 See above, p. 131 *et seq.*

thereof should not be recognised within the territory of that Party as valid." [101]

In the 1967 Draft Convention, apparently also on United States initiative,[102] the whole Section was deleted. All that remained was a cryptic and innocuous note in the 1967 Commentary that "questions concerning recognition by a Party of measures contrary to the provisions of the Convention shall be determined in accordance with such principles of international law as may apply." [103]

9—Termination

In the Abs-Shawcross Draft Convention the question of withdrawal from the Convention was left open.

Under Article 13 of the two O.E.C.D. Draft Conventions,[104] a Party may terminate the Convention in relation to itself or any dependent territory to which it has extended the application of the Convention under Article 11, by notification to a depositary organisation or government yet to be determined.

In principle, the termination takes effect one year after the receipt of such notification. Yet, in respect of property acquired or investments made before the date on which the termination takes effect, the provisions of Articles 1 to 12 of the Convention are to continue to apply for a further period of fifteen years from that date.

10—Evaluation

Comparisons between the Abs-Shawcross Draft Convention and the O.E.C.D. Draft Conventions of 1962 and 1967 indicate the change in climate during the last decade and the decreasing self-confidence of the private and official quarters concerned with safeguarding capital exports.

The contents of the substantive rules involved are the least of the problems raised by the drafting of such multilateral conventions. The real difficulties arise over getting beyond the point of conflicting auto-interpretations in the case of concrete disputes and over the enforcement of agreed rules or awards under such conventions.

The gradual retreat of the vested interests concerned from their initial positions and the restraining influence exercised on them by their own and other governments of capital-exporting States have reduced these draft

[101] *Loc. cit.* above, p. 153, note 4, p. 25.
[102] See above, p. 164.
[103] *Loc. cit.* above, p. 154, note 5, p. 32.
See also the Commentary on this point in the 1962 Draft Convention (*loc. cit.* above, p. 153, note 4, p. 27).
[104] *Loc. cit.* above, p. 153, note 4, p. 51, and *loc. cit.* above, p. 154, note 5, p. 55.

Conventions to their bare minimum or as, with some justice may be argued, below this point.

Even so, two questions remain wide open. First, will any but the least significant among the capital-importing countries find it politically feasible—or necessary—to become parties to such conventions? Secondly, if any of them did, would it make much difference for the protection of investments made on such terms?

CHAPTER 11

AN INTERNATIONAL INVESTMENT INSURANCE AGENCY?

EXPERIENCE has proved that capital-importing States are hardly less reluctant to become parties to multilateral treaties than to bilateral conventions on the protection of foreign investments.[1] Similarly, capital-importing States which are parties to the I.B.R.D. Convention on the Settlement of Investment Disputes tend to accept merely the bare minimum of obligations.[2] This state of affairs must leave any prudent investor wondering whether it is worth his while to invest in countries which are so hesitant to subscribe to even liberally framed international conventions on the subject.

On the national level, the United States of America, followed by Japan, Germany and other European capital-exporting States, decided to experiment with another approach to the problem: insurance against typical non-commercial risks run by investors abroad.[3] Realisation of the wastefulness of the multiplication of the administrative costs of such unilateral efforts and the attractiveness of solutions based on wide participation by other capital-exporting and capital-importing States inspired a number of projects for an international investment insurance agency.[4] Such an international agency may be envisaged as an alternative to, or a complement of, the multilateral conventions discussed in the preceding Chapters.

The latest of these schemes is the Draft of November 30, 1966, on the Articles of Agreement of the International Investment Insurance Agency, prepared by the staff of the International Bank for Reconstruction and Development. So far, this document is in the preliminary phase of circulation for purposes of comments by the member States of the International Bank and organisations with consultative status in relation to the Bank.[5]

1 See above, pp. 109 and 153 *et seq.*

2 See above, p. 135 *et seq.*

3 See, further, below, p. 173 *et seq.*; the Staff Report of the International Bank for Reconstruction and Development on *Multilateral Investment Insurance* (1962), p. 24 *et seq.*; A. A. Fatouros, *Government Guarantees to Foreign Investors* (1962); W. C. Brewer, 58 A.J.I.L. (1964), p. 62 *et seq.*; Lillich (1965), p. 147 *et seq.*; H. Aufricht in J. G. Starke (ed.), *The Protection and Encouragement of Private Foreign Investment* (1966), p. 23 *et seq.*; *Whiteman Digest*, Vol. 8, p. 1130 *et seq.*, and, on United Kingdom practice regarding the insurance of export credits, C. Schmitthoff, *The Export Trade* (1962), p. 235 *et seq.*

For illustrations, see the Investment Guarantee Agreement of October 15, 1964, between Germany and India, 4 I.L.M. (1965), p. 491 *et seq.*, and the Investment Guarantee Agreement of February 6, 1965, between Brazil and the United States of America, 4 *ibid.*, p. 296 *et seq.*

4 See, further, the I.B.R.D. Staff Report of 1962, *loc. cit.* above, note 3, p. 30 *et seq.*

5 For comments on the Draft Articles by the International Chamber of Commerce, see the (unclassified) document of the Economic and Social Council of May 2, 1967 (U.N.Doc. E/C.2/653).

See also the I.B.R.D. Reports on the status of I.B.R.D. studies on multilateral

(*ctd. overleaf*)

Until this Draft has matured into a formal draft convention, it is advisable to concentrate on the wider issues raised by such proposals for multilateral investment insurance: membership of the agency; organisation; insurance operations; financial aspects; sanctions in case of default of obligations under the convention and provisions for the settlement of disputes.

1—Membership

Three possible variants in the membership structure of an international insurance agency appear to be especially pertinent: limitation of membership to capital-exporting or capital-importing States and membership extending to capital-exporting and capital-importing States.

The first variant would imply acceptance of an assumption which cannot be lightly made. It is that capital-exporting States have a greater interest than capital-importing States in the encouragement of private investments in capital-importing States. If this were so, it might be preferable to forgo this type of foreign investment. As capital is always a scarce commodity, it is probably cheaper and safer to invest it on less favourable terms in other capital-exporting States or, even, leave it unemployed rather than chase chimeras of high yields which are most likely to lead to disappointment regarding capital and profits.

Reflections on these lines appear to recommend the second type of agency. Let capital-importing States exert themselves by providing such an international self-help service and make investments in their countries more attractive to foreign investors. Another attraction of this pattern would be that it would assist in increasing the self-respect of countries suffering from the inevitable psychological and moral drawbacks of being indefinitely recipients of unrequited gifts and soft loans.

In the abstract, probably more is to be said for the second variant than for either of the others. Yet, most capital-importing States find it difficult even to maintain the state of development they have reached.[6] Thus, they may well argue that they lack the necessary capital for any further effort and the manpower for running by themselves such an international insurance agency.

What is certain is that the Bretton Woods type of membership structure—membership of capital-exporting *and* capital-importing States—offers the line of least psychological resistance.

In proposals for an international investment insurance agency, in which capital-exporting countries are envisaged as being responsible for the whole

(*Note 5 ctd.*)
investment guarantees (September 20, 1965 (UNCTAD, TD/B/55—TD/B/C.3/17) and July 27, 1966 (TD/B/98)).

On the O.E.C.D. Report of June 18, 1965, on the Establishment of a Multilateral Investment Guarantee Corporation, see *ibid.*, UNCTAD, TD/B/55, TD/B/C.3/17, p. 7 *et seq.*

6 See, further, below, pp. 179 and 185 *et seq.*

of the Agency's aggregate of insurance,[7] these countries are also described as sponsor countries, and capital-importing countries as host countries.

Some countries may be exclusively or predominantly in the one or the other camp. If one category of members of the contemplated Agency were to assume greater burdens than the other, the distinction between these two types of members would become as material as it is in the International Development Association.[8] Yet, a number of capital-importing countries are also capital-exporting countries. Thus, it would be advisable to avoid undue rigidity and, subject to suitable safeguards, allow any member State to change over from the one category to the other or, as the case requires, act as a sponsor or host country. Admittedly, any such flexible scheme would complicate loss-sharing arrangements, which are limited to one or the other category of members or affect the two categories differently.[9]

If the Agency were to become associated with the Bretton Woods institutions, this would not necessarily mean that, from the outset, it would have to operate on a universalist scale. It might be possible to subdivide the areas of the Agency's activity on a regional basis and start with one or more regions where, at least comparatively, the moral risks, which have to be considered in any type of insurance, are lower than in other parts of the world.

2—Organisation

If, as is most likely, the contemplated Agency is to come into existence under the aegis of the International Bank for Reconstruction and Development, its constitution might appropriately be modelled on the two youngest and smallest of the Bretton Woods institutions: the International Development Association[10] and the International Centre for Settlement of Investment Disputes.[11]

At the most, such an Agency appears to require three organs: a members' meeting (suitably misdescribed as a Board of Governors or Council), an executive committee (enhanced in status by being termed Board of Directors) and a Secretary-General (elevated, if necessary, to the rank of Managing Director) in charge of the rest of the Agency's staff.

What matters more is the representation of the member States in the actual decision-making body. If the Agency were to be financed primarily by the capital-exporting States, it would be in accordance with the Bretton Woods pattern that these States should have a majority on the executive organ, and the capital-importing States be limited to a substantial minority.

[7] This would be the total of the aggregates of insurance sponsored by all sponsor States.
[8] See Articles of Agreement of I.D.A., Schedule A (Cmnd. 1244 (1961), p. 19). See also above, p. 16.
[9] See below, p. 177 *et seq.*
[10] *Loc. cit.* above, note 8.
[11] Cmnd. 2745 (1965). See also above, p. 138 *et seq.*

It would be reasonable to expect that, in determining the representation of capital-exporting States in the executive committee, the percentage which any such State would contribute to the Agency's aggregate of insurance [12] should be taken into account.

Once the members' meeting has elected the executive committee by separate electorates with weighted votes, it would be safe, in all routine matters, to follow the usual Bretton Woods procedure of one vote for each member and decision by simple majority in all the organs of the Agency. On matters as important as the suspension of a member in default,[13] the approval of agreements for the settlement of accounts with a member who has decided to withdraw from the Agency, the cessation of operation and liquidation of the Agency and the amendment of its constitution, qualified majorities or even unanimity—as for any suggested modification of the right of withdrawal from the Agency—appear appropriate.

As in the cases of the International Finance Corporation, the International Development Association and the International Centre for Settlement of Investment Disputes, the President of the International Bank for Reconstruction and Development is likely to be *ex officio* Chairman of the executive body, but without a vote or with merely a casting vote.

3—Insurance Operations

The two major issues under this head are the scope of protection granted to insured investments and the types of investment eligible for insurance.

(a) The Scope of Protection

Ultimately, any decision on the optimal scope of protection to be granted to foreign investments is based on a series of metalegal assumptions. They range from views held on the future of most capital-importing States, threatened as they are with population explosions, internal ethnical strife, endemic corruption and political instability,[14] to opinions on a more effective organisation of relations between capital-exporting States, co-existence with the Communist sector of the world and the feasibility of a world order under law.

Any scheme of insurance to protect investors abroad against all the risks they are likely to run in capital-importing States would be prohibitive. Wide agreement exists that ordinary commercial risks should not be insurable by the Agency. Similarly, there is strong pressure to exclude risks insurable privately or under national schemes for export and export credit insurance.

Leaving aside the less calculable non-commercial risks run by investors in capital-importing States, four typical non-commercial risks remain:

12 See above, p. 172, note 7.
13 See below, p. 178.
14 See, further, below, p. 185 *et seq.*, and *Power Politics*, p. 488 *et seq.*

(1) the outbreak of international and internal armed conflicts;
(2) the introduction of exchange regulations, limiting or excluding the transfer of capital and income abroad;
(3) devaluation and depreciation of the currency of the host State, possibly coupled with measures declaring invalid gold-value clauses or provisions creating duties of repayment of the capital and interests in freely convertible currencies;
(4) acts of open confiscation and creeping nationalisation in breach of international customary law or engagements entered into by the host State, including undertakings to submit investment disputes to arbitration.

The inclusion of any of these risks in a multilateral international insurance scheme is open to objections.

In relation to the *first* category, it has been justly argued that international and internal armed conflicts are not the monopoly of capital-importing States. Yet, at least in so far as internal armed conflicts are concerned, capital-importing States appear to show a greater proneness to such calamity risks, as they have also been called.

The risks in the *second* and *third* categories are closely linked with the weakness of the monetary international quasi-order of the International Monetary Fund. It is arguable that the encouragement of capital exports should be limited to countries which are willing to participate in a drastically overhauled international monetary system.

As this event may yet be far off, a consensus appears to be emerging to include the transfer risks mentioned under (2), but to exclude, on sometimes contradictory grounds, the devaluation risks enumerated under (3).

General agreement exists that the nationalisation risks summarised under (4) are the core of insurable risks in the minds of the sponsors of multilateral investment insurance.[15]

(b) Eligible Investments

For purposes of insurance, it is advisable to distinguish more strictly than is otherwise done in this book between foreign property and investments and to treat property as the wider term, including but not limited to investments.[16]

Whether an investment is made in monetary or non-monetary form is immaterial for purposes of insurance. It is, however, advisable to exclude from insurable investments short-term foreign loans and short-term suppliers' credits. It is a matter for discussion what is to be understood

[15] See, further, the I.B.R.D. Staff Report of 1962, *loc. cit.* above, p. 170, note 3, p. 6 *et seq.*

On types of insurance available under national insurance schemes, see also Sections 87 and 88 of the ECOSOC Report of March 6, 1967 (E/4293).

[16] See above, pp. 17 and 114.

by "short-term." [17] It has also been suggested that securities issued or guaranteed by governments, but not necessarily securities issued or guaranteed by government-owned enterprises, should be excluded.

Further questions which will require settlement in the convention are whether insurable investments should include public investments or be limited to those of a private character, and whether the coverage should extend to existing investments or be restricted to new investments, that is, investments made after the convention comes into force or the Agency begins its operations.

In the latter case it would be possible to canalise investments by making eligible only certain types of new investments. For instance, investments in this category could be restricted to those of a "developmental" character. It would also be possible to give to the States concerned a direct influence on the size and object of such investments. This could be done, for example, by treating as insurable only investments sponsored by a member State in the category of capital-exporting States and approved by a member State in the category of host State.

If eligible investments are restricted to developmental capital exports, a suggestion made by the International Chamber of Commerce deserves consideration. It is that, to an amount corresponding to the input of new resources eligible for insurance coverage, existing investments should be included in the permissible coverage. A relaxation of the "new investments" rule would also be advisable for the additional reason that when new resources have been added to previously made investments, it is difficult to distinguish any longer between the two types of investment.[18]

On the assumption that capital-importing States were exempted from any loss-sharing arrangement,[19] both the inclusion and exclusion of existing investments might equally tempt capital-importing States to do the very thing against which insurance is intended to protect foreign investors.

If old investments are included in the insurance, a temptation exists to interfere with such property and refer the owner to his sponsor State. Admittedly, the same argument may also apply to new investments. Yet, those who advocate the distinction do not only argue that the inclusion of old investments would impose intolerable burdens on the sponsor States or the investors, but also that, in the eyes of capital-importing States, new investments are less tarred by the ex-imperialist and ex-colonialist brush, because they are freely negotiated by "sovereign and equal" host States or, at least, are made with their blessing.

If old investments are ineligible for insurance, the distinction operates against them hardly less than if they are included in the insurance scheme. By being declared ineligible for insurance coverage, their status may appear to have been devalued and they may become more easily than before the object of depredation by less than scrupulous host States.

[17] See above, p. 17.
[18] See, further, below, p. 179 *et seq.*, and *loc. cit.* above, p. 170, note 5 (1967), p. 2.
[19] See below, p. 177 *et seq.*

To some extent, it may be possible to counteract these dangers by linking participation in multilateral conventions for the protection of foreign property [20] and the settlement of investment disputes [21] with eligibility of potential host States as members of the Agency [22] or with preferential premiums available for investments in countries which are parties to such conventions.[23]

Finally, the problem of multinational investments calls for examination. It appears sensible that so long as the home States of the nationals concerned do not object, a State should be able to sponsor projects in which the nationals of other States participate. All that is needed to achieve this object is to provide for due notice to be given of the contemplated sponsorship by the sponsor State or the Agency to the home States concerned.

A reservation has to be made regarding flight capital. Under the cover of multinational investments, such capital might be repatriated to host States in circumstances in which an investor attempted to secure in this way international protection against his own home State. Host States may welcome or wish to guard against such a contingency.

4—Financial Aspects

Contributions by member States, premiums, the use of profits and liability for losses call for consideration.

(a) Contributions by Member States

Proposals on the sources of initial payments to provide the Agency with a working capital and funds for its administrative expenses, and on the Agency's authorised capital, vary widely.[24]

If the Agency is to be established within the Bretton Woods framework, capital-importing States are likely to be exempted from participation in initial payments and calls for administrative expenses. While this may be a realistic Bretton Woods policy, good reasons—even from the point of view of such potential host States—can be advanced against what may be an embarrassing discrimination in their favour.[25] Yet, the general atmosphere prevailing in the Bretton Woods institutions appears to be that, for the relatively paltry amounts involved,[26] it would be hardly worth while to risk impairing the good working relations existing in these institutions between capital-exporting and capital-importing States.

20 See above, p. 153 *et seq.*
21 See above, p. 135 *et seq.*
22 See above, p. 171 *et seq.*
23 See below, p. 177.
24 See, further, the I.B.R.D. Staff Report of 1962, *loc. cit.* above, p. 170, note 3, pp. 34–35.
25 See above, p. 171, and below, pp. 177 and 180.
26 The more realistic figures for the initial capital contributions by each member in gold or convertible currencies vary between $750,000 and $1,500,000.

(b) Premiums

Three chief patterns are available: premiums should be paid—exclusively or jointly and, in this case, perhaps in varying proportions—by the sponsor State, the investor or the host State.

The exclusive payment of premiums by the sponsor State or investor would perhaps indicate an excessive interest of capital-exporting States and their nationals in investments in capital-importing States. Moreover, in most of the insurable contingencies,[27] the host State is in a better position than the sponsor State or investor to prevent the occurrence of the risks insured.

In fixing premiums, the Agency ought to have the necessary discretionary powers to bear in mind a number of relevant considerations: the need to earn enough to meet its own administrative expenses and accumulate appropriate reserves, and the possibility of differential premiums according to the character of the risk insured and the probability of the risk materialising in any particular host country.

(c) Profits

At least in theory, provision will have to be made regarding the use of profits. They could be employed, for instance, to pay interest or make amortisation payments to capital-contributing members, create or strengthen reserve funds, reduce premiums or extend the scope of protection under insurance policies.

(d) Liability for Losses

The basic issue is whether all members should take part in loss-sharing arrangements or whether, for this purpose, different categories of members should be created.

If the Agency is to be associated with the Bretton Woods organisations, considerations similar to those discussed in relation to initial capital payments[28] are likely to be pressed to exempt host States collectively and individually from even nominal liability. In this case, sponsor States might be made liable for all losses *pro rata* to their capital contributions, or they could be held liable merely for losses suffered by individuals or corporations sponsored by them and refunded by the Agency.

If, in the case of payment made by the Agency to an investor, the Agency were subrogated for the investor in relation to the host State, and a firm duty were imposed on the Agency to proceed against the debtor in default, such a provision might reduce the ultimate liability of sponsor States.

However ingenious any loss-sharing arrangement limited to sponsor States may be, individually or collectively the sponsor States underwrite

[27] See above, p. 173.
[28] See above, p. 176.

a contingent—or not so contingent—further obligation of assistance to capital-importing States.

5—Sanctions

If financial liabilities are limited to sponsor States, a number of sanctions are available against a sponsor State in default: the suspension of payments for losses under insurances sponsored by the member State concerned, the suspension of the issue of new insurances to nationals of the defaulting member or the suspension of other membership rights. It has also been suggested that other Bretton Woods organisations might add their own forms of appropriate pressure.[29]

In all likelihood, more important than any formal sanctions in moulding the behaviour of member States will be the reluctance of sponsor and host States alike to jeopardise such reputation as they have in relation to the International Bank and the International Monetary Fund. This invisible sanction of the fear of international credit-unworthiness and loss of financial prestige is probably the Agency's most effective means of pressure.

6—The Settlement of Disputes

If the Agency were to become one of the Bretton Woods institutions, it would be likely that disputes on the interpretation and application of the constituting instrument between the Agency and member States and between member States would be settled on the distinctive pattern evolved for such purposes by these institutions.

The pattern has two characteristic features:

(1) in disputes between the institution concerned with or between active members, preference for a quasi-judicial rather than arbitral judicial, settlement of any disagreement by the Executive Directors, with a right of appeal by the member State concerned to the Board of Governors, that is, the members' meeting;

(2) in disputes between the institution and a member which has withdrawn or during the liquidation of the institution, arbitral settlement by a tribunal of three arbitrators, one appointed by the institution concerned, another by the member or former member State involved, and an umpire appointed, for instance, by the President of the International Court of Justice.[30]

[29] See the I.B.R.D. Staff Report of 1962, *loc. cit.* above, p. 170, note 3, pp. 36–37.
On the desirability of a provision imposing a positive duty on the Agency to take appropriate action against defaulting member States and host States which have caused losses under the Agency's policies, see *loc. cit.* above, p. 170, note 5.

[30] See, further, above, p. 144; Article XVIII of the I.M.F. Agreement (December 27, 1945—Cmd. 6885 (1946), p. 25); Article IX of the I.B.R.D. Agreement (December 27, 1945—*ibid.*, p. 51); Article VIII of the I.F.C. Agreement (May 25, 1955—Cmnd. 1377 (1961), p. 14) and Article X of the I.D.A. Agreement (January 29, 1960—Cmnd. 1244 (1961), p. 17) and I. Seidl-Hohenveldern in *Domke Symposium*, pp. 324–325.

Disputes between the Agency and investors, arising from contracts of insurance, are matters for international trade arbitration.[31] It would be advisable that, as is emphasised by the International Chamber of Commerce, whatever method for the scrutiny and settlement of claims made by investors is adopted, the Agency should avoid being judge and party in its own cause, and any provisional assessment of damages by the Agency should be subject to independent review.[32]

7—Evaluation

It is possible to take different views of the desirability and feasibility of the proposed International Investment Insurance Agency. The questions which such a project poses are not primarily legal or organisational: they are essentially political and psychological.

At this formative stage of the discussion, what matters most is to try to see the problem in a commensurate perspective. In this context, three metalegal doubts may be raised:

(1) The more national schemes of insurance come into operation during the present deliberative phase, especially if co-ordinated with well selected host States, the more difficult it will probably become to generate and maintain interest in the project in sponsor countries.

(2) A point made in an earlier staff paper of the International Bank for Reconstruction and Development deserves to be recalled. It was there persuasively suggested that such an agency might itself be a cause of misdirection of capital exports.

Investors might be attracted by countries which follow inflationist policies and, therefore, offer small immediate business risks and the expectation of high profits. The legitimate fears of a potential investor that, in the end, such policies will lead to the imposition or extension of exchange restrictions and ultimate devaluation may be overcompensated by the possibility of insurance against the risk of non-transferability of the profits earned in such overheated economies.[33]

(3) It is questionable whether, as widely expected, the establishment of such an agency would constitute a third ring in the protection of foreign investments, supplementing property-protection conventions on the lines of the O.E.C.D. Draft Convention of 1967 or the I.B.R.D. Convention on the Settlement of Investments Disputes. The very existence of this project may be construed as evidence of anxiety to find an alternative to ineffective insistence on compliance with the substantive rules of international law on the protection of foreign property. In particular, any distinction between old and new investments, unavoidable as it may be, may well increase

[31] See above, p. 135, note 4; Spofford, *ibid.*, p. 152 *et seq.* and, further, M. Domke (ed.), *International Trade Arbitration* (1958) and R. David and B. A. Wortley in *Domke Symposium*, pp. 56 and 348 *et seq.*

[32] *Loc. cit.* above, p. 170, note 5 (1967), p. 5.

[33] I.B.R.D. Staff Report of 1962, *loc. cit.* above, p. 170, note 3, p. 5.

this danger. It may be too clever by half to expect that this distinction will lead to the indirect extension of protection to old investments once these have become indistinguishable from new investments which, for instance, are granted for purposes of the modernisation and improvement of existing plants.

One unexpected development may create a new interest in capital-importing countries in an international investment insurance agency run predominantly or exclusively by themselves. Organisations on lines of the United Nations Conference on Trade and Development, the United Nations Industrial Development Organisation and the United Nations Capital Development Fund, as well as the rapidly growing spate of resolutions of the General Assembly of the United Nations on topics such as permanent sovereignty over national resources [34] appear to produce one overall effect: they tend to create a less than flattering image of the poor countries. It is some consolation that the more far-sighted among the leaders of these countries appear to become increasingly aware of the risks of such policies of aggressive self-pity.

The reaction to such policies in capital-exporting countries is almost predestined. Even for circles which, in the past, were in favour of non-discriminatory world trade or of exceptions on preferential terms for poor countries, another alternative becomes increasingly attractive. It is acceptance of the permanency of autarkist rather than socialist economies in countries such as the Soviet Union and China, resignation to the inward-looking character of the European Communities and their neo-imperialist hinterlands in south-east Europe and Africa, and wistful thinking on the potentialities of an Atlantic free trade area.

To counter such trends, what could be more impressive than an international investment agency run predominantly or exclusively by capital-importing States? For a change, it would be a poor man's international institution in which the operators do not exhaust themselves in the launching of verbose but meaningless resolutions or the production of blue-prints which are to be financed by the objects of persistent denigration,[35] but try to think about constructive contributions they themselves can make to attract capital to their countries.

Any such effort at collective self-criticism and self-help would be likely to take resigned or mildly irritated capital-exporting countries so much by surprise that they would give almost enthusiastic support in manpower and initial capital outlay to the up-bringing of the wonder child.

It would be a legitimate repartee to this suggestion that, in terms of the political and psychological realities of the "third world," [36] any such

[34] See below, p. 189, note 22.
[35] On UNCTAD, see also R. N. Gardner, 22 *International Organization* (1968), p. 99 *et seq.*, and S. Mihailovic, 19 *Review of International Affairs* (Belgrade), March 20, 1968, p. 5 *et seq.*
[36] See, further, *Power Politics*, p. 430 *et seq.*

proposal is unrealistic in the extreme. If this were so, the reasons for this state of affairs would be an accurate measure of the even more utopian expectation that, in such a climate, further export of private capital on any major scale to the majority of capital-importing States could be more than the worst type of gift—one unintended by the donor.

CONCLUSIONS

Chapter 12

CHOICES BEFORE INVESTORS

Creditors anxious to bolster up dubious claims and debtors unable or unwilling to settle their commitments are perennial phenomena on the domestic and international scenes. Even in the context of decolonisation and " new " States, it all happened before in the nineteenth century in the period following the liquidation of the Spanish and Portuguese colonial empires in Latin America.[1]

Latin American countries of the pre-1914 era protested as violently as any subsequent champions of non-intervention against debt collection by naval forces and marines. The joint naval intervention by Germany, Great Britain and Italy in Venezuela had all the features of what in those years came to be termed gunboat diplomacy.[2] Similarly, United States disapproval during this period of European strong-arm techniques in her own hegemonial hinterland has a familiar ring.[3]

These and other European interventions sparked off characteristic exercises in *ad hoc* international law to suit debtors in default. The Drago Doctrine and Calvo Clause offer splendid illustrations of such ideologies.[4] In the Porter Convention of 1907 a sensible compromise was reached on the subject of forcible debt collection. In principle, willingness to submit to the peaceful settlement of investment disputes and to carry out awards was accepted as a substitute for unilateral and forcible debt collection by the home State of the creditors concerned.[5]

A quantitative difference exists between the pre-1914 and post-1945 situations. Then, decolonisation was the exception to the rule, and vast colonial empires continued to span the globe. Moreover, more openly than today, even formally independent States were the objects of informal understandings on spheres of exclusive influence, exercised by one or more great Powers.

1 See, for instance, E. Borchard and W. H. Wynne, *State Insolvency and Foreign Bondholders* (1951), Vol. II, p. 3 *et seq.*, and, on corresponding issues arising from the grant of independence to Belgium, P. H. Laurent, 15 I.C.L.Q. (1966), p. 395 *et seq.*

2 See, further, Vol. II (1968), p. 40 *et seq.*; the *Venezuelan Preferential Claims* case (1904) (J. B. Scott, *The Hague Court Reports*, Vol. 1 (1916), p. 55 *et seq.*), and above, p. 24.

3 On the phenomenon of hegemonial intervention to the exclusion of intervention by States other than the hegemonial Power in a particular area, see, further, 10 C.L.P. (1957), p. 284 *et seq.*; 13 Y.B.W.A. (1958), p. 236 *et seq.*

4 See, further, L. M. Drago, 1 A.J.I.L. (1907) p. 692 *et seq.*, D. R. Shea, *The Calvo Clause* (1955), p. 14 *et seq.* and H. Accioly, Hague *Recueil*, Vol. 96 (1959), p. 427 *et seq.*

5 See Hague Convention II of 1907 on the Limitation of the Employment of Force for the Recovery of Contract Debts (J. B. Scott, *The Hague Conventions and Declarations of 1899 and 1907* (1915), p. 89 *et seq.*).

In the post-1919 period, the colonialist and imperialist system of the pre-1914 era began to decline and, in the post-1945 period, this process accelerated. The active participation of non-white armies in the defeat of the Central Powers, the Soviet Revolution of 1917, the growth of Western-educated middle classes in colonial and imperialist dependencies, and the spread around the world of the virus of Western nationalism, all played their part in completing the decolonisation of most of the remaining overseas empires.

The process of decolonisation led to a paralysing atomisation of power on a world scale, comparable to that in Europe during earlier phases of its evolution and known in the pre-1914 period as Balkanisation.[6] Yet, simultaneously power continued to concentrate in a decreasing number of States.

The international environment of investments abroad has become even more complicated by the peculiar way in which post-1945 world society is organised.[7] One of the by-products of this system of power politics in disguise is that, in bodies such as the General Assembly of the United Nations, the compact majority of States, most of which have yet to prove their power of survival in adverse circumstances, attempt to exercise an influence on the formulation of international policies which is somewhat disproportionate to their position as objects in the world power game. While organs such as the General Assembly of the United Nations lack law-making powers in the strict sense, there comes a point when, even in such bodies, ineffective opposition or abstention by minorities tends to be transformed into acquiescence.[8]

Moreover, in the Charter of the United Nations, the outlawry of force as an instrument of national policy has been carried further than provision for the indispensable concomitants of such a sublimation of force: corresponding advances in the fields of the pacific settlement of international disputes, collective security and disarmament. Thus, a situation has been created in which a small-Power law-breaker in the economic sphere may rely on his auto-interpretation, however outrageous, of his own international obligations and take refuge behind the Charter against any threat or use of armed force otherwise than in self-defence against armed attack.[9]

This is the situation in which public and private investors have to consider the advisability of investments abroad and the value of the various forms of protection available to them. Some of these patterns have been fully considered in previous Chapters. To round off the picture some others also call for discussion.

[6] See, further, *Power Politics*, p. 110 *et seq.* and 19 Y.B.W.A. (1965), p. 223 *et seq.*
[7] See, further, *Power Politics*, p. 249 *et seq.*
[8] See, for instance, R. Higgins, *The Development of International Law through the Political Organs of the United Nations* (1963); M. Virally, 9 *Annuaire français* (1963), p. 508 *et seq.* and, further, *Inductive Approach*, p. 108 *et seq.*
[9] See above, p. 26, the Resolutions of the General Assembly of the United Nations on Non-Intervention (Resolutions 2131 (XX) of December 21, 1965 and 2225 (XXI) of December 19, 1966), and, further, Vol. II (1968), p. 50 *et seq.*

This can conveniently be done in a survey of the eight chief patterns at the disposal of investors abroad: the classical pattern, the good-faith pattern, the good-conduct pattern, the conciliation and arbitration pattern, the guarantee and insurance pattern, the pattern of counter-nationalisation, the pattern of international institutional investment and the pattern of economic self-sufficiency or autarky.

1—The Classical Pattern

In the post-1945 period, the rules of international customary law were reaffirmed, with minor reformulations which do not affect them in substance.[10] The principal means employed to this end were bilateral treaties concluded by the United States and other capital-exporting States with a number of capital-importing countries.[11]

Further attempts made to underpin the governing rules of international customary law by basing them on equivalent general principles of law recognised by civilised nations and alleged rules of natural law[12] carried matters little further. Yet, they were symptomatic of a growing uneasiness in Western countries about the willingness of the new States to comply with existing international law and were soon answered by hardly more convincing counter-exercises in *ad hoc* international law.[13]

The real difficulty was that the efforts made in the post-1945 period by capital-exporting States to revitalise the classical pattern lacked credibility. If a country in a suitable geographical position turned communist—and, in the case of Cuba, this feat was successfully accomplished at the very doorstep of the United States—it could defy with impunity its foreign creditors and their home States.

In the worst case, Western creditor countries could be relied upon to agree to lump-sum settlements which reduced the debt burden incurred by previous regimes to fractions of the capital and accumulated interest of the foreign investments concerned.[14] Policies of vicarious appeasement, such as those adopted by the Anglo-Saxon Powers towards Netherlands investments in Indonesia and the wholesale expulsion of Netherlands citizens, further drove home another lesson: how easy it was to frighten Western

[10] See above, p. 7 *et seq.*

[11] See above, p. 32.

[12] For a critical discussion, see R. B. Schlesinger and H.-J. Gündisch, 28 Z.A.I.P.R. (1964), p. 4 *et seq.*, and W. Friedmann, *The Changing Structure of International Law* (1964), p. 78.

[13] For summaries of some of these positions, see I. Seidl-Hohenveldern, 7 A.J.C.L. (1958), p. 541 *et seq.*, S. P. Sinha, 14 I.C.L.Q. (1965), pp 128 and 130–131, P. D. Weinstein, 5 I.J.I.L. (1965), p. 113 *et seq.*, R. P. Anand, 15 I.C.L.Q. (1966), p. 63 *et seq.*, and S. D. Metzger, *Law of International Trade*, Vol. I (1967), p. 105 *et seq.*

In this context, see also D. Dölle and Others, *Internationale Betrachtungen zur Dekolonisierung* (1964), and, critically, 19 Y.B.W.A. (1965), p. 281, and I. Seidl-Hohenveldern, *Juristenzeitung* (1964), p. 489 *et seq.*

See also, R. Bystricky in M. K. Nawaz and Others, *The Legal Principles Governing Friendly Relations and Co-operation Among States* (1966), pp. 109–110.

[14] See above, p. 40 *et seq.*

Powers with the threat of alignment with Moscow or Peking and reassure them with vague promises regarding the safety of the investments of their own nationals. The wholesale confiscations of Anglo-French property in Egypt in the post-Suez period, followed by humiliating attempts of these Powers to salvage what they could from the fiasco of their half-hearted intervention policies, further contributed to undermine respect for foreign investments.[15]

In any case, what is the point in adopting firm attitudes towards potential or actual defaulters if, for political reasons, the same States qualify for "development" aid in the inter-bloc competitions for their favours? To raise this question does not necessarily imply a negative answer. It is possible to combine assistance to poor countries with insistence on respect for the classical pattern.

If a debtor State is unwilling to submit a claim to arbitration, a capital-exporting State remains free to submit such a claim to scrutiny by one or more persons of generally recognised authority and integrity, publish their findings and, on this quasi-judicial basis, reduce its contemplated aid to the defaulting State by a corresponding amount.[16] If a number of capital-exporting States were prepared to join in any such scheme, the effectiveness of such set-off policies would increase even further.

2—The Good-Faith Pattern

National investment codes, offering guarantees for the protection of foreign capital on the level of constitutional law and immunity from, or limitation of, taxation, have been promulgated with growing liberality to attract foreign investors. A potential investor may well wonder whether the willingness to pass such statutes tends to stand in inverse ratio to the credit-worthiness of the country concerned.

Actually, this pattern has a long pedigree in the history of International Economic Law. For a prolonged period, the word and honour of princes were the pledges on which foreign merchants had to rely, and they were as secure as the personalities and fortunes of such high and mighty lords. Similarly, the equation of investment codes with national constitutions conjures up memories of short-lived Latin American and Balkan constitutions of the pre-1914 period and corresponding Afro-Asian specimens of the post-1945 era.

If ever a concession agreement contained in a cumulative form all imaginable safeguards any capital-importing State can possibly offer, it was the Anglo-Iranian Oil Concession of 1933.[17] Yet, this did not save it from being torn up by the Iranian Government. It would be unduly sanguine to assume that, after Iranian oil sovereignty had been restored,

[15] See above, pp. 84 and 100 *et seq.*
[16] On the United States practice since 1955 of preadjudication in comparable cases and similar legislation in the United Kingdom, see above, pp. 43 and 56.
[17] See above, p. 73 *et seq.*

such unilateral action had become past history. To disabuse one's mind of any such illusion, it suffices to draw attention to the Award by the Sole Arbitrator in *Sapphire International Petroleums Ltd.* v. *National Iranian Oil Company* (1963).[18]

Even greater difficulties may arise in relation to joint ventures between territorial sovereigns and foreign investors. In the typical case, such companies are incorporated in capital-importing States and, increasingly, the holdings of the foreign nationals or companies involved are likely to be limited to minority interests.[19] Even on formal grounds, effective intervention of the home State of foreign shareholders becomes more difficult in the cases of such companies incorporated in their host States.[20]

Ultimately, reliance on the good-faith pattern is a question of confidence in the stability and promises of the particular capital-importing country involved and correct analysis of the long-range trends in the world's poor South.[21] In this context, it is worth reflecting on one aspect of the basic Resolution on Permanent Sovereignty over Natural Wealth and Resources, passed by the General Assembly of the United Nations.[22] It had to be expressly reaffirmed that foreign investment agreements, even if "freely entered into" by or between sovereign States, should be observed in good faith.

3—The Good-Conduct Pattern

Various attempts were made in the post-1945 period to re-establish some standards of good conduct regarding the treatment of foreign investments

[18] See above, p. 145, and, further, J. F. Lalive, 19 *Annuaire suisse* (1964), p. 273 *et seq.*, or 13 I.C.L.Q. (1964), p. 1002 *et seq.*, D. Suratgar, 3 *Columbia Journal of Transnational Law* (1964), p. 152 *et seq.* and *The Economist*, March 2, 1968, pp. 47–48.
See also above, p. 147, note 60.

[19] See, further, W. Friedmann and G. Kalmanoff, *Joint International Business Ventures* (1961), pp. 194, 219 and 281 *et seq.*, M. Kidron, *Foreign Investment in India* (1965) and U.N.Doc. E/4293 of March 6, 1967 (Sections 48–54, pp. 21–23); also above, p. 150.

[20] See, further, above, pp. 27 and 112.
It is significant that, under the Hickenlooper Amendment, section 620 (e) of the United States Foreign Assistance Act of 1961 (as amended), which enjoins the President of the United States in certain cases to suspend assistance under the Act, applies only against States which have illegally interfered with property owned by any United States citizen or by any "corporation, partnership, or association not less than 50 per cent. beneficially owned by United States citizens." See, further, A. Chayes in Southwestern Legal Foundation, *Rights and Duties of Private Investors Abroad* (1965), p. 347 *et seq.*, and Lillich (1965), p. 17 *et seq.*
For the difficulties that can arise if foreign capital has a majority shareholding in a pipeline, but, under municipal law, the operating company must have a majority of directors of the nationality of the territorial sovereign, see *The Times* (London), March 10 and 28, 1966.

[21] See above, p. 186, note 6, below, p. 198 (under 8) and, further, International Commission of Jurists, *The Dynamic Aspects of the Rule of Law in the Modern Age* (1965).
On the external debts of countries such as Ghana, Indonesia and the United Arab Republic, see above, pp. 50 and 90 *et seq.*
For an illustration of common investment policies of capital-importing States embodied in a multilateral convention, see the Central African Convention on Investments of December 14, 1965, 7 I.L.M. (1968), p. 221 *et seq.*

[22] 1803 (XVII)—December 14, 1962. See also Resolution 2158 (XXI)—November 25, 1966, and, for symptomatic studies, M. A. Mughrabi, *Permanent Sovereignty over Oil* (*ctd. overleaf*)

in capital-importing States. Actually, all the sponsors of such projects could hope to achieve was, in more circuitous ways, to attain the objectives of the classical pattern.[23]

A number of States, with the United States of America in the lead, attempted to revive the classical pattern on a bilateral basis.[24] In relation to a limited number of relatively stable capital-importing States, with which, on historical or other grounds, particular capital-exporting States have established or intend to establish especially close relations, this pattern may be all that is needed.

If the object is to commit the vast number of capital-importing countries, especially new States, to clear-cut rules of international law on a consensual basis, the multilateral approach to the problem is, on the surface, more rational and likely to lead to quicker results.

So far, experience has failed to bear out these expectations. It appears that capital-importing States as a group are more difficult to handle than a particular capital-importing State which is anxious to obtain its *quid pro quo*. Even when, as at the Havana Conference of 1947–48, the group of independent capital-importing States was yet considerably smaller than it is today, their opposition sufficed to produce a result that fell considerably short of the protection of foreign property under international customary law.[25]

In the Abs-Shawcross Draft Convention, the position was redressed with a vengeance. This stiffening of the rules was, however, attained at the price of leaving the resulting Draft Convention still-born.[26] Whether its muted version—the O.E.C.D. Draft Convention of 1967—will become acceptable to, at least, the few capital-importing States who are members of the Organisation remains to be seen.[27]

Actually, the lack of trade union spirit among potential capital-exporters is their own worst enemy. Far from forming a united capitalist

(*Note 22 ctd.*)
Resources (1966); V. I. Sapozhnikov, *Soviet Year-Book of International Law* (1964–1965), p. 93 *et seq.*, and G. Brehme, *Souveränität der jungen Nationalstaaten über Naturreichtümer* (1967).

The summary and conclusions of the United Nations Secretariat study on *Financing of Economic Development—Promotion of Private Foreign Investment in Developing Countries* of March 6, 1967 (E/4293) contain a significant passage: "Even in the field of natural resources extraction, where large amounts of capital must be invested over a long period of time, it would be hard to find many important concession agreements which, though originally concluded for twenty, thirty, fifty years or more, have remained without substantial change for as long as ten years" (p. 35).

See also above, pp. 59 and 137.

23 See above, p. 187 *et seq.*

24 See above, p. 32 *et seq.*

25 See Article 11 of the Havana Charter (not in force), March 24, 1948, Cmd. 7375 (1948), pp. 12–13, and above, p. 136.

On similarly vague references to the protection of foreign investments in the also abortive Economic Agreement of Bogota, May 2, 1948, see A. A. Fatouros, *Government Guarantees to Foreign Investors* (1962), pp. 72–73.

For a further exercise in saying little in many words in this field, see the General Assembly Resolution on the Encouragement of Private Investments in Underdeveloped Countries (824 (IX)—December 11, 1954).

26 See above, p. 109 *et seq.*

27 See above, p. 153 *et seq.*

front, private capital, ready to be lured by high yields, is abundant; would-be investors appear to be as credulous and uninformed as ever, and pragmatic considerations combine with ex-colonial guilt complexes in capital-exporting countries to encourage further the grant of semi-soft and soft private loans.

In these circumstances, it is hardly surprising that capital-importing countries should be reluctant to commit themselves to subscribe to any standards of conduct, good or otherwise, regarding the treatment of foreign investments.

4—The Conciliation and Arbitration Pattern

Clauses for the arbitral or judicial settlement of disputes under treaties of commerce, navigation and establishment have been standard practice since the pre-1914 period. They also found their way into some of the bilateral investment treaties of the post-1945 era.[28]

The automatic arbitration of investment disputes occupied an even more central place in the Abs-Shawcross Draft Convention[29] and was coupled with far-reaching rights for the unilateral enforcement of awards.[30] These features of the Draft Convention probably contributed as much as any to deter capital-importing States.

The purely optional character of the arbitration of investment disputes in the O.E.C.D. Draft Convention of 1967[31] may increase its chances of emerging from the limbo of abortive draft conventions. Yet, the fact that the absence of automatic arbitration of investment disputes should be a decisive reason for a more auspicious augury is indicative of the political and psychological limitations of the conciliation and arbitration pattern in an age of highly developed national sensitivity and sovereignty-consciousness.

Willingness to respect this attitude, prevalent among, but not limited to, capital-importing States, assured the success of the I.B.R.D. Convention on the Settlement of Investment Disputes. Yet, whether, in any actual dispute, a capital-importing State will accept the jurisdiction of a conciliation commission or arbitral tribunal under the Convention will ultimately depend on a quiet exercise in legal realism: how, in a conciliation or arbitral organ composed of three members, the president of the tribunal or third member is likely to vote.[32]

In any case in which the government of the capital-importing State concerned has any mental reservation about its future ability or willingness to live up to its undertakings, the third member's vote is predictable with

28 See above, pp. 38 and 135 *et seq.*
29 See above, p. 123 *et seq.*
30 See above, p. 126 *et seq.*
31 See above, p. 165 *et seq.*
32 See above, pp. 140 and 145.

reasonable certainty, and so is the unwillingness of any such capital-importing State to submit itself for purposes of any concrete case to the jurisdiction of the International Centre for Settlement of Investment Disputes.

5—The Guarantee and Insurance Pattern

In discussing the problems raised by proposals for an international investment insurance agency, doubts have been raised regarding an international institution of this type, which is to be financed exclusively or predominantly by capital-exporting States.[33]

These objections would apply to a lesser degree to an international agency run by the capital-importing States as an experiment in collective self-help,[34] or to national insurance schemes, run by individual capital-exporting States.[35]

In the former case, the electrifying effects of a serious attempt by the capital-importing States as a group to exert themselves in this way would appear to outweigh any arguments to the opposite effect. In the latter case, the capital-exporting States involved must be allowed to be the judges of their own national interest. In particular, the use of the guarantee or insurance pattern may suit them and their counterparts as a convenient cover for public aid. If such aid is dispensed behind the facade of private "enterprise," the guarantee and insurance pattern may offer a suitable camouflage for neo-imperialist ventures and constitutes a form of financial aid less compromising than any open subsidy to a precariously poised government at the other end of the financial chain.

Even in cases in which insurance schemes are intended to serve genuinely economic ends, they suffer from a major drawback. They tend to bring about the evil they are intended to avoid and demoralise debtors further than may otherwise be the case. They hold out a continuous temptation to hard-pressed governments of capital-importing States to default on their obligations, to advise the foreign nationals or companies affected to recoup themselves at home under their insurance policies and to sit back to argue out matters in due course with the governments of the investors concerned.

In the practice of some capital-exporting States, especially the United States of America—but only with the prior consent of the capital-importing State involved[36]—the State of the creditor becomes subrogated for the private creditor satisfied under the national insurance scheme. This device is also relevant for the next pattern to be examined.

[33] See above, p. 176 *et seq.*
[34] See above, pp. 171 and 180.
[35] See above, p. 170.
[36] See, further, the Staff Report of 1962 of the International Bank for Reconstruction and Development, *loc. cit.* above, p. 170, note 3, p. 8, and Lillich (1965), p. 73.

6—The Pattern of Counter-Nationalisation

The term "counter-nationalisation" is intended to convey the possibility of viewing both private and public investments abroad from their angle as national assets. This pattern involves the substitution of the home State as the creditor of loans or owner of property abroad by legislation or agreement with the nationals concerned.

This type of situation differs from that in assignments such as the Litvinov assignment to the United States Government of claims of the Soviet Union against United States citizens.[37] It comes closer to the assignment of claims to the government of private investors under investment guarantee agreements.[38] It differs from both these devices in that assignments for purposes of counter-nationalisation are more likely to be effective if they take place prior to and, perhaps, in anticipation of interference abroad with foreign property or loans than if such measures are taken after the event.

The function of the pattern of counter-nationalisation would be to provide an alternative to more traditional ways of securing the assets of nationals in a number of contingencies. It would make possible the protection of:

(1) rights which, before, during and immediately after independence, the governments of capital-importing States accepted as being free from imperialist or colonialist taints,[39] but which more sanguine successors of theirs decide to treat retrospectively in this light;

(2) rights which, owing to gradual deterioration in the political or economic equilibrium of a foreign country, tend to fade away;

(3) rights which can be conveniently protected by treating compensation due for their violation as charges on credits or loans promised under financial assistance agreements.[40]

The experiences in recent years of majority or controlling government holdings in foreign companies—the former Anglo-Iranian Oil Company[41] and the Suez Canal Company[42]—appear to suggest an, at most, limited usefulness of this pattern. Do they not imply that it makes little difference whether a government directly controls companies which give hostages to fortune by the fixed location of their assets or whether it takes up

[37] See, for instance, *United States* v. *Belmont*, 301 U.S. 324 (1936), and *United States* v. *Pink*, 315 U.S. 203 (1942), and, further, D. G. Bishop, *The Roosevelt-Litvinov Agreements* (1965), p. 140 *et seq.*

[38] See above, p. 192.

[39] See above, p. 16.

[40] On the advisability of such links, see, for instance, C. J. Olmstead and W. G. Brown, *A.S.I.L. Proceedings* 1964, p. 205 *et seq.* See also R. B. Lillich, 17 *Rutgers L.Rev.* (1963), p. 405 *et seq.*

On the suspension of assistance by the United States of America to Ceylon in 1963, see 2 I.L.M. (1963), p. 386 *et seq.*

[41] See above, p. 66 *et seq.*

[42] See above, p. 84 *et seq.*

diplomatically cases of investments which it has acquired through measures of counter-nationalisation?

It would probably be advisable to bear in mind conditioning factors in each of the two above-mentioned cases: the limitations imposed by the United States as the Western hegemonial Power on policies pursued by her junior partner or partners in relation to Iran and Egypt; the geographical position of Iran and Egypt which, as marginal States in world-frontier areas, were able effectively to manoeuvre between the world camps, and the justified expectation of the United States that, in Iran, any defeat suffered by the Anglo-Iranian Oil Company was likely to give long-sought chances there to United States oil interests.[43]

In such extreme cases it makes little difference how a middle Power proceeds in protecting its national assets abroad. In other cases, however, acceptance of the primacy of politics over economics,[44] increasingly stressed by non-aligned countries,[45] is likely to assist in decreasing the potency of the ideological element in international economic conflicts. When nationalisation is seen to be employed as a mere technique of defending national assets rather than as a creed, it is likely to lose some of its present emotional appeal as a symbol of anti-Western identification.

Moreover, this pattern appears to respond to two major trends in national economies. The one is the growing coalescence of the public and private sectors in the majority of capital-exporting States and the development of mixed national economies, with increasing emphasis on the public sectors.[46] The other is the political instability and economic "non-viability" of a growing number of capital-importing States.[47]

7—The Pattern of International Institutional Investment

On the universalist level, the Bretton Woods organisations can show remarkable achievements. In the context of foreign investments, the value of organisations such as the International Bank for Reconstruction and

[43] See above, p. 66 *et seq.*

[44] See, further, *Power Politics*, pp. 125 and 420 *et seq.*

[45] See, for instance, R. L. Friedheim, 18 *World Politics* (1965), pp. 23 and 33.

[46] See, for instance, R. A. Brady, *Business as a System of Power* (1943), G. W. Stocking and M. W. Watkins, *Cartels or Competition?* (1948), A. Shonfield, *Modern Capitalism. The Changing Balance of Public and Private Power* (1965), pp. 71 and 239 *et seq.*, E. W. Hawley, *The New Deal and the Problem of Monopoly* (1966), and W. Friedmann, 22 C.L.P. (1969).

On the significant letter addressed by the United Kingdom Chancellor of the Exchequer to the chairmen of over 200 British companies, asking them to co-operate voluntarily in the redirection of British overseas investments, see *The Times* (London), May 11, 1966, and, for a United States counterpart, the letter by the Secretary of Commerce of January 14, 1966 (5 I.L.M. (1966), p. 235 *et seq.*). See also *ibid.*, p. 9 *et seq.*, and, on the mandatory controls of U.S. investments abroad of April 25, 1968, 7 *ibid.* (1968), p. 579 *et seq.*

For a critical view of the short-term benefits accruing from new overseas investments for the economy of the United Kingdom, see the *Reddaway Report* (1968), as summarised in *The Times* (London), August 26, 1968.

[47] See above, pp. 186 and 189, and below, p. 198 *et seq.*

Development and its three affiliates, the International Finance Corporation, the International Development Association and the International Centre for Settlement of Investment Disputes [48] may be summarised in seven propositions:

(1) The fact that, in these institutions, specialists from capital-exporting and capital-importing States co-operate informally, privately and on a footing of equality has created an atmosphere which is exceptionally congenial for constructive co-operation between otherwise more antagonistic States and groups of States.[49]

(2) United States predominance in these institutions has been sublimated in fact, if not in law, so as to jeopardise less than might be expected the success of the operations of these institutions.

(3) In this international institutional and public framework, capital-importing States appear willing to accept a degree of interference with their economic independence, including international investigations of credit-worthiness and arbitration, that, these days, is elsewhere less readily attainable.[50]

(4) The division of labour between the International Bank for Reconstruction and Development and its affiliates greatly increases confidence in the bonds issued by the International Bank. The International Finance Corporation may invest in suitable private enterprises, and the International Development Association employs the contributions subscribed by its members to finance projects which, at least from the point of view of convertibility, are intended to include " soft " loans. In contrast, the International Bank gives credits only for financially sound projects of member governments and other bodies whose commitments are guaranteed by the governments of the member States concerned.

(5) The limitation of private investors to purchasing bonds allows their capital to participate in the development of technologically backward areas of the world and reap a reasonable profit from such enterprises. Yet, the direction and administration of such capital is left to an independent

[48] See, further, and also on relevant activities of related economic international institutions such as the International Monetary Fund, Kirdar, *loc. cit.* above, p. 16, note 52, p. 100 *et seq.*, J. Salmon, *Le rôle des organisations internationales en matière de prêts et d'emprunts* (1958), p. 80 *et seq.*, E. Black, *The Diplomacy of Economic Development* (1961), Ch. H. Alexandrowicz, *World Economic Agencies* (1962), p. 203 *et seq.*, and *Robert McNamara, Banker, The Economist,* June 8, 1968, p. 70.

On corresponding regional institutions such as the European Investment Bank and the Inter-American Development Bank, see, *e.g.*, L. Nurick in South-Western Legal Foundation, *Private Investments Abroad* (1959), Vol. I, p. 253 *et seq.*

See, however, J. J. Kaplan, *The Challenge of Foreign Aid* (1967), p. 364 *et seq.*, and S. J. Rubin, *The Conscience of the Rich Nations. The Development Assistance Committee and the Common Aid Effort* (1966), and 62 A.J.I.L. (1968), p. 217.

[49] It suffices to recall the contributions made by I.B.R.D. to the settlement of the Indus Water dispute between India and Pakistan and the compensation of the shareholders of the former Suez Canal Company.

See also above, pp. 66 and 88.

[50] See above, p. 135 *et seq.*, and, further, A. Broches, Hague *Recueil*, Vol. 98 (1959), p. 316 *et seq.*, and C. J. Olmstead, *loc. cit.* above, p. 193, note 40, p. 208.

international civil service with a remarkable fund of experience and a large reservoir of available expertise.[51]

(6) In areas in which closer political and economic integration on lines of functional federalism is possible, as in the European Economic Community,[52] institutional devices such as the European Development Fund and the European Development Bank may be employed for similar purposes. Admittedly, such closer ties may also serve to further the object of aligning backward areas in South-Eastern Europe and Africa in ways which it would be hard to distinguish from other forms of neo-imperialism.[53]

(7) On a world scale, participation of the Soviet camp in the Bretton Woods organisations in an era of growing common hostility to China,[54] and consequent easing of tensions between the West and the Soviet Union, would mean a considerable step forward. It would assist in eliminating wasteful competitive development aid and limit financial aid on a bilateral basis, which is more likely to lead to forms of economic dependence. Time alone can tell whether this hypothesis will be borne out by events, or whether the invasion of Czechoslovakia in 1968 by the Soviet Union and four of the Warsaw Pact States will lead to a reopening of the East-West rift.[55]

Like any other pattern, that of international institutional investment is open to objections.

It is true that the interposition of international institutions on any large scale would separate capital-importing countries from the managerial and technological skill which some industrial investors are able and willing to offer. Yet, even if by exchange restrictions or other devices, capital-exporting States were to control tightly direct industrial investment abroad,[56] capital-importing States and international institutions would remain free to hire the expertise of particular enterprises or individuals for the communication of their technological skill. In appropriate cases, capital-exporting States might also be willing, as they have been in the past,[57] to consider making such knowledge available as part of their programmes for development aid.

[51] See, for instance, A. Waterston, *Development Planning: Lessons of Experience* (1965).

[52] See, further, above, p. 195, note 48, and 16 C.L.P. (1963), p. 17 *et seq.*

[53] See also above, p. 16, and below, p. 198 *et seq.*

For the Yaoundé Convention of July 20, 1963, between E.E.C. and the African and Malagasy States, see 2 I.L.M. (1963), p. 971 *et seq.*, and, further, *The Economist*, April 27, 1968, p. 70.

By 1968 23 African countries were linked by special trade preferences with E.E.C. (*The Economist*, August 3, 1968).

[54] See also below, p. 199.

[55] See, further, 21 Y.B.W.A. (1967), p. 179 *et seq.*, M. Howard, *The Listener*, Vol. 80 (1968), No. 2057, p. 272 *et seq.* and C. Burnham, 23 Y.B.W.A. (1969).

[56] See above, p. 194, note 46.

[57] See, for instance, the Agreement for Technical Co-operation of July 13, 1951, between the United Kingdom and the United States of America regarding British dependent territories (Cmd. 8346—1951); the Exchange of Notes between the same regarding Technical Assistance for the Caribbean Area, January 12/20, 1954, Cmd. 9143 (1954); the Exchange of Notes between the same regarding Technical Assistance for British

(*ctd. overleaf*)

It is also a fair comment that the bonds issued by the International Bank are competitive with other issues only at rates which make loans given on the basis of such capital influx more expensive than they might be if directly negotiated between the parties concerned. In cases in which funds for direct investment are available on terms acceptable to the parties concerned, no problem arises. Yet, the overall trend appears to be one of decline of private foreign investments in capital-importing countries.

The question is whether international institutions on the Bretton Woods model and capital-importing States can make bond issues of the World Bank and similar institutions more interesting to potential investors. It should, however, be recalled that, for the time being, even the International Bank lends money on terms more favourable than those on which it can borrow itself on the international capital market. Thus, unless the position on the international capital market changes, these institutions would have to earn the difference between borrowing and lending terms in other ways, raise their own rates of lending or rely on further funds from their wealthier member States.

In any case, to attract private investors on a larger scale, the conditions of the bonds issued by the International Bank—or by regional institutions such as the Inter-American, Asian or African Development Banks—would have to be improved. At present, the I.B.R.D. bonds are exposed to the risks of inflation and devaluation of the currencies in which they are issued. While, in a number of countries, legislative, judicial or administrative difficulties may have to be overcome,[58] a suitably worded maintenance-of-value clause is probably the only commensurate answer. It might also be possible, by way of premiums, to let bondholders participate in profits of the enterprises financed with the proceeds of the stock concerned. Finally, to make special tax concessions to holders of such bonds might be one of the less wasteful forms of assistance to capital-importing States.

If the implementation of any of these proposals would involve a closer assimilation of the activities of the International Bank to those of commercial banking than the Bank considers advisable, the issue becomes one of priorities between the Bank's anxiety not to trespass on the preserves of private bankers and, thus, to jeopardise their goodwill and a more effective stimulation of private investment in capital-importing countries.

(*Note 57 ctd.*)
Guiana, June 29/July 12, 1954 (Cmd. 9342—1954) and June 22/29, 1964 (Cmnd. 2484—1964), the Agreement for Co-operation in the Field of Applied Science and Technology of August 9, 1967, between the United Kingdom and Hungary, Cmnd. 3457 (1967) and U.N.Doc. E/4293 (March 6, 1967), Section 109 (pp. 39–40).

58 See, further, G.-R. Delaume, *Legal Aspects of International Lending and Economic Development Financing* (1967), p. 257 *et seq.*, and, on gold-value clauses, A. Nussbaum, *Money in the Law* (1950), p. 262 *et seq.*, and F. A. Mann, *The Legal Aspect of Money* (1953), p. 119 *et seq.*

For a relevant clause, dealing with fluctuations in the value of the Pound Sterling, see Article 10 (V) of the A.I.O.C. Concession of 1933, Cmd. 8425 (1951), p. 13.

8—The Pattern of Economic Self-Sufficiency

If it were permissible to presume that an investor or his financial or legal advisers were to read this Chapter, he would be fully entitled to draw rather pessimistic conclusions from the study of the seven patterns sketched in the previous sections.

He might conclude that the *classical* pattern lacked in credibility and effectiveness. In particular, it fails to provide for the possibility of automatic verification by an independent third party of alleged facts in any concrete dispute and enforcement of its rules.

He might dismiss the *good-faith* pattern as an appeal made once too often to credulous investors and point to the series of broken promises made even by respectable governments of capital-exporting States regarding the non-devaluation of their currencies.

He might express sympathy in the abstract with the *good-conduct* pattern, but qualify it by an understandable reluctance to act until draft conventions based on this pattern had become operational, and capital-importing countries in which he was especially interested had become parties to such conventions.

He might admire the ingenuity displayed in the I.B.R.D. Convention on the Settlement of Investment Disputes, in implementing the *conciliation and arbitration* pattern. He might, however, wish to be assured that any particular capital-importing country in which he might contemplate investing had not only become a party to the Convention, but had also undertaken, or was willing to undertake, such further commitments under the Convention as are required to make it applicable to investment disputes between himself and the State party concerned.

He might find proposals of national or international *insurance* attractive but make his decision dependent on a number of considerations. In particular, would any available insurance scheme cover the contingencies of which he was most afraid and, if so, would the premiums due cancel out surface advantages as compared with investments in more stable countries?

He might consider the pattern of *counter-nationalisation* distasteful to the point of refusing to understand its meaning. In any case, he might find it objectionable on grounds of ingrained capitalist ideologies. Yet, he might grudgingly accept it as a circuitous means of repatriating the whole or, at least, part of his capital already invested abroad.

In particular, if he was an institutional investor, he might be attracted by the yields of bonds under schemes for *international institutional investments*. Yet, he might find that he could do even better by investing in equities available on the world's leading stock markets, especially if he was anxious to protect his investments against further inflation.

Action on such cautious lines might not be in the spirit of the merchant adventurers, nor represent an act of faith in the objects embodied in the preambles of the constitutions of universalist institutions nor be " progressive " in the sense attached to the term by the professional " men of good will." Yet, the mid-twentieth century picture of merchant adventurers may be more romantic than the reality of these adventurers of old. In any case, they were tougher types than the typical investor of our age.

Similarly, the objects of constitutions such as the Bretton Woods organisations or the Organisation for Economic Co-operation and Development may be admirable. Yet, unless an investor wishes to act on faith rather than experience, decisions on preferences regarding investments ought to be based on more calculable considerations, such as the safety of the capital involved, the rate of the promised yields and the probability of these expectations being fulfilled.

This sceptical view of the seven patterns available to investors abroad can be further supported on more general grounds. It is borne out by powerful trends in contemporary world society towards the formation of strong macro-economies with markedly autarkist features in the capitalist and socialist sectors of the world. From this point of view, the second UNCTAD Conference of New Delhi (1968) was a moment of truth. It highlighted some stark if unpalatable realities. Unchecked population explosions, waste of financial aid in capital-importing States on prestige projects, the maintenance of armed forces and civil services beyond capacity and need, widespread corruption, the hoarding of gold and other valuables by the upper strata of poor countries and the surreptitious export of flight money as nest eggs to capital-exporting States were bound to lead to a predictable result: the majority of the "developing" countries are standing still or developing backwards,[59] with inevitable effects on the precarious stability of their fragile State edifices.

If the point has not yet been reached, it cannot be long before capitalist and socialist capital-exporters realise that their competitive development aid is becoming largely a misdirection of always scarce resources. On this ground alone, and for even more compelling reasons of global strategy, understandings between those whom capital-importing States would wish to play off indefinitely against one another may become an increasingly attractive alternative to the present position.[60]

Subject to reservations arising from the Russian invasion of Czechoslovakia in 1968, a Northern alignment, extending from the United States to the Soviet Union, might make advisable financial aid to capital-importing States which was planned jointly or on parallel lines. Yet, such decisions would be primarily of a political character and, even in the world's capitalist portion, best left to the governments concerned.

[59] See, for instance, the Survey for 1967 of the United Nations Commission for Latin America (1968), indicating a balance of payments deficit in the areas of about $1,600 million.

[60] See, further, *Power Politics*, pp. 549–550.

For co-ordination of bilateral aid within the framework of O.E.C.D., see Kaplan, *loc. cit.*, above, p. 195, note 48, p. 372 *et seq.*

In such a situation, the advantages for investors resulting from the colonialism and imperialism of bygone days—a reasonably assured continuity of public order and an effective legal system producing a favourable investment climate—might reproduce themselves in a new context: the background presence of the joint might of the two super-Powers. Yet, it would be more likely that the world Powers so aligned would prefer not to spoil even more their less than lily-white images by fostering such a form of super-imperialism.

In these unsettled conditions, an investor may choose to rely, hope against hope, on any of the patterns designed for more sanguine investors. Yet another alternative remains always open to him. He can resign himself to foreign investments in parts of the world where such investments are backed by favourable legal systems, supported if required by the whole of the political, economic and military power of capital-exporting States.[61]

The potential area of investment in such circumstances of maximal security and, possibly, minimal yields extends to the countries which are technologically most advanced and those of their hinterlands as are linked beyond the point of no return with one or other of the most highly industrialised countries in tightly organised common markets or free trade areas. In all but name, these areas are territorial units of preferential international trade and macro-economic systems of an actually or potentially autarkist character, more similar to their counterparts in the communist sectors of the world in outlook than ideologists on either side of the fence would lightly admit.

This pattern may justly be summarised in the motto: "*Caveat investor.*" Advice on such lines may also be fairly challenged as being pessimistic in the extreme. Yet, is not a pessimist a man who distinguishes himself from his opposite number by never wanting to be right but, on an empirical basis, being more likely right than wrong and, on occasion, being agreeably disappointed by being proved wrong?

[61] For evidence of powerful trends in this direction, see, for instance, the hesitation of United States private investors since 1963 to export capital to Latin America. See, further, 4 I.L.M. (1966), p. 25.

Equally significant is the change in the investment policy of the formerly Congo-based *Union Minière*. See, further, *The Economist*, August 31, 1968, p. 64.

For purposes of the long-term growth of the most highly developed industrialised nations, fresh capital of about £17 billion is required each year (T. A. Wise, *The Times* (London), August 19, 1968).

If confirmation of a policy of extreme caution on the part of private investors were required, it was furnished by the Charter of Algiers, adopted at the Ministerial Meeting of 77 developing countries on October 24, 1967. In this informative document it is pointed out that " the lot of more than a billion people of the developing world continues to deteriorate " and that, to remedy this situation, *inter alia*, it is necessary to adopt " suitable measures . . . for alleviating the debt-servicing burdens of developing countries by consolidation of their external debts into long-term obligations on low rates of interest. In case of imminent difficulties, speedy arrangements should be made for refinancing and re-scheduling of loan on ' soft ' terms and conditions " (7 I.L.M. (1968), p. 177, at p. 191).

SELECTED BIBLIOGRAPHY
ON
FOREIGN INVESTMENTS
AND INTERNATIONAL LAW

Compiled by

A. M. SUTTON, LL.M.

Assistant Lecturer in International Law
University College, London

INTRODUCTION

Chapter 1—FUNDAMENTALS

A.—*GENERAL*

Accioly, H.: *Principes Généraux de la Responsabilité Internationale d'après la Doctrine et la Jurisprudence*, 96 Hague *Recueil* (1959)

Amerasinghe, C. F.: *State Responsibility for Injuries to Aliens*, 1967

——: *The Rule of Exhaustion of Domestic Remedies in the Framework of International Systems for the Protection of Human Rights*, 28 Z.A.Ö.R.V.R. (1968)

Bagge, A.: *Intervention on the ground of damage caused to nationals, with particular reference to exhaustion of local remedies and the rights of shareholders*, 34 B.Y.I.L. (1958)

Basdevant, S.: *Théorie générale de la condition de l'étranger* in A. de la Pradelle and J. P. Niboyet (eds.): *Répertoire de droit internationale*, Vol. VIII (1930)

Berman, H. J., and Others: *Aspects juridiques du commerce avec les pays d'économie planifiée*, 1961

Birke, W.: *Die Konfiskation ausländischen Privatvermögens, etc.*, 1960

Borchard, E. H.: *Diplomatic Protection of Citizens Abroad*, 1928

——, and Wynne, W. H.: *State Insolvency and Foreign Bondholders*, 1954 (2 vols.)

Brandon, M.: *Legal Aspects of Private Foreign Investments*, 18 *Federal Bar J.* (1958)

Carlston, K. S.: *Law and Organisation in World Society*, 1962 (useful bibliography)

Cavaré, L.: *La protection des droits contractuels reconnus par les États à des étrangers à l'exception des emprunts*, 1956

Christie, G. C.: *What Constitutes a Taking of Property under International Law?* 38 B.Y.I.L. (1962)

Delaume, G. R.: *Legal Aspects of International Lending and Economic Development Financing*, 1967

Domke, M.: *On the Nationalisation of Foreign Shareholders' Interests*, 4 *New York Law Forum* (1958)

Dunn, F. S.: *The Protection of Nationals*, 1938

Eagleton, C.: *The Responsibility of the State in International Law*, 1928

Fachiri, A. P.: *The Permanent Court of International Justice*, 1932

Ferretjans, J.-P.: *Essai sur la notion de propriété sociale*, 1962

Friedmann, W.: *The Changing Structure of International Law*, 1964 (Chap. 12)

——, and Pugh, R. C. (eds.): *Legal Aspects of Foreign Investment*, 1959

Gros, A.: *Observations sur les méthods de protection des intérêts privés à l'étranger*, in *Mélanges Rolin* (1964)

Guggenheim, P.: *Der völkerrechtliche Schutz von Investitionen im Ausland*, 13 *Annuaire suisse* (1956)

Haesler, Th.: *The Exhaustion of Local Remedies in the Case Law of International Courts and Tribunals*, 1968

Hammarskjöld, A.: *Juridiction internationale*, 1938

Hecke, G. A. van: *Confiscation and the Conflict of Laws*, 4 I.L.Q. (1951)

Hornsey, G.: *Foreign Investment and International Law*, 3 I.L.Q. (1950)

Hudson, M. O.: *The Permanent Court of International Justice*, 1934

——: *The Permanent Court of International Justice, 1920–1942*, 1943

Hyde, J. N.: *Economic Development Agreements*, 105 Hague *Recueil* (1962)

Institut de Droit International: *Les effets internationaux des nationalisations*, 44 (II) *Annuaire* (1952)

Institut de Sociologie de l'Université Libre (Brussels): *Le droit de propriété dans les pays de l'Est*, 1964

Jessup, Ph. C.: *A Modern Law of Nations*, 1948

——: *Transnational Law*, 1956

Kaeckenbeeck, G.: *The Protection of Vested Rights in International Law*, 17 B.Y.I.L. (1936)

——: *La Protection internationale des droits acquis*, 59 Hague *Recueil* (1937)

Kaiser, J. H., and Others: *Staat und Privateigentum*, 1960

Lalive, P. A.: *The Doctrine of Acquired Rights*, in Southwestern Legal Foundation, *Rights and Duties of Private Investors Abroad*, 1965

Langen, E.: *Studien zum internationalen Wirtschaftsrecht*, 1963 (Chap. 5)

Lauterpacht, E.: *Confiscatory Taxation*, B.P.I.L. (1964) II, 202.

Lauterpacht, Hersch: *The Development of International Law by the International Court*, 1958

Lillich, R. B.: *The Protection of Foreign Investments. Six Procedural Studies*, 1965

Mann, F. A.: *Betrachtungen über ein Völkerhandelsrecht*, 1962

——: *The Law governing State Contracts*, 21 B.Y.I.L. (1944)

——: *Reflections on a Commercial Law of Nations*, 33 *ibid.* (1957)

——: *The Proper Law of Contracts concluded by International Persons*, 35 *ibid.* (1959)

McDougal, M. S.: *Some Basic Theoretical Concepts about International Law*, 4 *Conflict Resolution* (1960)

——, and Others: *Studies in World Public Order*, 1960

——: *Theories about International Law: Prologue to a Configurative Jurisprudence*, 8 *Virg. J.I.L.* (1968)

McNair, Lord: *The General Principles of Law Recognised by Civilised Nations*, 33 B.Y.I.L. (1957)

Metzger, S. D.: *International Law, Trade and Finance*, 1962

——: *Law of International Trade*, Vol. I, 1966

Miller, R. S., and Stanger, R. J. (eds.): *Essays on Expropriation*, 1967

Reeves, W. H.: *Act of State Doctrine and the Rule of Law*, 54 A.J.I.L. (1960)

Riad, F. A. M.: *L'entreprise publique et semi-publique en droit international privé*, 108 Hague *Recueil* (1963)

Rosenne, S.: *The Law and Practice of the International Court*, 1965 (2 vols.)

Schelling, F. W. von: *Investitionen*, 2 *Strupp-Schlochauer*

Schindler, D.: *Gleichberechtigung von Individuen als Problem des Völkerrechts*, 1957

Schmitthoff, C. M. (ed.): *The Sources of the Law of International Trade*, 1964

——: *The Law of International Trade and Investments*, 6 *Il Diritto negli Scambi Internazionali* (1967)

Schwarzenberger, G.: *The Fundamental Principles of International Law* (Chap. V: *The Principle of Good Faith*), 87 Hague *Recueil* (1955)

——: *The Principles and Standards of International Economic Law*, 117 Hague *Recueil* (1966)

Seidl-Hohenveldern, I.: *Investitionen in Entwicklungsländern und das Völkerrecht*, 1963 (exhaustive bibliography)

——: *Nationalisation*, 2 *Strupp-Schlochauer*

——: *Privatvermögen in Ausland*, 2 *ibid.*

Shaw, C. (ed.): *Legal Problems in International Trade and Investment*, 1962
Shawcross, Lord: *The Problems of Foreign Investment in International Law*, 102 Hague *Recueil* (1961)
Sohn, L. B., and Baxter, R. R.: *Responsibility of States for Injuries to the Economic Interests of Aliens*, 55 A.J.I.L. (1961)
South-Western Legal Foundation: *Proceedings of the 1959 Institute on Private Investments Abroad*, 1959
——: *Proceedings of the 1960 Institute on Private Investments Abroad*, 1960
——: *Rights and Duties of Private Investors Abroad*, 1965
Starke, J. G. (ed.): *The Protection and Encouragement of Private Foreign Investment*, 1966
Veith, W., and Boeckstiegel, K.-H.: *Der Schutz von ausländischen Vermögen im Völkerrecht*, 1962
Verdross, A.: *Les règles internationales concernant le traitement des étrangers*, 37 Hague *Recueil* (1931)
——: *Les principes généraux de droit dans le système des sources du droit international public*, in *Mélanges Guggenheim*
Verzijl, J. H. W.: *The Jurisprudence of the World Court*, 1965 (2 vols.)
Visscher, Ch. de: *Aspects récents du droit procédural de la Cour International de Justice*, 1966 (Chap. IV, Section II: Exhaustion of Local Remedies)
——, P. de: *La protection diplomatique des personnes morales*, 102 Hague *Recueil* (1961)
Wetter, J. G.: *Diplomatic Assistance to Private Investment*, 29 *Univ. Chicago L.R.* (1961–62)
Wortley, B. A.: *The General Principles of Private International Law*, 94 Hague *Recueil* (1958—Chap. VII: *The Protection of Property in Private International Law*)
Zander, M.: *The Act of State Doctrine*, 53 A.J.I.L. (1959)

B.—*EXPROPRIATION, CONFISCATION, NATIONALISATION AND RELATED MEASURES*

Adriaanse, P.: *Confiscation in Private International Law*, 1956
Albrecht, A. R.: *The Taxation of Aliens under International Law*, 29 B.Y.I.L. (1952)
Asian-African Legal Consultative Committee: *Immunity of States in respect of Commercial Transactions* (Colombo Session—1960)
Bindschedler, R. L.: *Verstaatlichungsmassnahmen und Entschädigungspflicht nach Völkerrecht unter besonderer Berücksichtigung der schweizerischen Praxis über den Schutz schweizerischer Vermögenswerte im Ausland*, 1950
——: *La protection de la propriété privés en droit international public*, 90 Hague *Recueil* (1956)
Birke, W.: *Die Konfiskation ausländischen Privatvermögens*, 1960
Borchard, E. M.: *The Minimum Standard in the Protection of Aliens*, 33 *A.S.I.L. Proceedings* (1939)
Brandon, M.: *Sovereign Immunity of Government-Owned Corporations and Ships*, 39 *Cornell L.Q.* (1954)
Carlston, K. S.: *Nationalisation: An Analytical Approach*, 54 *Northwestern Univ.L.R.* (1959)
Charpentier, J.: *De la Non-discrimination dans les investissements*, 9 *Annuaire français* (1963)

Cheng, B.: *Expropriation in International Law*, 21 *The Solicitor* (1954)
——: *The Rationale of Compensation for Expropriation*, 44 *Grotius Transactions* (1958–59)
Christie, G. C.: *What Constitutes a Taking of Property under International Law?* 38 B.Y.I.L. (1962)
Cohn, E. J.: *Memorandum on the Application of the German Land Reform Legislation to Property of Non-German Nationals*, 1951
Dawson, F. G., and Weston, B. H.: "*Prompt, Adequate and Effective*": *A Universal Standard of Compensation?* 30 *Fordham L.R.* (1962)
De Nova, R.: *L'esproprio in diritto internazionale*, 16 *Il Politico* (1951)
Domke, M.: *Enteigunung*, 1 *Strupp-Schlochauer*
——, Friedmann, W., and Henkin, L.: *Act of State*, 3 *Col.J. Transnational Law* (1964)
Fachiri, A. P.: *Expropriation and International Law*, 6 B.Y.I.L. (1925)
——: *International Law and the Property of Aliens*, 10 B.Y.I.L. (1929)
Falk, R. A.: *The Role of Domestic Courts in the International Legal Order*, 1964
——: *The Complexity of Sabbatino*, 58 A.J.I.L. (1964)
Fawcett, J. E. S.: *Some Foreign Effects of Nationalisation of Property*, 27 B.Y.I.L. (1950)
Foighel, I.: *Nationalisation*, 1957
Fouilloux, G.: *La Nationalisation et le droit international public*, 1962
Friedman, S.: *Expropriation in International Law*, 1953
Friedmann, W.: *National Courts and the International Legal Order: Projections on the Implications of the Sabbatino Case*, 34 *George Washington L.R.* (1966)
Gilmour, D. R.: *The Validity of the Act of State Doctrine*, 12 *Juridical Review* (1967)
Guggenheim, P.: *Der völkerrechtliche Schutz von Investitionen im Ausland*, 13 *Annuaire suisse* (1956)
Hecke, G. A. van: *Confiscation and the Conflict of Laws*, 4 I.L.Q. (1951)
Herz, H.: *Expropriation of Foreign Property*, 35 A.J.I.L. (1941)
Hjerner, L. A. E.: *The General Approach to Foreign Confiscations*, 2 *Scandinavian Studies in Law* (1958)
Hyde, C. C.: *Confiscatory Expropriations*, 32 A.J.I.L. (1938)
——: *Compensation for Expropriations*, 33 *ibid.* (1939)
International Law Association: *Report of the Committee on Nationalisation*, New York Conference 1958
Jaenicke, G.: *Diskriminierung*, 1 *Strupp-Schlochauer*
Jessup, Ph. C.: *Confiscation*, *A.S.I.L. Proceedings* (1927)
Katzarov, K.: *The Theory of Nationalisation*, 1964 (useful bibliography)
Kipp, H.: *Das Verbot der Diskriminierung im modernen Friedensvölkerrecht*, 9 A.V.R. (1962)
Lillich, R. B., and Christenson, G. A.: *International Claims: Their Preparation and Presentation*, 1962
Mann, F. A.: *The Legal Consequences of Sabbatino*, 51 *Virginia L.R.* (1965)
McNair, Lord: *The Seizure of Property and Enterprises in Indonesia*, 6 *Netherlands R.I.L.* (1959)
Metzger, S. D.: *Exchange Controls and International Law*, in T. O. Proehl (ed.), *Legal Problems of International Trade*, 1959
Mooney, E. F.: *Foreign Seizures: Sabbatino and the Act of State Doctrine*, 1967
Münch, F.: *The Effects of Nationalisation Abroad*, 98 Hague *Recueil* (1959)

Olmstead, C. J.: *Nationalisation of Foreign Property Interests*, 32 N.Y.U.L.Q.R. (1956)
Panebianco, M.: *Giurisdizione Interna e Immunità degli State stranieri*, 1967
Petrén, S.: *La confiscation des biens étrangers et les réclamations internationales auxquelles elle peut donner lieu*, 109 Hague *Recueil* (1963)
Pfeiffer, K.: *Gleichheitsgrundsatz und Reparationsentschädigung*, 1968
Quadri, R.: *Espropriazioni all'estero e ordine publico. Studi critici di diritto internazionale*, Vol. I, 1958
Ray, G. W.: *Law Governing Contracts between States and Foreign Nationals*, in South-Western Legal Foundation, *Proceedings of the 1960 Institute on Private Investments Abroad*, 1960
Rolin, H.: *Avis sur la validité des mesures de nationalisation décrétées par le gouvernement indonésien*, 6 *Netherlands R.I.L.* (1959)
Roth, A. H.: *The Minimum Standard of International Law applied to Aliens*, 1949
Rubin, S. J.: *Nationalisation and Compensation—A Comparative Approach*, 17 *Univ. Chicago L.R.* (1950)
Schnitzer, A. F.: *Mindeststandard*, 2 *Strupp-Schlochauer*
Scholz, W.: *Die Schlechterbehandlung des Ausländers bei der Heranziehung zu Geldleistungen*, in *Erler Festgabe*, 1965
Schwarzenberger, G.: *International Law*, Vol. I (3rd ed.), Chap. 12, Section 3 (*The Minimum Standard of International Law*)
Seidl-Hohenveldern, I.: *Internationales Konfiskations- und Enteignungsrecht*, 1952
——: *Zur Theorie der Verstaatlichung*, 7 *Osteuropa-Recht* (1961)
——: *Title to Confiscated Foreign Property and Public International Law*, 56 A.J.I.L. (1962)
——: *Zur Konfiskation von Aktionärsrechten*, 28 Z.A.I.P.R. (1964)
Simmonds, K. R.: *The Sabbatino Case and the Act of State Doctrine*, 14 I.C.L.Q. (1965)
Timberg, S.: *Expropriation Measures and State Trading*, 55 *A.S.I.L. Proceedings* (1961)
Tondel, L. M. (ed.): *The Aftermath of Sabbatino*, 1965
Troller, A.: *Internationale Zwangsverwertung und Expropriation von Immaterialgütern*, 1955
Verdross, A.: *The Status of Foreign Private Interests*, 9 Ö.Z.Ö.R. (1959)
Verzijl, J. H. W.: *The Relevance of Public and Private International Law Respectively for the Solution of Problems Arising from Nationalisation of Enterprises*, 19 Z.A.Ö.R.V.R. (1958)
Wetter, J. G.: *Diplomatic Assistance to Private Investment*, 31 *Acta Scandinavica* (1961)
White, G.: *Nationalisation of Foreign Property*, 1961
Williams, John Fischer: *International Law and the Property of Aliens*, 9 B.Y.I.L. (1928)
Wortley, B. A.: *Expropriation in Public International Law*, 1959
——: *The Protection of Property Situated Abroad*, 35 *Tulane L.R.* (1961)

C.—*PUBLIC CONTRACTS*

Amerasinghe, C. F.: *State Breaches of Contracts with Aliens and International Law*, 58 A.J.I.L. (1964)
Batiffol, H.: *Sur la signification de la loi designée par les contractants*, 1 *Scritti Perassi*

Borchers, K. G.: *Verträge von Staaten mit ausländischen Privatpersonen*, 1966
Calvert, H. G.: *The Law Applicable to Concessions*, 1 *University of Malaya L.R.* (1959)
Carlston, K. S.: *Concession Agreements and Nationalisation*, 52 A.J.I.L. (1958)
Delaume, G. R.: *The Proper Law of Loans concluded by International Persons*, 56 A.J.I.L. (1962)
Geck, W. K.: *Konzession*, 2 *Strupp-Schlochauer*
Guldberg, T.: *International Concessions. A Problem of International Economic Law*, 25 *Acta Scandinavica* (1955)
Hyde, J. N.: *Economic Development Agreements*, 105 Hague *Recueil* (1962)
Jennings, R. Y.: *State Contracts in International Law*, 37 B.Y.I.L. (1961)
——: *Rules governing Contracts between States and Foreign Nationals*, in Southwestern Legal Foundation, *Rights and Duties of Private Investors Abroad*, 1965
Kipp, H.: *Verträge zwischen staatlichen und nichtstaatlichen Partnern*, 5 *Berichte der deutschen Gesellschaft für Völkerrecht* (1964)
Lalive, J.-F.: *Contracts between States and a Foreign Company*, 13 I.C.L.Q. (1964)
Mann, F. A.: *The Law Governing State Contracts*, 21 B.Y.I.L. (1944)
——: *Die Verträge der Völkerrechtssubjekte und die Parteiautonomie*, in *Gutzwiller Festgabe*, 1959
——: *The Proper Law of Contracts concluded by International Persons*, 35 B.Y.I.L. (1959)
——: *State Contracts and International Responsibility*, 54 A.J.I.L. (1960)
Mosler, H.: *Wirtschaftskonzessionen bei Aenderung der Staatshoheit*, 1940
Olmstead, C. J.: *Economic Development Agreements*, 48 and 49 *Calif.L.R.* (1960–61)
Schwarzenberger, G.: *Die Kreuger-Anleihen*, 1931
Schwebel, S. M.: *International Protection of Contractual Arrangements*, 53 *A.S.I.L. Proceedings* (1959)
Suratgar, D.: *Considerations affecting Choice of Law Clauses in Contracts between Governments and Foreign Nations*, 2 *Indian J.I.L.* (1962)
Verdross, A.: *The Status of Foreign Private Interests stemming from Economic Development Agreements with Arbitration Clauses*, 18 Z.A.Ö.R.V.R. (1958)
——: *Protection of Private Property under Quasi-international Agreements*, in *Liber Amicorum J.P.A. François* (1959)
——: *Quasi-international Agreements and International Economic Transactions*, 18 Y.B.W.A. (1964)
——: *Gibt es Verträge, die weder dem innerstaatlichen Recht noch dem Völkerrecht unterliegen?* 6 *Zeitschrift für Rechtsvergleichung* (1965)
Zweigert, K.: *Verträge zwischen staatlichen und nichtstaatlichen Partnern*, 5 *Berichte der Deutschen Gesellschaft für Völkerrecht* (1964)

D.—*INTER-DISCIPLINARY ASPECTS*

Brady, R. A.: *Business as a System of Power*, 1943
Conan, A. R.: *Britain as Creditor, The Listener*, December 28, 1967
Mikesell, R. F.: *United States Private Investment and Government Investment Abroad*, 1962
Osborn, P. G., and Grandage, S. T.: *The Concise Commercial Dictionary*, 1966
United Nations, Department of Economic and Social Affairs: *The External Financing of Economic Development* (1968—E. 68. II. D. 10)
——: *Year Book of International Trade Statistics*

See also below, pp. 216 *and* 223.

Part One

THE PROTECTION OF INVESTMENTS ABROAD IN THE MIRROR OF BRITISH PRACTICE

Chapter 2—EVOLUTION AND SCOPE OF THE GOVERNING RULES

Amerasinghe, C. F.: *State Responsibility for Injuries to Aliens*, 1967

Beckett, Eric: *Diplomatic Claims in respect of Injuries to Companies*, 17 *Grotius Transactions* (1937)

Beemelmans, H.: *Die gespaltene Gesellschaft*, 1963

Brown, E. D.: *Eminent Domain in Anglo-American Law*, 13 C.L.P. (1965)

Buckland, W. W., and McNair, Lord (ed. by F. H. Lawson): *Roman Law and Common Law*, 1952

Clay, H. J.: *Recent Developments in the Protection of American Shareholders' Interests in Foreign Corporations*, 45 *Georgetown L.J.* (1956)

Cohn, E. J., and Simitis, C.: *"Lifting the Veil" in the Company Laws of the European Continent*, 12 I.C.L.Q. (1963)

Doeker, G.: *Der Abschluss völkerrechtlicher Verträge im traditionellen Commonwealth of Nations*, 14 A.V.R. (1968)

Drucker, A.: *The Confiscation of Corporations and the Conflict of Laws*, 234 *The Law Times* (1963)

Elias, T. O.: *British Colonial Law*, 1962

Franzke, H.-G.: *Schutzaktionen zugunsten der Staatsangehörigen im Ausland*, 1965

Goodhart, A. L.: *English Law and the Moral Law*, 1953

Graveson, R. H.: *The Restless Spirit of English Law*, in *Jeremy Bentham and the Law* (ed. by G. W. Keeton and G. Schwarzenberger), 1948

Hochepied, J.-P. de: *La protection diplomatique des sociétés et des actionnaires*, 1965

Holmes, O. W.: *The Common Law*, 1881

Keeton, G. W. (General Editor): *The British Commonwealth Series*, 1955–

Lauterpacht, E. (ed.): *The Contemporary Practice of the United Kingdom in the Field of International Law*, 5 I.C.L.Q. (1956)—10 (1961) and supplements covering 1962 (1962–63)

——: *British Practice in International Law*, 1963–

Lillich, R. B.: *International Claims: Postwar British Practice*, 1967

Lorz, R.: *Ausländische Enteignungsmassnahmen vor amerikanischen Gerichten*, 1954

Mann, F. A.: *Outlines of a History of Expropriation*, 75 L.Q.R. (1959)

——: *The Confiscation of Corporations, Corporate Assets and the Conflict of Laws*, 11 I.C.L.Q. (1962)

McNair, Lord, and Watts, A. D.: *The Legal Effects of War*, 1966

Mervyn Jones, J.: *Claims on Behalf of Nationals who are Shareholders in Foreign Companies*, 26 B.Y.I.L. (1949)

Parry, C.: *Nationality and Citizenship Laws of the Commonwealth and of the Republic of Ireland* (1957–60—2 vols.)

—— (ed.): *A British Digest of International Law*, 1965–

—— (ed.): *British International Law Cases*, 1964–67

——, in H. C. L. Merillat (ed.): *Legal Advisers and Foreign Affairs*, 1964

Platt, D. C. M.: *Finance, Trade and Politics in British Foreign Policy, 1815–1914*, 1968

Pollock, F.: *The Expansion of the Common Law*, 1904
Roth, A. H.: *The Minimum Standard of International Law applied to Aliens*, 1949
Schwarzenberger, G.: *The Frontiers of International Law* (Chapter 5: *International Law in Early English Practice* and Chapter 6: *The Protection of Human Rights in British Practice*), 1962
——: *The Protection of British Property Abroad*, 5 C.L.P. (1952)
Setalvad, M. C.: *The Common Law in India*, 1960
Sheridan, L. A.: *Repatriation of the Common Law*, 18 C.L.P. (1965)
Vallat, Sir Francis: *International Law and the Practitioner*, 1966
Visscher, P. de: *La Protection diplomatique des personnes morales*, 102 Hague *Recueil* (1961)
Wetter, J. G.: *Diplomatic Assistance to Private Investment. A Study of the Theory and Practice of the United States during the Twentieth Century*, 29 *Univ. Chicago L.R.* (1962)
Ziegel, T. S.: *Confiscation in English Private International Law*, 6 *McGill L.J.* (1959)

See also above, pp. 205 *and* 207, *and below*, pp. 211 *and* 217.

Chapter 3—POST-1945 BRITISH TREATY PRACTICE:

I—PEACE TREATIES—GENERAL ECONOMIC TREATIES

Almond, H. H.: *The Anglo-Japanese Commercial Treaty of 1963*, 13 I.C.L.Q. (1964)
Benton, S. A.: *The Protection of Property Rights in Commercial Treaties of the United States*, 25 Z.A.Ö.R.V.R. (1965)
Brooks, E. A. S.: *Registration of International Claims under the Foreign Compensation Act, 1950*, 44 *Grotius Transactions* (1959)
Collier, F. H.: "*Registered*" *Claims against the Egyptian Fund under the Foreign Compensation Acts*, 15 I.C.L.Q. (1966)
Connell, H. P.: *United States Protection of Private Foreign Investment through Treaties of Friendship, Commerce and Navigation*, 9 A.V.R. (1961)
Lauterpacht, E.: *Foreign Compensation Act 1950*, 4 I.L.Q. (1951)
Lillich, R. B.: *International Claims: Their Adjudication by National Commissions*, 1962
——: *International Claims: Post-War British Practice*, 1967
——: *Judicial Review and the Foreign Claims Settlement Commission*, 15 *Administrative L.R.* (1963)
——: *International Claims: A Comparative Study of United Kingdom and United States Practice*, 17 C.L.P. (1964)
McNair, Lord, and Watts, A. D.: *The Legal Effects of War*, 1966
Mosler, H., and Doehring, K.: *Die Beendigung des Kriegszustands mit Deutschland nach dem zweiten Weltkrieg*, 1963
Oppikofer, U.: *Der Schutz der schweizerischen Auslandsinvestitionen*, 1958
Preiswerk, R.: *La protection des investissements privés dans les traités bilateraux*, 1963
——: *Les accords de co-opération technique avec les pays en voie de développement*, 21 *Annuaire suisse* (1964)
——: *New Developments in Bilateral Investment Protection*, 3 *Revue Belge de Droit International* (1967)
Rode, Z. R.: *The International Claims Commission of the United States*, 47 A.J.I.L. (1953)

Scheuner, U.: *Zweiseitige Handelsverträge und multilaterale Handelsvereinbarungen*, 52 *Friedenswarte* (1954)
——: *Die Rolle der Handelsverträge im internationalen Wirtschaftsrecht der Gegenwart*, in *Mélanges Kyriacopoulos* (1966)
Schwarzenberger, G.: *The Frontiers of International Law*, 1962 (Chaps. 4–6)
——: *International Law*, Vol. II (Part Nine: The Termination of Armed Conflicts), 1968
Solomon, E., in J. G. Starke (ed.): *The Protection and Encouragement of Foreign Investment*, 1966
Walker, H.: *Treaties for the Encouragement and Protection of Foreign Investment: Present United States Practice*, 5 A.J.C.L. (1956)
——: *Modern Treaties of Friendship, Commerce and Navigation*, 42 *Minnesota L.R.* (1958)
Wilson, R. R.: *United States Commercial Treaties and International Law*, 1960

See also above, pp. 203 *and* 207, *and below*, pp. 212 *and* 223.

Chapter 4—POST-1945 BRITISH TREATY PRACTICE:

II—NATIONALISATION AGREEMENTS

Baade, H. W.: *Baltische Staaten*, 1 *Strupp-Schlochauer*
Carlston, K. S.: *Interpretation of Peace Treaties with Bulgaria, Hungary and Roumania*, 44 A.J.I.L. (1950)
Christenson, G. A.: *United States-Rumanian Claims Settlement Agreement of March 30, 1960*, 55 A.J.I.L. (1961)
Dairaines, S.: *Les étrangers et les sociétés étrangères en France*, 1957
Déak, F.: *The Hungarian-Rumanian Land Dispute*, 1928
Doman, N. R.: *Postwar Nationalisation of Foreign Property in Europe*, 48 *Col. L.R.* (1948)
——: *Compensation for Nationalised Property in Eastern Europe*, 3 I.L.Q. (1950)
Domke, M.: *Foreign Nationalisations*, 55 A.J.I.L. (1961)
Drucker, A.: *The Nationalisation of United Nations Property in Post-War Europe*, 36 *Grotius Transactions* (1950)
——: *Compensation for Nationalised Property: The British Practice*, 49 A.J.I.L. (1955)
——: *The Protection of Foreign Investments. An addendum*, 16 I.C.L.Q. (1967)
Dunn, F. S.: *The Diplomatic Protection of Americans in Mexico*, 1933
Gaither, R. B.: *Expropriation in Mexico. The Facts and the Law*, 1940
Garcia Robles, A.: *La question de pétrole au Mexique et le droit international*, 1939
Gordon, W. C.: *The Expropriation of Foreign-Owned Property in Mexico*, 1941
Grünewald, J.: *Das Eigentum und das Eigentumsrecht in der sowjetischen Besatzungszone Deutschlands*, 1961
Gutteridge, J. A. C.: *Expropriation and Nationalisation in Hungary, Bulgaria and Roumania*, 1 I.C.L.Q. (1952)
Herman, S.: *War Damage and Nationalisation in Eastern Europe*, 16 *Law and Contemporary Problems* (1951)
Herzog, J. S.: *La expropriación del petróleo en Mexico*, 1963
Kuhn, A. K.: *The Mexican Supreme Court Decision in the Oil Companies Expropriation Cases*, 34 A.J.I.L. (1940)

Kunz, J. L.: *The Mexican Expropriations*, 17 N.Y.U.L.Q.R. (1940)
Langer, R.: *Seizure of Territory*, 1947
La Pradelle, A. de: *La réforme agraire tchécoslovaque devant la justice internationale*, 1929
Lillich, R. B.: *The Jurisprudence of the Foreign Compensation Commission: Eligible Claimants*, 13 I.C.L.Q. (1964)
——: *International Claims: Their Settlement by Lump Sum Agreements*, *Domke Symposium*
Martin, A.: *The Distribution of Funds under the Foreign Compensation Act 1950*, 44 *Grotius Transactions* (1958–59)
Moller, N. H.: *Compensation for British Owned Foreign Interests*, 44 *Grotius Transactions* (1958–59)
Puget, H.: *Les nationalisations en France et à l'étranger* (2 vols.—1950 and 1958)
Rado, A. R.: *Czechoslovakian Nationalisation Decrees: Some International Aspects*, 41 A.J.I.L. (1947)
Re, E. D.: *The Foreign Claims Settlement Commission and the Adjudication of International Claims*, 56 A.J.I.L. (1962)
——: *The Foreign Claims Settlement Commission and International Claims*, 13 *Syracuse L.R.* (1962)
——: *Domestic Adjudication and Lump-Sum Settlement as an Enforcement Technique*, 58 *A.S.I.L. Proceedings* (1964)
Rode, Z. R.: *The International Claims Commission of the United States*, 47 A.J.I.L. (1953)
Scamell, E. H.: *Nationalisation in Legal Perspective*, 5 C.L.P. (1952)
Sipkov, I.: *Postwar nationalisations and alien property in Bulgaria*, 52 A.J.I.L. (1958)
Siqueiros Prieto, J. C.: *Las reclamaciones internacionales por intereses extranjeros en sociedades mexicanas*, 1947
Steiniger, P. A.: *Oktoberrevolution und Völkerrecht*, 1967
Thomas, G. (ed.): *Nationalisations à l'étranger*, 1946
Woolsey, L. H.: *The Expropriation of Oil Properties by Mexico*, 32 A.J.I.L. (1938)
Wortley, B. A.: *The Mexican Oil Dispute 1938–1946*, 43 *Grotius Transactions* (1957)

See also above, pp. 205 *and* 207, *and below*, pp. 216 *and* 223.

Chapter 5—POST-1945 BRITISH TREATY PRACTICE: III—OTHER RELEVANT TREATIES

Antonopoulos, N.: *La jurisprudence des organs de la Convention Européene des Droits de l'Homme*, 1967
Bastid, S.: *L'action militaire franco-britannique en Egypte et le Droit des Nations Unies*, in *Mélanges Gidel*
Böckstiegel, K.-H.: *Die allgemeinen Grundsätze des Völkerrechts über Eigentumsentzierung. Eine Untersuchung zu Art. 1 des Zusatzprotokolls zur Europäischen Menschenrechtskonvention*, 1963
Briggs, H. W.: *Non-Recognition in the Courts: The Ships of the Baltic Republics*, 37 A.J.I.L. (1943)
Brownlie, I.: *International Law and the Use of Force by States*, 1963 (*see Index under* United Kingdom, Suez operations)

Caemmerer, E. von, and Others: *Wissenschaftliche Gesellschaft für Europarecht, Kolloquium der Fachgruppe Europarecht, Europäische Handelsgesellschaft und Angleichung des nationalen Gesellschaftsrechts*, 1968
Fawcett, J. E. S.: *Intervention in International Law*, 103 Hague *Recueil* (1961)
Hahn, H. J.: *Die Organisation für Wirtschaftliche Zusammenarbeit und Entwicklung—Das Wirtschaftsrecht des Verbandes und seine Systematik*, 13 A.V.R. (1967)
International Law Association: *The Effect of Independence on Treaties*, 1965
Kunzmann, K. H.: *Die Europäische Konvention über die friedliche Beilegung von Streitigkeiten*, 5 *Europa-Archiv* (1959)
Lauterpacht, H.: *An International Bill of the Rights of Man*, 1945
——: *International Law and Human Rights*, 1950
Lawford, H. J.: *The Practice concerning Treaty Succession in the Commonwealth*, 5 *Can.Y.B.I.L.* (1967)
McDougal, M. S., and Bebr, G.: *Human Rights in the United Nations* 58 A.J.I.L. (1964)
Monconduit, F.: *La Commission Européene de Droit de l'Homme*, 1965
Morrison, C. C.: *The Developing European Law of Human Rights*, 1967
Mosler, H.: *Wirtschaftskonzessionen bei Aenderung der Staatshoheit*, 1948
O'Connell, D. P.: *State Succession in Municipal Law and International Law*, 1967 (2 vols.)
——: *Economic Concessions in the Law of State Succession*, 27 B.Y.I.L. (1950)
Putterils, G. C.: *Les Travaux du Comité d'Experts chargé d'Elaborer un Projet de Convention Européenne sur le Traitement Réciproque des Nationaux* (1952–1955), 5 *Bulletin de Droit des Gens* (Brussels—1965)
Robertson, A. H.: *The Council of Europe*, 1961
Roberts-Wray, Sir Kenneth: *Commonwealth and Colonial Law*, 1966
Schmitthoff, C.: *The Export Trade*, 1962
——: *British Aid to Developing Countries*, 1 J.W.T.L. (1967)
Schwarzenberger, G.: *The Frontiers of International Law* (Chap. 7: *The Impact of the East–West Rift on International Law*), 1962
Schwelb, E.: *The Protection of the Rights of Property of Nationals under the First Protocol of the European Convention of Human Rights*, 13 A.J.C.L. (1964)
——: *Human Rights*, in *International Encyclopedia of the Social Sciences*, 1968
Seidl-Hohenveldern, I.: *Reprisals and the Taking of Private Property*, *Mélanges Kollewijn-Offerhaus*, 1962
United Nations: International Law Commission. First Report by M. Bedjaoui on *Succession of States in respect of Rights and Duties resulting from Sources other than Treaties* (A/CN4/204–1968)
Vasak, K.: *La convention européene des droits de l'homme*, 1964
Vellas, P.: *Droit International Economique et Social*, Vol. I: *Droit International Agricole*, 1965
——: *Les contrats de longue durée dans les relations internationales agricoles*, 3 *Annuaire français* (1957)
Wilson, R. R.: *The International Law Standard in Treaties of the United States*, 1953
——: *United States Commercial Treaties and International Law*, 1960
Zemanek, K.: *State Succession after Decolonisation*, 116 Hague *Recueil* (1965)

See also above, pp. 203 *and* 210, *and below*, pp. 216 *and* 223.

CHAPTER 6—TWO TEST CASES

Albaharna, H. M.: *The Legal Status of the Arabian Gulf States*, 1968
Baade, H. W.: *Permanent Sovereignty over Natural Wealth and Resources*, in R. S. Miller and R. J. Stanger (eds.), *Essays on Expropriations*, 1967
Broches, A.: *Quasi-Arbitration by the I.B.R.D.*, 55 *A.S.I.L. Proceedings* (1961—p. 72)
Broms, B.: *The Legal Status of the Suez Canal*, 1961
Cattan, H.: *The Evolution of Oil Concessions in the Middle East and North Africa*, 1967
——: *The Law of Oil Concessions in the Middle East and North Africa*, 1967
Cheng, B.: *The Anglo-Iranian Dispute*, 5 *World Affairs* (New Series—1951)
Deener, D. R. (ed.): *International Law and the Middle East Crisis*, 1957
Delson, R.: *Nationalisation of the Suez Canal Company*, 57 *Col.L.R.* (1957)
Domke, M.: *American Protection against Foreign Expropriation in the Light of the Suez Canal Crisis*, 105 *U.Pa.L.R.* (1957)
——: *Indonesian Nationalisation Measures before Foreign Courts*, 54 A.J.I.L. (1950)
Douglas-Home, Ch.: *Keeping the Peace to Protect the Supply of Oil*, *The Times* (London), November 14, 1967
Eden, A.: *The Full Circle* (Memoirs), Vol. II, 1960
El-Sayed, M.: *L'Organisation des Pays Exportateurs de Pétrole*, 1967 (useful bibliography)
Engler, R.: *La politica petrolera*, 1966
Fahmy-Abdou, A.: *La Nazionalizzazione della Società del Canale di Suez*, 1962
Farmanfarma, A..: *The Oil Agreement between Iran and the International Oil Consortium*, 34 *Texas L.R.* (1955)
Focsaneanu, L.: *L'accord ayant pour objet l'indemnisation de la compagnie de Suez nationalisée par l'Egypte*, 6 *Annuaire français* (1959)
Ford, A. W.: *The Anglo-Iranian Oil Dispute of 1951–1952*, 1954 (useful bibliography)
Frankel, J.: *The Anglo-Iranian Dispute*, 6 Y.B.W.A. (1952)
Friedmann, W., and Kalmanoff, G.: *Joint International Business Ventures*, 1961
Hartshorn, J. E.: *Oil Companies and Governments*, 1967
——: *Oil and the Middle East War*, 24 *The World Today* (1968)
Henkin, L.: *International Law and the Behaviour of Nations* (Chap. 3), 114 Hague *Recueil* (1965)
Hoveyda, F.: *Les aspects juridiques de la nationalisation des industries pétrolières en Iran*, 1 *Revue de droit international pour le Moyen-Orient* (1951–52)
Huang, T. T. F.: *Some international and legal aspects of the Suez Canal question*, 51 A.J.I.L. (1957)
Hurewitz, J. C.: *Diplomacy in the Near and Middle East*, 1956 (2 vols.)
Johnson, D. H. N.: *The Eden Memoirs and International Law*, 31 *Acta Scandinavica* (1961)
——: *Some Legal Problems of International Waterways, with particular reference to the Straits of Tiran and the Suez Canal*, 31 M.L.R. (1968)
Kazemzadeh, F.: *Russia and Britain in Persia 1864–1914: A Study in Imperialism*, 1968
alive, J. F.: *Recent Trends: Abrogation or Alternation of an Economic Development Agreement between a State and a Private Foreign Party*, 17 *Business Lawyer* (1962)

Lalive, J. F.: *Contracts between a State or a State Agency and a Foreign Company—Theory and Practice: Choice of Law in a New Arbitration Case*, 13 I.C.L.Q. (1964)
Lauterpacht, E. (ed.): *The Suez Canal Settlement*, 1960
Lawrence, T. J.: *Essays on Some Disputed Questions in Modern International Law*, 1884
Leeman, W. A.: *The Price of Middle East Oil*, 1962
Lenczowski, G.: *Oil and State in Middle East*, 1960
Liang, Yuen-Li: *The Question of Domestic Jurisdiction in the Anglo-Iranian Oil Dispute before the Security Council*, 46 A.J.I.L. (1952)
Lok Sabha Secretariat (New Delhi): *Suez Canal*, 1956
——: *Nationalisation and After*, 1956
Longrigg, S. H.: *Oil in the Middle East: Its Discovery and Development*, 1968
Lubell, H.: *Middle East Oil Crises and Western Europe's Energy Supplies*, 1963
Matthews, R. D.: *The Suez Canal Dispute: A Case Study in Peaceful Settlement*, 21 *International Organisation* (1967)
Mensbrugghe, Y. van der: *Les Guaranties de la Liberté de Navigation dans le Canal de Suez*, 1964
Mughrabi, M. A.: *Permanent Sovereignty over Oil Resources*, 1966
Nasr, M.: *Mineralölwirtschaft im Nahen Osten*, 1967
Obieta, J. A.: *The International Status of the Suez Canal*, 1960
O'Connell, D. P.: *A Critique of the Iranian Oil Litigation*, 4 I.C.L.Q. (1955)
Odell, P.: *Oil and the Middle East*, 3 *Journal of Contemporary History* (1968)
Penrose, E. T.: *The Large International Firm in Developing Countries. The International Petroleum Industry*, 1968
——: *Monopoly and Competition in the International Petroleum Industry*, 18 Y.B.W.A. (1964)
Petroleum Legislation. Basic Oil Laws and Concession Contracts, 5 Vols. 1963– (with supplements)
Pinto, R.: *L'affaire de Suez*, 2 *Annuaire français* (1956)
Ramazani, R. K.: *Choice of Law Problems and International Oil Contracts*, 11 I.C.L.Q. (1962)
Rauschning, D.: *Der Streit um den Suez Kanal*, 1956
Rouhani, F.: *International Agreements and Contracts in the Field of Petroleum*, 1962
Scelle, G.: *La Nationalisation du Canal de Suez et le droit international*, 2 *Annuaire français* (1956)
Shwadran, B.: *The Middle East, Oil and the Great Powers*, 1959
Skeet, T. H. H.: *The International Oil Industry*, 1 J.W.T.L. (1967)
Suratgar, D.: *The Sapphire Arbitration Award*, 3 *Col.J. Transnational Law* (1964)
Visscher, P. de: *Les aspects juridiques fondamentaux de la question de Suez*, 62 R.G.D.I.P. (1958)
Wall, E. H.: *The Iranian-Italian Oil Agreement of 1957*, 7 I.C.L.Q. (1958)
Watts, D. C.: *Documents on the Suez Crisis*, 1957
Williams, H. R., and Meyers, Ch. J.: *Forfeiture, Notice and Demand and Judicial Ascertainment Clauses in Oil and Gas Leases*, 1 *Natural Resources Journal* (1961)

See also above, pp. 205 *and* 211, *and below*, pp. 216 *and* 223.

CHAPTER 7—FURTHER CHALLENGES

Alisjahbana, S. T.: *Indonesia: Social and Cultural Revolution*, 1966
Amerasinghe, C.: *The Ceylon Oil Expropriations*, 58 A.J.I.L. (1964)
——: *L'expropriation des Compagnies pétrolières de Ceylan et le droit international*, 36 (I) R.G.D.I.P. (1965)
Balloch, M.: *Charter for Investors* [in Uganda], *The Times* (London), October 9, 1968
Bayer, H. W.: *Die Enteignungen auf Kuba vor den Gerichten der Vereinigten Staaten*, 25 Z.A.Ö.R.V.R. (1965)
Bienen, H. L.: *Tanzania: Party Transformation and Economic Development*, 1967
Brehme, G.: *Souveränität der jungen Nationalstaaten über Naturreichtümer*, 1967
Cardozo, M. H.: *Essays on Intervention*, 1964
Council of the Corporation of Foreign Bondholders, London: *Annual Reports* (1874–)
Cuba: *Nationalisation Law of July 6, 1960*, 55 A.J.I.L. (1961)
Cutajar, M. Z., and Franks, A.: *The Less Developed Countries in World Trade. A Reference Handbook*, 1967.
Domke, M.: *Foreign Nationalisations*, 55 A.J.I.L. (1961)
Fatouros, A. A.: *International Law and the Third World*, 50 *Virginia L.R.* (1954)
Friedmann, W.: *Social Conflict and the Protection of Foreign Investment*, *A.S.I.L. Proceedings* (1963)
——, and Kalmanoff, G. (eds.): *Joint International Business Ventures*, 1961
Gess, K. N.: *Permanent Sovereignty over Natural Resources*, 13 I.C.L.Q. (1964)
Haseeb, K.: *The National Income of Iraq 1953–1961*, 1964
Hofmannsthal, E. von: *Foreign Investments: Risky under International Law*, N.Y.U.L.Q.R. (1950)
Holpern, M.: *The Politics of Social Change in the Middle East and North Africa*, 1963
Hoskyns, C.: *Africa's Foreign Relations. The Case of Tanzania*, 44 *International Affairs* (1968)
Hyde, J. N.: *Permanent Sovereignty over Natural Wealth and Resources*, 50 A.J.I.L. (1956)
Kelsen, H.: *The Law of the United Nations*, 1950
Kidron, M.: *Foreign Investment in India*, 1965
Krishna, R.: *Quantitative Restrictions on Transfers of Income, etc.*, in J. G. Starke (ed.), *The Protection and Encouragement of Private Foreign Investment*, 1966
——: *India's Foreign Trade*, 1 J.W.T.L. (1967)
Kust, M. J.: *Foreign Investment in India: Laws and Policies*, 1964, and *Supplement*, 1966
Lieuwen, E.: *Venezuela* (2nd ed.), 1965
McNair, Lord: *The Seizure of Property and Enterprises in Indonesia*, 6 *Netherlands R.I.L.* (1959)
McVey, R. T.: *The Rise of Indonesian Communism*, 1965
Melford, D. C.: *Zambia: The Politics of Independence 1957–1964*, 1967
Mitchell, J. D. B.: *The Contracts of Public Authorities*, 1954
Mukharji, P. B.: *The Critical Problems of the Indian Constitution*, 1968
Nwogugu, E. I.: *The Legal Problems of Foreign Investment in Developing Countries*, 1965
O'Brien, P.: *The Revolution in Egypt's Economic System: From Private Enterprise to Socialism 1952–1965*, 1966

Parry, Sir David Hughes: *The Sanctity of Contracts*, 1959
Pearcy, G. E., and Stoneman, E. A.: *A Handbook of New Nations*, 1968
Pendle, G.: *Argentina* (3rd ed.), 1963
Pluvier, J. M.: *Confrontations: A Study in Indonesian Politics*, 1965
Proehl, P. O.: *Foreign Enterprise in Nigeria*, 1965
Rajan, M. S.: *United Nations and Domestic Jurisdiction*, 1961
Roeber, J.: *The Venezuelan Squeeze on the Oil Firms, The Times* (London), April, 30, 1968
Rolin, H.: *Avis sur la validité des mesures de nationalisation décritées par le gouvernement indonésien*, 6 *Netherlands R.I.L.* (1959)
Saab, G. S.: *The Egyptian Agrarian Reform 1952–1962*, 1967
Seidl-Hohenveldern, I.: *Investitionen in Entwicklungsländern und das Völkerrecht*, 1963
Shilleto, K.: *Shipping and the Closure of the Suez Canal*, 24 *The World Today* (1968)
Smith, S. A. de: *The New Commonwealth and its Constitutions*, 1964
——: *Judicial Review of Administrative Action*, 1968
Suckow, S.: *Nigerian Law and Foreign Investment*, 1966
TANU: *The Arusha Declaration and TANU'S Policy on Socialism and Self-Reliance* (Dar-es-Salaam—1967)
Tinker, H.: *The Union of Burma: A Study of the First Years of Independence*, 1967
Tugendhat, C.: *Oil: The Biggest Business*, 1968
Tuncel, E.: *L'Exécution des décisions de la Cour Internationale de Justice selon la Charte des Nations Unies*, 1960
United Nations: *International Tax Agreements*, 1948–
——: *Investment Laws and Regulations in Africa*, 1965
Verdross, A.: *Die Nationalisierung niederländischer Unternehmungen in Indonesien im Lichte des Völkerrechts*, 6 *Netherlands R.I.L.* (1959)
Wilson, Ch.: *Unilever, 1945–1965*, 1968
Wolf, Ch.: *Foreign Aid—Theory and Practice in Southern Asia*, 1960
Wortley, B. A.: *Indonesian Nationalisation Measures—An Intervention*, 55 A.J.I.L. (1961)
Wurfel, S. W.: *Foreign Enterprise in Colombia: Laws and Politics*, 1965
See also above, pp. 205 *and* 211, *and below*, pp. 219 *and* 223.

PART TWO

MULTILATERAL APPROACHES

CHAPTER 8—THE ABS-SHAWCROSS DRAFT CONVENTION ON INVESTMENTS ABROAD

Abs, H. J.: *Proposals for Improving the Protection of Private Foreign Investments*, 1958
Baade, H. W.: *Die Anerkennung im Ausland vollzogener Enteignungen*, 3 *Jahrbuch für Internationales Recht* (1954)
——: *Gesetzgebung zum Förderung ausländischer Kapitalanlagen*, 1957
——: *Indonesian Nationalisation Measures before Foreign Courts—A Reply*, 54 A.J.I.L. (1960)
Boyle, D. A. V.: *Some Proposals for a World Investment Convention*, J.B.L. (1961)

Brandon, M.: *Legal Deterrents and Incentives to Private Foreign Investments*, 43 *Grotius Transactions* (1957)
——: *An International Investment Code: Current Plans*, J.B.L. (1959)
——: *Recent Measures to Improve the International Investment Climate*, 9 J.P.L. (1960)
Castberg, F.: *De l'effet extraterritorial des décrets d'expropriation et de réquisition*, in 2 *Scritti Perassi*
Cohn, E. J.: *Die Auslandsenteignung im englischen Internationalen Privatrecht* in *Janssen Festschrift*, 1958
Cowles, W. B.: *Treaties and Constitutional Law. Property Interference and Due Process of Law*, 1941
Dicey, A. V., and Morris, J. H. C.: *Conflict of Laws*, 1967
Fatouros, A. A.: *An International Code to Protect Private Investments—Proposals and Perspectives*, 14 *Un. Toronto L.J.* (1961)
Gesellschaft zur Förderung des Schutzes von Auslandsinvestitionen: *International Convention for the Mutual Protection of Private Property Rights in Foreign Countries*, 1957
Gihl, T.: *Two Cases concerning Confiscation of Foreign Property*, in *Liber Amicorum A. Bagge*
Graveson, R. H.: *The Conflict of Laws*, 1965
Haynes, C. O.: *The Revival of Natural Law Concepts*, 1930
Hofmannsthal, E. von, and Sulzberger, M.: *A Convention against Traffic in Confiscated Goods*, 1960
Larson, A.: *Recipients' Rights under an International Investment Code*, 9 J.P.L. (1960)
Lipstein, K.: *Recognition of Governments and the Application of Foreign Laws*, 35 *Grotius Transactions* (1949)
Mann, F. A.: *The Doctrine of Jurisdiction in International Law*, 111 Hague *Recueil* (1964)
Mann, M., and Lauterpacht, E.: *The Dissolved Foreign Corporation*, 18 M.L.R. (1955)
Metzger, S. D.: *Multilateral Conventions for the Protection of Private Foreign Investment*, 9 J.P.L. (1960)
——: *Reply to Professor Seidl-Hohenveldern's Comments on the Round Table on the Abs-Shawcross Draft Convention*, 10 J.P.L. (1961)
Miller, A. S.: *Protection of Private Foreign Investment by Multilateral Convention*, 53 A.J.I.L. (1959)
Morgenstern, F.: *Foreign Acts Contrary to International Law*, 4 I.L.Q. (1951)
Niederer, W.: *Einige Grenzfragen des ordre public in Fällen entschädigungsloser Konfiskation*, 11 *Annuaire suisse* (1954)
Parliamentary Group for World Government: *A World Investment Convention?* 1959
Re, E. D.: *Foreign Confiscations in Anglo-American Law*, 1951
Round Table on *The Proposed Convention to Protect Private Foreign Investments* (M. Brandon, R. N. Gardner, A. Larson, S. D. Metzger and G. Schwarzenberger), 9 J.P.L. (1960)
Schlochauer, H.-J.: *Die extraterritoriale Wirkung von Hoheitsakten*, 1962
Schwarzenberger, G.: *International Law as Applied by International Courts and Tribunals*, Vol. II (1968—Chap. 27)
——: *Uses and Abuses of the "Abuse of Rights" in International Law*, 42 *Grotius Transactions* (1956)
——: *The Abs-Shawcross Draft Convention on Investments Abroad: A Critical Commentary*, 9 J.P.L. (1960), or 14 C.L.P. (1961)

Seidl-Hohenveldern, I.: *Extraterritorial Effects of Confiscations and Expropriations*, 49 *Mich. L.R.* (1950–51)
——: *Eigentumsschutz durch Resolutionen internationaler Organisationen* in *Janssen Festschrift* (1958)
——: *The Abs-Shawcross Draft Convention to Protect Private Foreign Investment*, 10 J.P.L. (1961)
——: *Title to Confiscated Foreign Property and Public International Law*, 56 A.J.I.L. (1962)
Walker, H.: *Law and International Agreements*, 42 *Minnesota L.R.* (1958)
White, J.: *West German Aid to Developing Countries*, 41 *International Affairs* (1965)

See also above, pp. 205 *and* 211, *and below*, pp. 222 *and* 223.

CHAPTER 9—THE I.B.R.D. CONVENTION ON THE SETTLEMENT OF INVESTMENT DISPUTES

Amadio, M.: *Le Contentieux international de l'investissement privé et la convention de la Banque mondiale du 18 mars 1965*, 1967
Atkey, R. J.: *Foreign Investment Disputes*, 9 *Can.Y.B.I.L.* (1967)
Becker, E.: *Die Rechtsprechung der sowjetischen Aussenhandelsschiedskommission*, 1964
Benjamin, P. I.: *Inter-institutional Agreements designed to extend existing facilities for international commercial arbitration*, 8 I.C.L.Q. (1959)
——: *The European Convention on International Commercial Arbitration*, 37 B.Y.I.L. (1961)
——: *The Developing Nations and Certain Legislative Obstacles in the Field of International Commercial Arbitration*, in *Domke Symposium*
Böckstiegel, K.-H.: *Arbitration of Disputes between States and Private Enterprises in the International Chamber of Commerce*, 59 A.J.I.L. (1965)
Brandon, M.: *The World Bank Convention on the Settlement of Investment Disputes*, 6 *Il Diritto negli Scambi Internazionali* (1967)
Broches, A.: *International Legal Aspects of the Operations of the World Bank*, 98 Hague *Recueil* (1959)
——: *Development of International Law by the International Bank for Reconstruction and Development*, 33 *A.S.I.L. Proceedings* (1965)
——: *The Convention on the Settlement of Investment Disputes between States and Nationals of other States: Applicable Law and Default Procedure*, in *Domke Symposium*
Carabiber, Ch.: *L'arbitrage international de droit privé*, 1960
——: *L'évolution de l'arbitrage commercial international*, 99 Hague *Recueil* (1960)
Carlston, K. S.: *Psychological and Sociological Aspects of the Judicial and Arbitration Processes*, in *Domke Symposium*
Cohn, E. J.: *The Rules of Arbitration of the International Chamber of Commerce*, 14 I.C.L.Q. (1965)
——: *The Rules of Arbitration of the United Nations Economic Commission for Europe*, 16 *ibid.* (1967)
David Davies Memorial Institute: *The Peaceful Settlement of International Disputes. Report of a Study Group*, 1966
David, R.: *Arbitrage et droit comparé*, 11 *Revue internationale de droit comparée* (1959)
Dawson, F. G.: *International Law and the Procedural Rights of Aliens before National Tribunals*, 17 I.C.L.Q. (1968)

Delaume, G. R.: *Convention on the Settlement of Investment Disputes between States and Nationals of Other States*, 1 *The International Lawyer* (1966) or 93 *Journal du droit international* (1966)

Domke, M.: *The Law and Practice of Commercial Arbitration*, 1968

——: *The Settlement of International Investment Disputes*, 12 *Business Lawyer* (1957)

—— (ed.): *International Trade Arbitration*, 1958

——: *The Settlement of Disputes in International Trade*, in P. O. Proehl (ed.), *Legal Problems of International Trade*, 1959

——: *Arbitration between Governmental Bodies and Foreign Private Firms*, 17 *Arbitration Journal* (N.S.—1962)

——: *American Arbitral Awards: Enforcement in Foreign Countries*, in University of Illinois *Law Forum* on *International Trade, Investment and Organisation*, 1965

——: *Progress in International Commercial Arbitrations*, 1 *New York Univ. Journal of International Law and Politics* (1968)

Fouchard, F.: *L'arbitrage commercial international* (2 vols.), 1965

François, J. P. A.: *La liberté des parties de choisir les arbitres dans les conflits entre les Etats*, in *Domke Symposium*

Gardner, R. N.: *The United Nations Conference on Trade and Development*, 22 *International Organisation* (1968)

Geimer, R.: *Zur Prüfung der Gerichtsbarkeit und der internationalen Zuständigkeit bei der Anerkennung ausländischer Urteile*, 1966

Goldman, B.: *Arbitrage international privé*, 109 Hague *Recueil* (1963)

Hallier, H.-J. (ed.): *Internationale Gerichte und Schiedsgerichte*, 1961

——: *Völkerrechtliche Schiedsinstanzen für Einzelpersonen*, 1962

Hazard, J. N.: *Flexibility of Law in Soviet State Arbitration*, in *Domke Symposium*

Heydte, F. A. von der: *L'individu et les tribunaux internationaux*, 107 Hague *Recueil* (1962)

Hyde, J. N.: *Economic Development Agreements*, 105 Hague *Recueil* (1962—Chap. 5)

International Law Association: *Report of the Committee on the Juridical Aspects of Nationalisation and Foreign Property*, Hamburg (1960) and Brussels (1962) Conferences

Jenks, C. W.: *The Prospects of International Adjudication*, 1964 (Chap. 12)

Johnson, D. H. N.: *The Constitution of an Arbitral Tribunal*, 30 B.Y.I.L. (1953)

——: *Arbitration in English Law and International Law*, 41 *Grotius Transactions* (1955)

Kelly, G. B.: *Eastern Arabian Frontiers*, 1964 (Chaps. 6 and 7)

Kipp, H.: *Verträge zwischen staatlichen und nichtstaatlichen Partnern*, 5 *Berichte der deutschen Gesellschaft für Völkerrecht* (1964)

Kopelmanas, L.: *The Settlement of Disputes in International Trade*, 61 *Col.L.R.* (1961)

Kos-Rabcowicz-Zubkowski, L.: *Le droit commercial international dans les rapports Est-Ouest*, 5 *Can.Y.B.I.L.* (1967)

Lauterpacht, E.: *The World Bank Convention on the Settlement of International Investment Disputes*, in *Mélanges Guggenheim*

Lazarus, N. Y., and Others: *Resolving Business Disputes*, 1965

Lipstein, K.: *Conflict of Laws before International Tribunals*, 27 *Grotius Transactions* (1942) and 29 *ibid.* (1944)

Mann, F. A.: *Lex facit Arbitrum*, in *Domke Symposium*

McMahon, J. F.: *Settlement of Disputes in Special Fields*, in David Davies Memorial Institute, *Report of a Study Group on the Peaceful Settlement of International Disputes*, 1966

Nantwi, E. K.: *The Enforcement of International Judicial Decisions and Arbitral Awards in Public International Law*, 1966

Pisar, S.: *The United Nations Convention on Foreign Arbitral Awards*, J.B.L. (1959)

Ramzaitsev, D.: *The Law of Trade in the New Soviet Legislation*, J.B.L. (1963)

Re, E. D.: *The Presettlement Adjudication of International Claims*, in *Domke Symposium*

Riedberg, P.: *Der amiable compositeur im internationalen privaten Schiedsgerichtsverfahren*, 1962

Rodley, N. S.: *Some Aspects of the World Bank Convention on the Settlement of Investment Disputes*, 4 *Can.Y.B.I.L.* (1966)

Roulet, J. D.: *La Convention du 18 mars 1965 pour le règlement des différends relatifs aux investissements entre Etats et ressortissants d'autres Etats*, 22 *Annuaire suisse* (1965)

Russell, F. (ed. by A. Walton): *The Law of Arbitration*, 1963

Sanders, P.: *ECAFE Rules for International Commercial Arbitration*, in *Domke Symposium*

Sarojini, K. P.: *Arbitration of Trade Controversies between Governments and Foreign Firms*, 1 *Indian J.I.L.* (1961)

Sarre, D. A. G.: *European Commercial Arbitration*, J.B.L. (1961)

Sassoon, D. M.: *Convention on the Settlement of Investment Disputes*, J.B.L. (1965) or 1 *Israel L.R.* (1966)

Schachter, O.: *Enforcement of International Decisions*, 54 A.J.I.L. (1960)

——: *Conciliation Procedures in the United Nations Conference on Trade and Development*, in *Domke Symposium*

Schlesinger, R. B., and Gündisch, H.-J.: *Allgemeine Rechtsgrundsätze als Sachnormen in Schiedsgerichtsverfahren*, 28 Z.A.I.P.R. (1964)

Schwarzenberger, G.: *The Arbitration Pattern and the Protection of Property Abroad*, in *Domke Symposium*

Schwebel, S. M., and Wetter, J. G.: *Arbitration and the Exhaustion of Local Remedies*, 60 A.J.I.L. (1966)

Seidl-Hohenveldern, I.: *Judicial Protection of Foreign Investments*, 2 *Mélanges Séfériadès*

Simpson, J. L., and Fox, H.: *International Arbitration*, 1959

Snyder, E.: *Foreign Investment Protection: Is Institutional Arbitration an Answer?*, 40 *North Carolina L.R.* (1962)

——: *Foreign Investment Protection: The Dispute Solving Aspect*, 3 *Col. J. Transnational Law* (1964)

Spofford, Ch. M.: *Third-Party Judgment and International Economic Transactions*, 113 Hague *Recueil* (1964)

Starke, J. G. (ed.): *The Protection and Encouragement of Private Foreign Investment*, 1966 (Chap. 1)

Suratgar, D.: *The Sapphire Arbitration Award*, 3 *Col. J. Transnational Law* (1964)

Szászy, I.: *International Civil Procedure*, 1967

Union International des Avocats (Rapporteur Général F. Ch. Jeantet): *Les juridictions internationales*, 1959

—— (Rapporteur Général P. Sanders): *Arbitrage international commercial* (no date)

United Nations: *A Survey of Treaty Provisions for the Pacific Settlement of International Disputes 1949–1962*, 1966

—— Economic Commission for Europe: *Handbook of National and International Institutions Active in the Field of International Commercial Arbitration*, 1958

Verdross, A.: *Die Sicherung von ausländischen Privatrechten aus Abkommen für wirtschaftliche Entwicklung mit Schiedsklauseln*, 18 Z.A.Ö.R.V.R. (1957–8)

——: *Quasi-International Agreements and International Economic Transactions*, 18 Y.B.W.A. (1964)

——: *Zwei Schweizer Schiedssprüche über quasi-völkerrechtliche Verträge*, 21 *Annuaire suisse* (1964)

Walker, H.: *Commercial Arbitration in United States Treaties*, 11 *Arbitration J.* (1956)

Wortley, B. A.: *Quelques développements modernes qui touchent les controversies entres les particuliers et les Etats et les entités étatiques*, in *Domke Symposium*

See also above, pp. 207 *and* 217, *and below*, p. 223.

Chapters 10–11—THE O.E.C.D. DRAFT CONVENTION OF 1967 ON THE PROTECTION OF FOREIGN PROPERTY—AN INTERNATIONAL INVESTMENT INSURANCE AGENCY

Brewer, B. C.: *The Proposal for Investment Guarantees by an International Agency*, 58 A.J.I.L. (1964)

Broches, A.: *International Investment Guarantees: Possibilities and Problems*, 56 *A.S.I.L. Proceedings* (1962)

Collins, L. A., and Etra, A.: *Policy, Politics, International Law and the United States Investment Guaranty Program*, 4 *Col.J. Transnational Law* (1966)

Emde Boas, M. J. van: *The O.E.C.D. Draft Convention on the Protection of Foreign Property*, 1 C.M.L.R. (1963–64)

Fatouros, A. A.: *Government Guarantees to Foreign Investors*, 1962 (useful bibliography)

——: *The Quest for Legal Security of Foreign Investments*, 17 *Rutgers L.R.* (1963)

Hecke, G. A. van: *Le projet de convention de l'O.C.D.E. sur la protection des biens étrangers*, 68 R.G.D.I.P. (1964)

International Bank for Reconstruction and Development. Staff Report: *Multilateral Investment Insurance*, 1962

Rubin, S. J.: *The Investment Guaranty Program of the United States*, 56 *A.S.I.L. Proceedings* (1962)

Seidl-Hohenveldern, I.: *Internationale Organisationen und der Schutz des Privateigentums*, 90 *Journal du Droit International* (1963)

Suy, E.: *La guarantie des investissements privés*, *Industrie, Revue mensuelle de la Fédération des Industries Belges* (September, 1963)

Wilner, G. M.: *Contract Guarantees in International Law*, 3 *Indian J.I.L.* (1963)

See also above, pp. 217 *and* 219, *and below*, p. 223.

Chapter 12—CHOICES BEFORE INVESTORS

Alexandrowicz, Ch. H.: *World Economic Agencies*, 1962

Amman, U.: *Der Schutz ausländischer Privatinvestitionen in Entwicklungsländern aus volkswirtschaftlicher und betriebswirtschaftlicher Sicht*, 1967

Anand, R. P.: *Attitudes of the Afro-Asian States towards Certain Problems of International Law*, 15 I.C.L.Q. (1966)

Baldwin, D. A.: *The International Bank in Political Perspective*, 18 *World Politics* (1965)

Balekjian, W. H.: *Legal Aspects of Foreign Investment in the European Economic Community*, 1967

Balog, N.: *Legal Relations concerning Foreign Investment in Yugoslav Economic Organisations*, 18 *The New Yugoslav Law* (1967)

Bing, G.: *Reap the Whirlwind*, 1968

Black, E.: *The Diplomacy of Economic Development*, 1961

Boyd Orr, Lord, and Lubbock, D.: *The White Man's Dilemma*, 1967

Brandon, M.: *Investment Encouragement Legislation in the Developing Countries*, J.B.L. (1963)

British Institute of International and Comparative Law: *The Encouragement and Protection of Investment in Developing Countries*, 1961

Broches, A.: *International Legal Aspects of the Operations of the World Bank*, 98 Hague *Recueil* (1959)

Broderick, M.: *Associated Statehood—A New Form of Decolonisation*, 17 I.C.L.Q. (1968)

Brown, W. G.: *The Use of Foreign Aid as an Instrument to Secure Compliance with International Obligations*, 58 *A.S.I.L. Proceedings* (1964)

Brownlie, I.: *Principles of Public International Law*, 1966 (Part Nine)

Buron, R.: *Some Basic Realities of Development Assistance*, 42 *International Affairs* (1966)

Bystricky, R.: *On the Principle of Obligatory Co-operation of States*, in N. K. Nawaz and Others: *The Legal Principles Governing Friendly Relations and Co-operation among States*, 1966

Castberg, F.: *De l'effet extraterritorial des décrets d'expropriation et de réquisition*, 1 *Scritti Perassi*

Chayes, A.: *United States Policy towards Private Investments Abroad*, in Southwestern Legal Foundation: *Rights and Duties of Private Investors Abroad*, 1965

Darja, K. H. R.: *The Rule of Law and Economic Inequalities among Nations*, 1 *Indian J.I.L.* (1960–61)

Delaume, G.-R.: *Legal Aspects of International Lending and Economic Development Financing*, 1967

Dölle, D., and Others: *Internationale Betrachtungen zur Dekolonisierung*, 1964

Drago, L. M.: *State Loans in their Relation to International Policy*, 1 A.J.I.L. (1907)

Dugard, C. I. R.: *The Organisation of African Unity and Colonialism*, 16 I.C.L.Q. (1967)

Esman, M. J., and Cheever, R.: *The Common Aid Effort*, 1967

Falk, R. A.: *The New States and International Legal Order*, 118 Hague *Recueil* (1966)

Fatouros, A. A.: *Obstacles to Private Foreign Investment in Underdeveloped Countries*, 2 *Current Law and Social Problems* (1961)

——: *International Law and the Third World*, 50 *Virg.L.R.* (1964)

Feldman, H.: *Aid as Imperialism?*, 43 *International Affairs* (1967)

Friedheim, R. L.: *The "Satisfied" and "Dissatisfied" States Negotiate International Law: A Case Study*, 18 *World Politics* (1965)

Friedmann, W.: *Methods and Policies of Principal Donor Countries in Public International Development Financing*, 1962
——: *Social Conflict and the Protection of Foreign Investment*, 57 *A.S.I.L. Proceedings* (1963)
——: *The Relevance of International Law to the Processes of Economic and Social Development*, 60 *A.S.I.L. Proceedings* (1966)
——, Kalmanoff, G., and Meagher, R. F.: *International Financial Aid*, 1967
——: *Public Enterprise*, 22 C.L.P. (1969)
Gess, K. N.: *Permanent Sovereignty over Natural Resources*, 13 I.C.L.Q. (1964)
Gosovic, B.: *UNCTAD : North-South Encounter*, 568 *International Conciliation* (1968)
Hawley, E. W.: *The New Deal and the Problem of Monopoly*, 1966
Hellmann, R.: *Auslandsinvestitionen und europäische Souveränität*, 18 *Europa Archiv* (1968)
Higgins, R.: *The Development of International Law through the Political Organs of the United Nations*, 1963
——: *Conflict of Interests*, 1965 (Part II)
Howard, M.: *Reflections on the Russian Invasion*, 80 *The Listener* (1968—No. 2057)
Hyde, J. N.: *Permanent Sovereignty over Natural Wealth and Resources*, 50 A.J.I.L. (1956)
International Commission of Jurists: *The Dynamic Aspects of the Rule of Law in the Modern Age*, 1965
Jenks, C. W.: *Mutual Aid in International Law*, 14 *Indian Y.B.I.A.* (1967)
Johnson, H. G.: *The World Economy at the Crossroads*, 1965
——: *Economic Policies towards Less Developed Countries*, 1967
—— (ed.): *Economic Nationalism in Old and New States*, 1968
Kahn, Ph.: *Les problèmes juridiques des investissements étrangers dans les pays en voie de développement*, in I.L.A., Helsinki Conference (1966)
Kaplan, J. J.: *The Challenge of Foreign Aid*, 1967
Kay, D. A.: *The Politics of Decolonisation : The New Nations and the United Nations Political Process*, 21 *International Organisation* (1967)
Kirdar, U.: *The Structure of United Nations Economic Aid to Underdeveloped Countries*, 1966
Kretzschmar, W. W.: *Auslandshilfe als Mittel der Aussenwirtschaftsund Aussenpolitik*, 1964
Lachmann, K. E.: *The Role of International Business in the Transfer of Technology to Developing Countries*, J.B.L. (1967)
LaFave, W. R., and Hay, P. (eds.): *International Trade, Investment and Organisation*, 1967
Larson, A.: *Recipient's Rights under an International Investment Code*, 9 J.P.L. (1960)
Laurent, P. H.: *State Responsibility : A Possible Historic Precedent to the Calvo Clause*, 15 I.C.L.Q. (1966)
Lillich, R. B.: *The Protection of Foreign Investment and the Foreign Assistance Act of 1962*, 17 *Rutgers L.R.* (1963)
——: *The Protection of Foreign Investments and the Hicklenlooper Amendment*, 112 *U.Pa.L.R.* (1964)
Lissitzyn, O. J.: *International Law Today and Tomorrow*, 1965
Little, I. M. D., and Clifford, J. M.: *International Aid*, 1965
Lloyd, P. J.: *International Trade Problems of Small Nations*, 1968
Mason, E. S.: *Foreign Aid and Foreign Policy*, 1964
Meier, G. M.: *Legal-Economic Problems of Private Foreign Investment in Developing Countries*, 33 *Univ. Chicago L.R.* (1965–66)

Meissner, H. G.: *Das Entwicklungsgeschäft: Theoretische Grundlagen, Betriebliche Probleme, Weltwirtschaftliche Zusammenhänge*, 1966
Metzger, S. D. *Regulation of International Trade*, 60 A.J.I.L. (1966)
Mihailovic, S.: *Confrontation without Real Solutions*, 19 *Review of International Affairs* (Belgrade), March 20, 1968
Mikesell, R. F.: *Public Foreign Capital to Private Enterprise in Developing Nations* (Princeton University, *Essays in International Finance*, No. 52), 1966
Miles, C.: *Trade and Aid: The Second UNCTAD*, 24 *The World Today* (1968)
Montgomery, J. D.: *The Politics of Foreign Aid*, 1962
Myrdal, G.: *Asian Drama: An Enquiry into the Poverty of Nations*, 1968 (3 vols.)
Nkrumah, K.: *Neo-Colonialism*, 1965
Nurick, L.: *International Agencies Aiding or Affecting Foreign Investment*, in Southwestern Legal Foundation: *Institute on Private Investments Abroad*, 1959
Nwogugu, E. I.: *The Legal Problems of Foreign Investment in Developing Countries*, 1965
O'Brien, W. V. (ed.): *The New Nations in International Law and Diplomacy*, 1965
Olmstead, C. J.: *Foreign Aid as an Effective Means of Persuasion*, 54 *Col.L.R.* (1966)
Pineus, J. A.: *Reshaping the World Economy: Rich and Poor Countries*, 1968
Preiswerk, R.: *La réciprocité dans les négociations entre pays à systèmes sociaux ou à niveaux économiques différents*, 94 *Journal du Droit International* (1967)
Reid, E.: *The Future of the World Bank*, 1965
Röling, B. V. A.: *International Law in an Expanded World*, 1960
Rubin, S. J.: *Private Foreign Investment. Legal and Economic Realities*, 1956
——: *The Conscience of the Rich Nations. The Development Assistance Committee and the Common Aid Effort*, 1966
Sahovic, M.: *Influence des Etats nouveaux sur la conception du droit international*, 12 *Annuaire français* (1966)
Salmon, J.: *Le rôle des organisations internationales en matière de prêts et d'emprunts*, 1958
Sapozhnikov, V. I.: *Sovereignty over Natural Resources*, *Soviet Yearbook of International Law* (1964–1965)
Schwarzenberger, G.: *Decolonisation and the Protection of Foreign Investments*, 20 C.L.P. (1967)
Schwebel, S. M.: *The Story of the United Nations Declaration on Permanent Sovereignty over Natural Resources*, 49 *Am. Bar Assn. J.* (1963)
Seidl-Hohenveldern, I.: *Communist Theories on Confiscation and Expropriation*, 7 A.J.I.L. (1958)
Shea, D. B.: *The Calvo Clause*, 1955
Shonfield, A.: *Modern Capitalism. The Changing Balance of Public and Private Power*, 1965
Sinha, S. P.: *Perspective of the Newly Independent States on the Binding Quality of International Law*, 14 I.C.L.Q. (1965)
Stocking, G. W., and Watkins, M. W.: *Cartels or Competition?*, 1948
Strange, S.: *Changing Trends in World Trade*, 16 Y.B.W.A. (1962)
——: *A New Look at Trade and Aid*, 42 *International Affairs* (1966)
——: *Debts, Defaulters and Development*, 43 *ibid.* (1967)
United Nations: *Report of the Commission on Permanent Sovereignty over Natural Resources*, 1962

United Nations Secretariat: *The Status of Permanent Sovereignty over Natural Wealth and Resources*, 1962

——: Study on *Financing of Economic Development—Promotion of Private Foreign Investment in Developing Countries*, 1967

Virally, M.: *Droit International et Décolonisation devant les Nations Unies*, 9 *Annuaire français* (1963)

——: *Vers un droit international du développement*, 11 *ibid.* (1965)

Waterston, A.: *Development Planning: Lessons of Experience*, 1965

Weinstein, P. D.: *The Attitude of the Capital-Importing Nations Towards the Taking of Foreign-owned Private Property*, 5 *Indian J.I.L.* (1965)

Westring, G.: *Cooperation for Development*, 37 *Acta Scandinavica* (1967)

Williams, S.: *Negotiating Investment in Emerging Countries*, 43 *Harv.Bus.Rev.* (1965)

Wolf, Ch.: *Some Aspects of the "Value" of Less-Developed Countries to the United States*, 15 *World Politics* (1963)

See also above, pp. 214 *and* 216.

AUTHORS' INDEX

SUBJECT INDEX

The London Institute of World Affairs

Founded 1934

THORNE HOUSE
4–8 ENDSLEIGH GARDENS, LONDON, W.C.1

OFFICERS

President and Treasurer:

Professor G. W. Keeton

Vice-Presidents:

H.E. Dr. F. T. Cheng
Sir Kenneth G. Grubb
Professor Georg Schwarzenberger
Professor Quincy Wright

Council:

L. Aird
W. Burmeister
Dr. J. W. Burton
Professor B. Cheng
Dr. E. J. Cohn
R. M. Forrest
Professor J. Frankel
Professor L. C. Green
Dr. D. Malaiperuman
Maurice W. Maxwell
Dr. C. M. Rigby

Director:

Professor Georg Schwarzenberger

Assistant Director:
F. Parkinson

Secretary:
E. D. Brown

Organising Tutor:
A. M. Sutton

Official Publishers:
Stevens & Sons, Limited, London

THE LONDON INSTITUTE OF WORLD AFFAIRS

Founded 1934

OBJECTS

The LONDON INSTITUTE OF WORLD AFFAIRS is a self-governing, independent research and teaching organisation for the study of world affairs.

The Institute seeks to achieve this object by the promotion of conferences, lectures, discussion groups and research upon the main problems of world affairs, and by its various publications. It is an unofficial body committed to no particular party and no particular ideology.

The membership of the Institute is international, and its activities are financed by the subscriptions and donations of its members, and by income from its various activities.

The minimum subscription is £3 3s. 0d. ($7.80) *per calendar year.*

Members receive the *Year Book of World Affairs* free of charge and post free, and are entitled to purchase volumes in the Library of World Affairs at a reduction of twenty-five *per cent.* below the published price, provided that such copies are ordered from the Secretary of the Institute.

The Institute is responsible for the full teaching programme in connection with the University of London Diploma in International Affairs, which extends over two years, and organises one-year courses for advanced students leading to the Associateship of the Institute. In addition, the Institute awards a Diploma in Air and Space Law on the basis of an approved course of study.

THE INSTITUTE'S TEACHING PROGRAMME

DIPLOMA IN INTERNATIONAL AFFAIRS

This is a Diploma in the Humanities of the Extramural Department of the University of London, and the lectures for the day course are the responsibility of the London Institute of World Affairs.

The Diploma course extends over two years, the subjects for the first year being:

International Economics
International Law
Modern International History
Advanced English.

In the second year the subjects studied are:

International Economic Law
International Institutions
International Relations.

The fees for the course are thirty Pounds each year.

Candidates for the Diploma are required to attend twenty-four lectures and discussion classes in each subject, and are expected to do such written work as will be prescribed. At the end of each year students are required to take an examination in each of the prescribed subjects, and on the results of these examinations the Diploma is awarded.

ASSOCIATESHIP OF THE LONDON INSTITUTE OF WORLD AFFAIRS

A course leading to the Associateship is offered to certain categories of advanced students. The course extends over at least one session and the Associateship is awarded on the basis of a thesis which candidates are required to prepare under the supervision of a teacher appointed by the Director.

THE INSTITUTE'S TEACHING PROGRAMME

DIPLOMA IN AIR AND SPACE LAW

This is a Diploma awarded by the London Institute of World Affairs on the basis of examinations held annually by the Institute. The examination is divided into two Parts, which may be taken separately:

Part I: General Principles of Air and Space Law.

Part II: Selected Problems of Air and Space Law.

Candidates for the Diploma must have pursued a recognised course of study in order to qualify for admission to the examination.

Full details and application forms for both Diploma and Associateship courses may be obtained from:

The *Organising Tutor*,
The London Institute of World Affairs,
Thorne House,
4–8 Endsleigh Gardens,
London, W.C.1

THE LIBRARY OF WORLD AFFAIRS

1. *Making International Law Work.* By George W. Keeton and Georg Schwarzenberger. Second Edition. (*Out of print.*)
2. *China Moulded by Confucius: The Chinese Way in Western Light.* By His Excellency Dr. F. T. Cheng. Illustrated. (*Out of print.*)
3. *A Manual of International Law.* By Georg Schwarzenberger. Fifth Edition. £4 18s.
4. *The Crisis in the Law of Nations.* By H. A. Smith. (*Out of print.*)
5. *Great Britain, the United States and the Future.* By J. E. Tyler. (*Out of print.*)
6. *China, The Far East and the Future.* By George W. Keeton. Second Edition. (*Out of print.*)
7. *Czechoslovakia between East and West.* By W. Diamond. (*Out of print.*)
8. *The Allied Military Government of Germany.* By W. Friedmann. (*Out of print.*)
9. *The Law and Custom of the Sea.* By H. A. Smith. Third Edition. (*Out of print.*)
10. *Charter of the United Nations.* By L. M. Goodrich and E. Hambro. Second Edition. (*Out of print.*)
11. *The Law of the United Nations: A Critical Analysis of its Fundamental Problems.* By Hans Kelsen. With supplement. (*Out of print.*)
12. *The North Atlantic Treaty, the Brussels Treaty and the United Nations Charter.* By Sir W. Eric Beckett. (*Out of print.*)
13. *Finland: The Adventures of a Small Power.* By Hugh Shearman. With maps. (*Out of print.*)
14. *The World of the Slavs.* By A. Mousset. (*Out of print.*)
15. *Russia and the United States.* By P. A. Sorokin. Second Edition. (*Out of print.*)
16. *The International Law of Recognition.* By T. C. Chen. (*Out of print.*)
17. *International Law through the Cases.* By L. C. Green. Second Edition. £4 18s.
18. *Power Politics: A Study of World Society.* By Georg Schwarzenberger. Third Edition. £4
19. *International Economic Organizations.* By C. H. Alexandrowicz. (*Out of print.*)
20. *Expropriation in International Law.* By S. Friedman. (*Out of print.*)
21. *The General Principles of Law as applied by International Courts and Tribunals.* By Bin Cheng. (*Out of print.*)
22. *The Law of Nations: Cases, Documents and Notes.* By H. W. Briggs. Second Edition. £6 6s.
23. *Law and Social Change in the U.S.S.R.* By J. N. Hazard. (*Out of print.*)
24. *The British Commonwealth in International Law.* See No. 61.
25. *International Relations: The World Community in Transition.* By N. D. Palmer and H. C. Perkins. Second Edition. (*Out of print.*)
26. *The Communist Theory of Law.* By Hans Kelsen. (*Out of print.*)
27. *Organising for Peace: International Organisation in World Affairs.* By D. S. Cheever and H. Field Haviland, Jr. (*Out of print.*)
28. *Nationality and Statelessness in International Law.* By P. Weis. (*Out of print.*)
29. *Germany and the North Atlantic Community: A Legal Survey.* By M. Bathurst and J. L. Simpson. (*Out of print.*)
30. *Law and Structures of Social Action.* By K. S. Carlston. (*Out of print.*)
31. *Cases and Materials on International Law.* By L. B. Orfield and E. D. Re. (*Out of print.*)
32. *The Council of Europe: Its Structure, Functions and Achievements.* By A. H. Robertson. Second Edition. (*Out of print.*)
33. *The Trusteeship System of the United Nations.* By C. E. Toussaint. (*Out of print.*)
34. *International Relations.* By M. Margaret Ball and Hugh B. Killough. (*Out of print.*)
35. *The International Protection of Trade Union Freedom.* By C. Wilfred Jenks. £5 10s.

THE LIBRARY OF WORLD AFFAIRS

36. *Cases on United Nations Law.* By Louis B. Sohn. (*Out of print.*)
37. *Basic Documents of the United Nations.* By Louis B. Sohn. (*Out of print.*)
38. *Democratic Institutions in the World Today.* Edited by Werner Burmeister. (*Out of print.*)
39. *Aggression and World Order: A Critique of United Nations Theories of Aggression.* By Julius Stone. (*Out of print.*)
40. *The Legal Framework of World Trade.* By V. A. Seyid Muhammad. (*Out of print.*)
41. *The Common Law of Mankind.* By C. Wilfred Jenks. £4 8s.
42. *The Uniting of Europe: Political, Social and Economic Forces, 1950–1957.* By Ernst B. Haas. (*Out of print.*)
43. *The Legality of Nuclear Weapons.* By Georg Schwarzenberger. (*Out of print.*)
44. *European Institutions.* By A. H. Robertson. Second Edition. £4 4s.
45. *NATO and the European Union Movement.* By Margaret Ball. (*Out of print.*)
46. *Rivers in International Law.* By F. J. Berber. (*Out of print.*)
47. *The Law of International Air Transport.* By Bin Cheng. (*Out of print.*)
48. *The United Nations.* By L. M. Goodrich. £3 12s.
49. *Human Rights and International Labour Standards.* By C. Wilfred Jenks. £1 14s.
50. *Consular Law and Practice.* By Luke T. Lee. £6 10s.
51. *Comparative Law.* By Rudolf B. Schlesinger. Second Edition. (*Out of print.*)
52. *Consensus Formation in the Council of Europe.* By Ernst B. Haas. (*Out of print.*)
53. *International Transactions and Relations.* By Milton Katz and Kingman Brewster, Jr. (*Out of print.*)
54. *Dual Nationality.* By N. Bar-Yaacov. (*Out of print.*)
55. *The European Common Market.* By Isaiah Frank. £3 8s.
56. *The International Status of the United Nations.* By Guenter Weissberg. (*Out of print.*)
57. *Nationalisation of Foreign Property.* By Gillian White. £4
58. *Judicial Control of the European Communities.* By Gerhard Bebr. £3 5s.
59. *The Frontiers of International Law.* By Georg Schwarzenberger. £5 4s.
60. *The Law of International Institutions.* By D. W. Bowett. Second Edition. £3 15s. (Hardback). £2 (Paperback)
61. *The British Commonwealth in International Law.* By J. E. S. Fawcett. £3 12s.
62. *The Interpretation of Ambiguous Documents by International Administrative Tribunals.* By Alan H. Schechter. £3
63. *The International Monetary Fund: Legal Bases, Structure, Functions.* By Hans Aufricht. (*Out of print.*)
64. *Comparative Survey of Central Bank Law.* By Hans Aufricht. £3 18s.
65. *The Structure, Function and Law of a Free Trade Area: The European Free Trade Association.* By John S. Lambrinidis. £4 15s.
66. *International Controls for Antarctica.* By John Hanessian. (*In preparation.*)
67. *The Inductive Approach to International Law.* By Georg Schwarzenberger. £3 2s.
68. *Foreign Investments and International Law.* By Georg Schwarzenberger. £3 18s.

Members of the Institute who wish to obtain publications in the Library at the special reduced price (25% less than the published prices) should order them from *the Secretary of the Institute.*

Non-Members should address orders to Messrs. Stevens & Sons Limited, the official publishers of the Institute.

(*Addresses are on the Order form overleaf.*)

APPLICATION FOR MEMBERSHIP

TO THE SECRETARY,
THE LONDON INSTITUTE OF WORLD AFFAIRS
THORNE HOUSE,
4–8 ENDSLEIGH GARDENS, LONDON, W.C.1.

I enclose £............................ * as membership subscription to THE LONDON INSTITUTE OF WORLD AFFAIRS for the year 19......

BLOCK CAPITALS PLEASE

Name ....

Address ....

....

Date ....

* Minimum Annual Subscription £3 3s. ($7.80).

ORDER FOR PUBLICATIONS*

MEMBERS

To The Secretary,
The London Institute of World Affairs,
Thorne House,
4–8 Endsleigh Gardens, London, W.C.1.

NON-MEMBERS

To Stevens & Sons, Ltd.,
North Way,
Andover, Hants
[*Tel.: Andover 62141*
Telex 47214.]

(Please delete address which does not apply)

Please send the following books in the Library of World Affairs Nos. ....

and the Year Book of World Affairs for the year(s) ....

(Members receive this automatically)

BLOCK CAPITALS PLEASE

Name ....

Address ....

....

Date ....

Overseas postage, packing and insurance is charged at the following rates:

Orders of value up to £1: . . . 3s. postage.
Orders in excess of £1:
first £1: . . . 3s. postage.
each additional £1: . . . 1s. 6d. extra.

Inland postage, 2s. 6d. for each book ordered.

☐ Remittance enclosed ☐ Charge to account

* See note on page vii.

THE EASTERN PRESS LTD.